Secret Selves

Secret Selves

A History of Our Inner Space

Stephen Prickett

BLOOMSBURY ACADEMIC
NEW YORK · LONDON · OXFORD · NEW DELHI · SYDNEY

BLOOMSBURY ACADEMIC
Bloomsbury Publishing Inc
1385 Broadway, New York, NY 10018, USA
50 Bedford Square, London, WC1B 3DP, UK
29 Earlsfort Terrace, Dublin 2, Ireland

BLOOMSBURY, BLOOMSBURY ACADEMIC and the Diana logo are trademarks
of Bloomsbury Publishing Plc

First published in the United States of America 2021

Cover design by Daniel Benneworth-Gray

Library of Congress Cataloging-in-Publication Data

Names: Prickett, Stephen, author.
Title: Secret selves / Stephen Prickett.
Description: New York, NY : Bloomsbury Academic, 2021. | Includes bibliographical references and index. | Summary: "Our secret, inner, sense of self – what we feel makes us distinctively 'us' – seems a natural and permanent part of being human, yet in fact it is surprisingly new. Over the last 2,000 years we have increasingly felt old sources of identity, such as family, tribe, or social status, as intensely personal, even unique to us. Confessional religious writings and novels, from Augustine to Jane Austen, or diaries even of 20th-century holocaust victims, took the same path to self-discovery and exploration inwards – as did the cinema. Artistic realism began with internalization. In the last few centuries our inner space has expanded far beyond any possible personal experience. Our knowledge of history, other cultures, the world, and the cosmos, and has vastly enhanced our capacity not merely to write about what we have never seen, but even to create fantasies and impossible fictions around them. Yet our secret selves can also be a source of terror. Dreamers and visionaries often fear rather than delight in what they have uncovered. We all have specific nightmares. Identity theft has a long history – going back at least to 15th century Florence. Mystics and poets, from Dante to Newman or Hopkins, sought God in their secret spaces not least because they feared the 'abyss beneath'. The medieval three-storey universe reappears in modern psychoanalysis. The fringes of our secret selves are often porous, ill-defined, and, if some wilder prophecies of cyborgs or reincarnation have any validity, open to frightening forms of external control"– Provided by publisher.
Identifiers: LCCN 2021000618 (print) | LCCN 2021000619 (ebook) | ISBN 9781501372469 (hardback) | ISBN 9781501372476 (ebook) | ISBN 9781501372483 (pdf)
Subjects: LCSH: Self. | Psychology. | Identity (Psychology)
Classification: LCC BF697 .P6949 2021 (print) | LCC BF697 (ebook) | DDC 155.2—dc23
LC record available at https://lccn.loc.gov/2021000618
LC ebook record available at https://lccn.loc.gov/2021000619

ISBN: HB: 978-1-5013-7246-9
         ePDF: 978-1-5013-7248-3
         eBook: 978-1-5013-7247-6

Typeset by RefineCatch Limited, Bungay, Suffolk
Printed and bound in the United States of America

To find out more about our authors and books visit www.bloomsbury.com
and sign up for our newsletters.

Contents

Figures

Plates

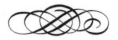

Acknowledgements

My thanks are due to many friends who read all or parts of the manuscript and made helpful suggestions: Robin Gill, Simon Haines, Christopher Herbert, Peter Hill, Elisabeth Jay and Ruth Prickett. For specialist expertise, I have to thank Philip Knight for his unrivalled knowledge of Etty Hillesum.

Above all is my debt to my wife, Patricia Erskine-Hill, who not merely worked through the text, line by line, finding innumerable typos, not to mention errors of fact, but also was able mentally to distance herself sufficiently from the detail to make a number of illuminating further suggestions.

Introduction:
A self-conscious story

Knowing that she would shortly be on her way to the gas chambers in 1943, Etty Hillesum, a young Dutch Jew, wrote in her diary:

> What was it like this morning just before I woke up? An almost tangible feeling, just as if there were all sorts of spaces and distances locked up inside me which now wanted to break out to unfold into ever wider spaces and distances. As if the distances were tangible things I had to let out. Like stamping and pawing horses from a crowded stable. That special feeling within me is very strong ... As if infinite steppes lay spread out inside me – I can see them and feel them and move over them.[1]

Etty Hillesum (1914–43) was in many ways an extraordinary young woman, but most of us today can recognize that sense of a seemingly vast space within her own mind. Speak of an 'inner world' and we all know what she means. Her description may be unusually vivid, but we can all understand and even empathize with what she is describing. At its centre was an overwhelming sense of her own individuality. This is essentially a secret space; only shared by invitation. Those 'infinite steppes' are spread out *'inside'* her, and nobody else – and, tragically, they died with her. Nevertheless, we only know about them for the simple reason that she tried to describe her secret space by writing

---

[1] *Etty: The Letters and Diaries of Etty Hillesum 1941–1943 Complete and Unabridged.* Klaas A. D. Smelik (ed.). trs. Arnold J. Pomerans, Grand Rapids, MI, Eerdmans Publishing Company, 2002. p. 435.

about it. It remained 'secret', however, in the sense that such accounts were confined to her diary. She avoided talking about them. But if it was remarkable that her diary survived her imprisonment and was preserved, it is even *more* remarkable that she wrote it down in the first place – especially since the diary also recorded other private events, such as having sex with two different lovers on the same day.[2] With little idea of a potential readership, and, indeed, if what she wrote would *ever* find any readers at all, she clearly wanted to try and describe somehow that irreducible sense of freedom of her inner self. In her own words, this was part of an attempt to convey her 'inner landscape' – for her a matter of 'great wide plains, infinitely wide, with hardly a horizon in sight – one plain merging into the next. As I sit huddled up in this chair,' she wrote, 'my head bowed low, I roam across these bare plains . . .'[3] Though at one level this was a matter of recalling the unconscious images of her dreams, the mere act of writing turned them into a conscious creation.

Like St Augustine, one of her heroes,[4] she actively wanted to invite God to share her inner space. Whether that made her 'religious' in the normal sense is doubtful. Her last communication was written on a postcard thrown from the cattle truck that transported her from Westerbork in the Netherlands to Auschwitz, the site of her death. It was found and posted by a local farmer. 'Opening the Bible at random,' she writes, 'I find this: "The Lord is my high tower".' In the original Dutch (*de Heere is mijn hoog vertrek*) *vertrek* is a pun,[5] meaning either 'high tower' or a living 'inner space'. It can also refer to a point of departure for a journey – as from a railway platform. An alternative might be: 'As I depart on this train God is my inner room.'[6] Though she was Jewish

---

[2]Many of her published letters were smuggled out of the camp (she was also involved in smuggling out children into safe hiding). She continued to write a diary in the camp but these diaries (at least two) were burnt with her at Auschwitz. Her main diary, like that of Anne Frank, was left behind in Amsterdam but, unlike that of Anne Frank, with instructions to seek its publication should she not return. See Bettine Siertsema, 'New Light on Etty Hillesum's Actions in Camp Westerbork' in Klaas A. D. Smelik (ed.) *The Lasting Significance of Etty Hillesum's Writings*, Amsterdam: Amsterdam University Press, 2019, pp. 341–52.

[3]Smelik, *Etty*, p. 60.

[4]'I felt like climbing into bed for just an hour with St. Augustine.' Ibid., p. 387.

[5]See Denise De Costa et al., *Anne Frank and Etty Hillesum: Inscribing Spirituality and Sexuality*, New Brunswick: Rutgers University Press, 1998, pp. 236–9.

[6]7 September 1943. Ibid., pp. 658–9.

by birth, her unorthodox, deeply mystical and internalized idea of a 'God', who was both part of her inner space, and, at the same time, the supreme 'other', certainly did not fit comfortably into either Jewish or Christian traditions.

> To carry the other with one, always and everywhere privately within oneself, and to live with him there ... To draw the other into one's inner space and let him go on flourishing there, to assign him a place where he can grow and unfold. To live genuinely with another ... and allow him to go on living within you ... it makes for great responsibility.[7]

Yet, even as she was physically imprisoned, and knew that she would soon be killed, what evidence we have suggests that what she calls 'this great responsibility' of a secret space was something relatively new in human experience. What had once been, as it were, a purse, a handbag or a backpack had grown into an ever-larger holdall to be filled by each owner with his or her secret personal experiences and desires, and then finally into an illimitable interior space far greater than any possible personal experience.

Compare Etty Hillesum's vivid personal account, for instance, with the description of Abraham's servant, Eliezer, by the German novelist, Thomas Mann (1875–1955), writing *Joseph and His Brothers* in exile in America at almost precisely the same time in the 1940s. Here he is trying to convey the pre-modern state of mind of someone who has little sense of himself as being separate or different from his ancestors:

> the old man's ego was not quite clearly demarcated, that it opened at the back, as it were, and overflowed into spheres external to his own individuality both in space and time; embodying in his own experience events which, remembered in the clear light of day, ought actually to have been put into the third person ... The concept of individuality belongs after all to the same category as that of unity and entirety, the whole and the all; and in the days of which I am writing the distinction between spirit in general and individual spirit possessed not nearly so much power of the mind as in our

---

[7]Ibid., p. 281.

world of today ... It is highly significant that in those days there were no words for conceptions dealing with personality and individuality ...[8]

Even a cursory view of what we know of the history of consciousness shows a pattern of slow evolution. Indeed, so far from being a simple and easily traceable development, this idea of an evolving history of consciousness is itself ambiguous, complex and capable of many interpretations.[9] What we can say is that Mann's Eliezer has what modern social anthropologists would call a 'dividual' consciousness, as distinct from an 'individual' one. The best evidence we have is that for thousands of years – from the dawn of recorded time – most people thought and felt more like Mann's fictional Eliezer than the very real twentieth-century Etty Hillesum.[10] If they had a sense of personal identity, it was by reference to external things: their family, their clan, their tribe, even to their station in life as an aristocrat, a soldier, a hunter, a craftsman or a servant. Even one's fate in the afterlife was originally a collective one, and only later made personal.[11] As late as the classical Roman period an official classification of social ranks was widely recognized: senatorial (the natural rulers), equestrian (a military upper class), decurian (provincial and civic leaders and magistrates), plebeian (small traders and craftsmen), freedmen and slaves. Which may account for why, according to Mary Beard,[12] so many freed slaves who had become successful Roman citizens chose to describe themselves on their tombstones by their professions. If you were a woman, your identity would be even more tightly bound into your family or social group. People would commonly refer to themselves, by name, in the third person. In the Old Testament it is usually only God who says 'I'.[13] Those fortunate enough to

---

[8]Thomas Mann, *Joseph and His Brothers*, tr. H.T. Lowe-Porter, (Knopf, 1948) Penguin, 1988, p. 78.

[9]Erich Neuman's book, *The Origins and History of Consciousness* (1949), is more a speculative piece of Jungian psychology than a general historical account.

[10]Three very different writers who have taken up this theme are Erich Auerbach, *Mimesis: The Representation of Reality in Western Literature*, Princeton University Press, 1953; Owen Barfield, *Saving the Appearances*, Harcourt Brace, 1957; and Julian Jaynes, *The Origins of Consciousness in the Breakdown of the Bicameral Mind*, Boston: Houghton Mifflin, 1976.

[11]See Bart D. Ehrman, *Heaven and Hell: A History of the Afterlife*, Oneworld Books, 2020, p. xix.

[12]BBC TV Programme, *Meet the Romans*, 2012.

[13]There are, of course, exceptions to this. Psalm 3, traditionally ascribed to David, uses the personal 'I', as does Job – but David, of course, was also a King.

believe that they were being addressed by Him, tended to reply with suitably humble self-descriptions. Even in the New Testament, Simeon's joy at seeing the infant Jesus follows the accepted third-person self-description, saying, in the King James version of Luke's Gospel: 'Lord now lettest thou thy servant depart in peace . . .' Unlike some modern translations, the King James Bible is still close enough to this world to repeat the conventional 'externalized' view of the speaker. Nor was the classical world any different.

Julius Hare (1795–1855), a perceptive Victorian critic, notes that in *Medea*, a late Roman play by Seneca (died AD 65), Medea, the Queen of Colchis, deserted by her husband, Jason, says bitterly '*Medea superest*'. 'An English poet,' Hare writes, would hardly say 'Medea remains'. In contrast, what he rather contemptuously calls 'a modern' Italian opera has Medea reply to Jason's question '*Che mi resta?*' with the simple pronoun '*Io*' ('I'). 'An ancient poet could not have used the pronoun; a modern poet could hardly use the proper name.'[14] There are many traces of this even in Shakespeare. *Richard III*, one of his early plays, spans the transition more explicitly than most, where Richard, steadying himself (unsuccessfully) before the battle of Bosworth, uses the words 'Richard loves Richard; that is, I am I.' It is a mark of his own disintegration that it is hard here to define which is the royal, which the personal.

As in the Roman world, class still played a part in self-discovery well into the eighteenth century. Royalty might use the first person – either the singular 'I' or the political plural 'We' – but humbler subjects took some time to travel the same route. Part of the scandal in the reception of the *Figaro* trilogy by the French polymath Pierre-Augustin Caron de Beaumarchais (1732–99) was that the principal figure was an inferior – a servant – who runs rings around his aristocratic patrons. But in the Beaumarchais play, *The Marriage of Figaro*, and, even more famously, in the *largo al factotum* in Rossini's Italian opera, *The Barber of Seville* (1816), Figaro alternates between boastful arias, where he describes himself one moment in the third person, and then, more assertively, as 'I' in the next. This did not pass unnoticed. Louis XVI himself had taken great exception to Beaumarchais's text in the last act of *The Marriage*, where Figaro directly challenges the Count.

---

[14]Julius Hare, *Guesses at Truth* (1827), Vol. 1, pp. 116–17.

No, my lord Count, you shan't have her … you shall not have her! Just because you are a great nobleman, you think you are a great genius – Nobility, fortune, rank, position! How proud they make a man feel! What have *you* done to deserve such advantages? Put yourself to the trouble of being born – nothing more. For the rest – a very ordinary man! Whereas I, lost among the obscure crowd, have had to deploy more knowledge, more calculation and skill merely to survive than has sufficed to rule all the provinces of Spain for a century![15]

For 1786, only three years before the French Revolution, this was dangerous stuff. Georges Danton (1759–94), soon to be one of the revolutionary leaders, said that Beaumarchais's play had 'killed off the nobility'; Napoleon called it 'the Revolution in action'. The huge popularity of the Beaumarchais original, not to mention the da Ponte and Mozart opera, indicated just how dramatic was this shift in consciousness. That shift was all the more dramatic in that in the 1770s Beaumarchais had spent much of his time in London, in effect acting as a secret agent of Louis XVI during the American War. Now he had changed sides. Louis saw – and hated – what was happening, but signally failed to understand the consequences for himself …

Yet already the novel was exploring the emergence of secret spaces. *Pride and Prejudice* (1813) by Jane Austen (1775–1817) combines a keen awareness of social hierarchy even while quietly asserting the primacy and privacy of independent selfhood. This comes to its climax in the famous confrontation between Lady Catherine de Burgh and Elizabeth Bennet over her relationship to Lady Catherine's nephew, Mr Darcy. 'Miss Bennet,' says Lady Catherine, 'do you know who I am? … I am almost the nearest relation he has in this world, and I am entitled to know all his dearest concerns.' 'But,' replies Elizabeth, 'you are not entitled to know *mine*.'[16] This is by no means the first example, but there

---

[15]*Non, monsieur le comte, vous ne l'aurez pas … vous ne l'aurez pas. Parce que vous êtes un grand seigneur, vous vous croyez un grand génie! … noblesse, fortune, un rang, des places, tout cela rend si fier! Qu'avez-vous fait pour tant de biens? vous vous êtes donné la peine de naître, et rien de plus: du reste, homme assez ordinaire! tandis que moi, morbleu, perdu dans la foule obscure, il m'a fallu déployer plus de science et de calculs pour subsister seulement, qu'on n'en a mis depuis cent ans à gouverner toutes les Espagnes; et vous voulez jouter!* Le Mariage de Figaro, Act V, sc 111.

[16]*Pride and Prejudice*, Chatto & Windus, 1898, Vol. 2, pp. 205–6.

speaks the new voice. It is those who preserve their secret selves most guardedly who emerge as the heroines in Austen's novels.

Such shifts of consciousness have long been recognized, though not always understood in the same way. The eponymous hero of Mrs Humphry Ward's best-selling novel, *Robert Elsmere* (1888), delves into what she calls a 'history of testimony' – based on the evidence that people of different historical periods have understood and therefore described their worlds in radically different ways. For her, this meant that whereas early Christian and medieval saints lived in societies permeated by miracles, for the more scientifically sophisticated nineteenth century miracles did not happen, and, where necessary, more prosaic explanations of these events had to be found. Nevertheless, the awkward persistence of reported visions, miracles, and other extreme events into Mrs Ward's own era has since led to a more nuanced historical approach. Thus, we simply *cannot* say what exactly happened to the peasant girl, Bernadette Soubirous, near the French town of Lourdes in 1858 when she reported seeing the Virgin Mary. It constituted a 'singularity' not accessible to any historical investigation. We can invent speculative psychological 'explanations' but, in the end, they remain guesswork. They *explain* nothing. Whatever one may believe about her story, however, what *is* verifiable history is that her testimony was responsible for Lourdes becoming one of the world's most frequented sites of pilgrimage and religious tourism, receiving around six million visitors a year, making it the third most important site of international Catholic pilgrimage after Rome and Israel – with correspondingly important consequences for the transport system and hospitality industries of the entire region of France. Here, it would seem, something in the inaccessible inner space of Bernadette's mind has, nevertheless, radically transformed the economy of an entire French province.

If such an interaction of inner and outer worlds were not enough, more complicated still is what has been called 'double consciousness' – an awareness not merely of ourselves as individuals, but of ourselves *as if* we were external spectators of our own actions. An outer consciousness invades our original inner space so that we have, in effect, not one but *two* inner spaces. Everyone who has ever given a public lecture is aware of what it is like to watch themselves as they speak – checking for faults in delivery, audience response and planning where they are going next. But we have all, in some way or another, had the experience of watching ourselves. Sometimes it is the cause of acute embarrassment; less often – much less often! – a cause of self-congratulation; occasionally – very occasionally – a source of precious self-knowledge. As so often Rudyard Kipling (1865–1936) captures this perfectly in his 1890 poem 'Tommy Atkins':

> I WENT into a public 'ouse to get a pint o' beer,
> The publican 'e up an' sez, 'We serve no red-coats here.'
> The girls be'ind the bar they laughed an' giggled fit to die,
> I outs into the street again an' to myself sez I:
> O it's Tommy this, an' Tommy that, an' 'Tommy, go away';
> But it's 'Thank you, Mister Atkins,' when the band begins to play.

'To myself sez I . . .'. That capacity to narrate a story where an individual mentally addresses him or herself as someone separate from the speaker constitutes a particular kind of double consciousness. In this case, that the supposed speaker is very definitely working class – or, in the Duke of Wellington's telling phrase about his own troops, 'the scum of the earth enlisted for drink' – is equally revealing. This is a hundred years later than Figaro, and, now, even the common soldier (at least according to Kipling) exhibits a double consciousness once the sole preserve of the monarchy and aristocracy.

Such a double consciousness is central to our picture of ourselves.[17] It is the only chance we have to try and see ourselves as others see us. It creates a kind of residue, a memory, layer upon layer of who we are – and, perhaps, who we would like to be. Nowadays we automatically tend to think of memory as something individual. Much of it, then and now, clearly *is* personal, but if we are to believe psychologists like Jung, we may also have a 'race memory' going back thousands, if not hundreds of thousands of years. Fear of spiders and snakes, or a love of heights and broad open views, may even, according to some anthropologists, hark back to what might be called our 'ape-history', before our simian ancestors had descended from the trees – if they ever were

---

[17]We can, of course, also watch our selves watching ourselves, and so on in a kind of infinite regress, but this does not change the initial duality.

arboreal. Whether or not this is true, we can be much more certain about the role our own personal memories have played in constructing who, and what, we are. As we have seen in the contrast between ancient and modern consciousness, there is no doubt that human culture, in all its many and varied forms, plays a huge part in how we receive and structure the stuff of memory. What makes us remember some childhood experiences all our lives, and forget nearly all the rest? Indeed, a visitor from outer space might be interested in a culture that produces anthropologists interested in relating such preferences about spiders or aerial viewpoints to a speculative evolutionary history.

But if memory provides some of the content of that infinite inner space, much of the rest is the product of what, with post-Romantic secularity, we call 'imagination' – literally, the power to conjure up images of things not present to our senses. Even this word has its own cultural history, shifting almost imperceptibly from that original capacity to recall particular images to the modern sense of personal creativity. More precisely, for the Romantics that creativity is associated with a bringing together of the two levels of consciousness we have just been looking at in the form of symbols. According to the pre-historian Yuval Noah Harari, there seems to have been what he calls a 'cognitive revolution' about 70,000 years ago when a few members of *Homo sapiens*, a hitherto unremarkable member of the Ape family, but who probably already had language of some sort, developed the capacity to talk about things that they had never seen, touched or smelled.[18] This cognitive revolution included whole categories of abstractions, including the ideas of tribes, gods, stories, myths, legends, and various kinds of advance planning. In what might be called (at least in evolutionary terms) 'short order' people seem to have invented boats, oil lamps, bows and arrows, and needles (essential for making warm clothing) – and, in the long term, above all, art.[19] Harari makes it clear how vitally important this capacity for abstraction has turned out to be. It includes almost every form of human self-identification and collective groupings, from religions, to nations, political parties, and even limited liability companies. In a very entertaining exercise of de-familiarization, he has a section

---

[18]Yuval Noah Harari. *Sapiens: A Brief History of Humankind*, Penguin Random House, 2011. p. 27.
[19]Ibid., p. 23

on 'The Legend of Peugeot' – asking *where* exactly is this car company, 'Peugeot', to be found? Is it to be found in its managers? In its workers? In its factories and plant? On the stock exchange? Or even perhaps simply in the rampant lion on the front of cars?[20] The answer, of course, is that like so many things in our everyday lives, it is just one of thousands of imaginary but nevertheless real entities that surround us in our everyday lives. Indeed, our whole sense of who we are is largely composed of such membership of imaginary but very real entities – including our personal affiliations, our workplace, and even our spiritual values.

For some, however, even the idea of 'spiritual values' remains *essentially* unreal. The philosopher, Immanuel Kant, held that such objects of belief as God, the design of creation, the soul, and its freedom and immortality, because they have no physical component, are not properly objects of knowledge at all. William James – brother of the novelist, Henry James – commented rather tartly:

> Yet strangely enough they have a definite meaning for our practice. We can act as if there were a God ... consider Nature as if she were full of special designs, lay plans as if we were to be immortal; and we find then that these words make a definite difference to our moral lives ... So we have the strange phenomenon, as Kant assures us, of the mind believing with all its strength in ... a set of things of no one of which can it form any notion whatsoever.[21]

Perhaps rather alarmingly, many of the most important things in our lives are not merely unverifiable in practice, they cannot *ever* be verified. But that, of course, does not diminish their importance.

Such imaginary entities consist not merely of imaginary things, but no less importantly, imaginary *spaces*. St Augustine (AD 354–430), author of a spiritual autobiography known simply as the *Confessions*, calls these interior spaces 'caverns'. Though some caverns may be dark and gloomy, others are flooded with light and teeming with life. Though he starts by writing of them as part of

---

[20]Ibid., pp. 28–31.
[21]William James, *The Varieties of Religious Experience* [1902], Harvard University Press, 1985, pp. 52–3.

memory, he rapidly admits that memory and imagination run into one another in ways that are hard to distinguish. In this he was, as so often, anticipating modern psychology. There is abundant evidence, especially from what psychologists call the 'false-memory syndrome', that what we firmly believe to be memory alone is also shaped by imagination in ways we are often not even conscious of. A recent book on memory goes further, arguing that memory is *essentially* an imaginative process. It is 'not a PDF we open and reread on a computer, or a camera filled with high-definition images'. It seems to be 'more like live theatre, where there are constant new productions of the same pieces'.[22] Brain scans suggest that remembering something looks very similar to imagining it. Indeed, as we shall see, imagination lights up everything else we experience. If it illuminates the selections of memory, it draws also on what we have read, what others – parents, teachers, friends, the spoken and visual media – have told us about, but all this huge mass of stories, reading, acquired images, television, cinema, videos, things remembered and half-remembered, is invisibly given form, organized and structured by the world we have been brought up in. That environment organizes and tightly structures all of this huge mass of memories, sounds, images, tastes and smells. It shapes not just our conscious perceptions, but no less our unconscious ones. If we have visions or ecstatic experiences, Christians have 'Christian' visions, Buddhists have 'Buddhist' ones. It creates but also limits our imagination. We call it, quite simply, 'culture'. But because our culture so dominates who we are, and who we believe ourselves to be, it is difficult (though, as we shall see, not impossible) to step outside it.

For the poet Samuel Taylor Coleridge (1772–1834), who probably re-defined the word 'imagination' in its modern sense and did more to develop it than any of his generation, even the definition of the word rested on an essentially theological base. Though he would probably not have recognized the word in this sense, what we would now call his 'Romanticism' can itself be seen as a return to religious traditions that had tended to atrophy under the

---

[22]See Hilde Ostby and Ylva Ostby, *Adventures in Memory: The Science and Secrets of Remembering and Forgetting*, tr. Marianne Lindvalle, Greystone, 2018. p. 109. But, as so often, fiction precedes science. The last section of Doris Lessing's *Golden Notebook* (1964), describes memory in terms of a cinematic projection with constantly changing events and emphases. See below, Chapter 4.

Enlightenment.[23] In a world whose theories of perception and even psychology were to evolve from a combination of Newtonian experiments with light and Kant's theory of the mind, behind the Romantic experience of the self was at least two thousand years of spiritual evolution – some Christian, but before that, classical Greek and Jewish traditions stretching back even further into the past.

If we cannot so easily step outside our culture, we are even more constrained when it comes to source material. There are actually very few ways of trying to understand the past. Gene testing is one; archaeology provides another. There are even hints from pre-history – an obvious case would be the so-called Lion man of Ulm, at 35 to 40 thousand years old, probably the earliest known example of the creation of something that the creator can never have seen, and therefore the earliest known imaginary object.[24] We can even learn something from studying the art, symbolism and architecture of the more recent past. Genes will tell us a lot about our distant ancestry, migrations of people, interbreeding of races and, now it seems, even between various human species: Neanderthal, Denisovan, Florian etc. By digging up graves and what remains of buildings, archaeologists can learn a great deal about the way people once lived, where they came from, what they ate, and even how they died. Paintings, and other visual arts, major public buildings, including palaces, law courts, temples and the great cathedrals are often replete with the symbolism of their respective functions.[25]

None of these, however, valuable as they may be, gives us any information about the inner space of those former generations, if, indeed, they had any; nor how individual people thought and felt about themselves and the world around them. One of the more amusing aspects of archaeology-talk is the desperate attribution of anything that baffles the diggers to conjectural 'cults' or, more generally 'religion'. But, on the other hand, since so much of their work involves the excavation of graves, this may well be appropriate. Overwhelmingly however, our prime – *almost* our only – source of information on the history

---

[23]He would not, of course, have called it that. See Stephen Prickett, *Romanticism and Religion*, Cambridge University Press, 1976, and Louis Dupré, *The Quest of the Absolute: Birth and Decline of European Romanticism*, Notre Dame: University of Notre Dame Press, 2013.

[24]See Neil MacGregor, *Living with the Gods,* Penguin, 2018.

[25]See, for instance, Pamela Tudor-Craig, *One Half of Our noblest Art: A study of the sculptures of Wells west front* (1976).

of inner space in human consciousness is through writing: originally through religious texts, historical narratives, and, now above all in the last few hundred years, literary fiction. As we shall see, the newest intimate art-form, the cinema, though presented as a visual experience, almost always has behind it a written script – often adapted from a previous novel.

The *Epic of Gilgamesh* and some bits of the sacred Hindu texts are probably the oldest written texts we have, but much more comes from the so-called 'axial age', roughly the eighth to the third century BCE.[26] This would comprise, among others, the ideas of Confucius in China, Zoroaster in Persia, Buddha in India, the eighth-century prophets in Israel, and the Greek philosophers such as Socrates, Plato and Aristotle. For us, in the culture of Western Europe and North America, that tends to mean the Greek and Latin literature and the Bible. Even then, as we shall see, it is not easy to guess exactly what was part of the *inner* worlds of the participants, and what, for them at least, was felt to be 'external'. Certainly, what evidence we have from these early writings suggests that much of what we think of as internal, was experienced by them as external.

If, then, this investigation seems to rely more on works of literature over the past five hundred years than on other sources, there is a very good reason. For better or worse that is where the vast bulk of our evidence originates. Though there are rare individual exceptions (such as Augustine's *Confessions*), the novel, in all its various shapes, is the first popular art-form to concentrate primarily on the inner space of its characters. Indeed, thought of this way, we can say that not merely is the novel form essentially about inner worlds – about what are always and inevitably private spaces – but that inner worlds have themselves evolved with the development of fiction-writing. Which brings home very clearly the central paradox of all literature: that invented stories may tell us more about people than so-called 'true' stories do. 'All writers,' wrote Ernest Hemingway, 'are liars.' All fiction, he went on, 'is just lies made truer than the truth.' Hemingway was, perhaps, a bigger liar than most, but the claim rings true. Nevertheless, is this so very strange? By their very nature, *all* excursions into our inner worlds are 'fictions' in the obvious sense that no

---

[26]The term coined by German philosopher Karl Jaspers, in *The Origin and Goal of History* (*Vom Ursprung und Ziel der Geschichte*), 1949.

external verification is possible. We have no idea if what someone is telling us about themselves, their thoughts, their ideas, their aspirations, is true or false. Early novelists were very conscious of this problem. Not for nothing did many novels of the seventeenth and eighteenth centuries have some anecdotal preface to explain how they came to be written or published, and/or take the form of improbably lengthy letters from one of the protagonists to another to add some kind of further appearance of truth. Moreover, there is, of course, no sharp boundary between fiction and fact. All fiction, even fantasy, is drawn from somewhere: either from the personal experience of the writer, or from the writer's imagination – which, however distorted, has in turn roots somewhere in the real world – or from other writing. And this last category is probably the largest of all. The Anglo-Irish academic and popular writer, C.S.Lewis (1898–1963), for example, had an astonishingly original imagination, but he was also possessed of a truly astonishing capacity to draw on his reading and take the mythology of others, re-furbish it, dust it down, and use it in quite new contexts. Thus in the seven children's books about his imaginary world of Narnia he brings together the whole tradition of European literature into apparently seamless fantasy, and charges them with new depths of meaning. Any child who reads them has been introduced, unknowingly, to almost the whole of European literature and theology: though it may take that same child almost a lifetime to recognize what it has learned – and I use 'recognize' in the philosopher Plato's very particular sense that we *recognize* the truth when we encounter it, rather than have to discover or learn it.

What evidence we have, therefore, suggests that Christianity, combining Judaic and Greek roots in the early centuries of its growth, gave rise not merely to a stronger sense of individuality (and, therefore, of individual destiny) than any other civilization, but also to a correspondingly unique sense of inner space. As the French philosopher and confessional writer François-René de Chateaubriand (1768–1848) argued some two hundred years ago, it is now impossible to separate the ideas, values and patterns of thought in European civilization from their Christian base.[27] Even that arch-sceptic, Voltaire, as

---

[27] A point brilliantly made by Larry Siedentop, *Inventing the Individual: The origins of Western Liberalism*, Allen Lane (Penguin), 2014, and reiterated, no less brilliantly, but in a slightly different key by Tom Holland in *Dominion: The Making of the Western Mind*, Little, Brown, 2019.

Chateaubriand gleefully pointed out, was heir to that tradition – and his resistance to it was no more than might be expected of a culture that has always retained a self-critical (or perhaps, in theological terms, 'prophetic') element – a point effectively repeated by the theologian, David Bentley Hart in his recent critique of the most vocal contemporary atheists, such as Dawkins, Harris, Hitchins or Wilson.[28]

Byron, the Romantic poet, was certainly no friend to Christianity, but nevertheless deploys biblical imagery to proclaim an inner world not as promoting any kind of spiritual awareness but, on the contrary, as a barrier against the 'tyrannous threats' of an over-bearing religious establishment. In his play, *Cain*, Lucifer claims the Fall itself as the foundation of a new kind of 'inner world'.

> Think and endure, – and form an inner world
> In your own bosom – where the outward fails;
> So shall you nearer be the spiritual.
> Nature . . .[29]

If the Christian myth of the Fall had, indeed, originally helped to form such an inner world, that inwardness was always tensional, and – as Byron saw by invoking Lucifer – it was not so much the path into inner peace as providing a new area of conflict.

The long historical movement from externalized to internalized experience, from shame culture to guilt culture, from projection to contemplation, has been well traced by many critics, historians and social scientists. For many, St Augustine would seem to have been the first to show a modern consciousness of self; others have found similar milestones of interiority in Dante, Chaucer and Shakespeare.[30] Over the last two millennia there is a sense in which even the idea of what constituted an individual has itself changed – a point expressed brilliantly, if perhaps anachronistically, in Thomas Mann's portrait of Joseph in his novel *Joseph and His Brothers*. Whether or not the historical Joseph really

---

[28]David Bentley Hart, *Atheist Delusions: The Christian Revolution and Its Fashionable Enemies*, New Haven, Yale University Press, 2009.

[29]Byron: *Cain* II.ii. pp. 463–6.

[30]See Chapter 2, below.

possessed such a sharply modern consciousness,[31] in contradistinction to Eliezer, it is certainly true that a thousand years later those prepared to endure martyrdom in the various Roman persecutions of Christians must have had an extraordinarily strong sense of their own personal identity – even of their personal exceptionalism – to go to as they did to their very public deaths.

Such a sense of identity also gives a new spin to the common saying that 'history is written by the victors'. It is more often written by the losers. The Christian martyrs were unlikely to have seen themselves as 'victors' in anything but a spiritual sense, but it was their testimony, written either by them or their co-religionists, that *made* them into the victors. Similarly the Old Testament is a long record of the humiliations and defeats of the people of Israel, but simply being the forerunner of what was deemed to be the divinely-inspired story of Christianity gave it final authority until at least the end of the eighteenth century. In secular terms we note the virtual monopoly of novels from the Royalist side in the English Civil War, or from the Southern side in the American – most famously in *Gone with the Wind*. Who now reads Cromwell's accounts of his battles, or, apart from the Gettysburg Address, of Lincoln's? Winston Churchill's comment on his victory was suitably cynical: 'History will be kind to me, since I intend to write it myself.'

We take it for granted that we all have our own story to tell, and that story is what makes us, *us*. We can equally take it for granted that every single person we pass on the street has a complex interior world in their heads that we will know nothing of. Thus a recent popular novel, *One Day*, by David Nicholls, described the death of its heroine not in terms of the destruction of her physical body (in a road accident) but in terms of the instantaneous obliteration of her inner world: all her memories, ideas, hopes, fears and desires.[32] But when and how did this 'post-Eliezer' consciousness begin? It is probably too simple to say that this is a simply a literary creation. But it certainly coincides with literacy. More likely is that this is a two-way process of emergence. We read about the interior lives of others, and this, in turn, expands our own interior consciousness, which then becomes the subject of further writing. But this

---

[31]Mann himself admitted that his 'Joseph' incorporated elements of Roosevelt's 'New Deal' of the 1930s.
[32]David Nicholls, *One Day*, Hodder and Stoughton, 2009.

process begins with literacy itself. Learning to read is not merely a matter of mastering (in English) some 26 letters. We don't read by looking at the letters. We read by taking in whole words – when we meet an unfamiliar or new word we are usually stopped in our tracks for a moment. Reading automatically increases our vocabularies, and with enhanced vocabularies comes an increase in ideas, experiences, new ways of seeing and understanding the world. New words, new descriptions of things, give us experiences we would probably otherwise never have had. Not for nothing is it sometimes claimed that Shakespeare had the largest vocabulary of any English-speaking person. While this is probably untrue, it bears witness to the enormous range and depth of experiences covered by his writing.[33]

More first-hand evidence can be traced in the inexorable expansion of interiority through the Metaphysical poets, the Romantics, and poets such as Walt Whitman (1819–92) in America. In our post-Romantic world we acknowledge, perhaps even expect, complexity, uncertainty and often contradiction in biographies of real individuals and characters in novels. There is a sense in which the whole development of European (and, later, transatlantic) literature is concerned with exploring this unfolding and ever-growing interior world. As we shall be seeing in the following chapters, modern fiction is an art-form more or less constructed on the premise of the rich interior lives of the characters described.

As we shall see in Chapter 3, some art historians have seen a parallel to this process in terms of the growth of visual 'realism'. For them, realism was itself a *product* of internalization. Technical developments, such as perspective, important as these were, served rather than created the new style. A new religious practice, known as the *Devotio Moderna*, popular in the Burgundian Netherlands in the fifteenth century, found in visual realism a way of shaping a new kind of spirituality. As always, such a new spirituality uncovers corresponding terrors. Hieronymus Bosch (d. 1516) belongs to the same period and place. Though one can see a Renaissance painting of a Madonna, or a portrait of the artist's patron, as conventionally 'exterior', even here such realism can increasingly be read in terms of interior states of mind, as in Velazquez's famous portrait of Pope

---

[33] The latest discussion of this is John Kerrigan, *Shakespeare's Originality,* Oxford University Press, 2018.

Innocent X (1650), while, for instance, the paintings of Van Gogh (1853–90) or *The Scream* (1893) by Edvard Munch (1863–1944) offer much stronger evidence of a troubled interior consciousness.

If we accept the argument that the *Devotio Moderna* was a key element in the Reformation across northern Europe, which in turn was to inspire corresponding spiritual movements in literature, the idea that literary realism is *also* the product of internalization is worth exploring. It would, for instance, certainly go some way to explain a phenomenon that has often intrigued critics: that, contrary to obvious expectations, eighteenth-century novels often seem much more unrealistic than nineteenth-century ones. But this assumes a conventional movement from naïve realism towards what we now think of as the modernist and 'experimental' writing of the twentieth century. If, on the other hand, we see realism as essentially a by-product of an ever-greater sense of personal interiority, then the sequence seems much more logical. We recall that glorious comic moment in *Tristram Shandy*, by Lawrence Sterne (1713–68), where Tristram discovers that so detailed and tortuous is the description of his mental history that his autobiography is now proceeding more slowly than his real life!

Leonard Shlan (1937–2009) a medical scientist and historian, has pointed out how, at almost the same time in the sixteenth century, art, music and physics all came to recognize the need for a single favoured 'point of view'.

> In perspectivist art, the entire canvas was designed to be seen by a passive spectator, standing in the favoured location several feet in front of the painting. In physics, an external reality could be measured because the observer was peering at it through a telescope from a favoured position of absolute rest. In music, the principle of a single point of view became manifest in the form of key . . .[34]

Observing the external world now demands a viewpoint. As we shall see, especially in Chapter 3, inner space is both logically and historically prior to any representation of 'outer' space.

---

[34]Leonard Shlan, *Art and Physics: Parallel Visions in Space, Time and Light*, New York: William Morrow, 1991. See also Stephen Prickett, *Narrative, Religion and Science: Fundamentalism versus Irony 1700–1999*, Cambridge University Press, 2002, pp. 241–2.

For some members of a new wave of brain researchers, however, such philosophical niceties are irrelevant. For them consciousness is not so much a matter of interiorization as of electrical impulses in the brain. What is often dismissed as 'mysticism' must be an obvious waste of time, because consciousness, memory, and everything that takes place in the mind is, in the end, nothing more than a matter of synapses in the brain.[35] Such reductionism illustrates how separated various specialisms have now become. Few students of mystical – or, for that matter, any other specific states of mind – would dispute that there is a physical counterpart to any and every particular mental experience. The fact that all Shakespeare's work was a matter of neurones and synapses in his brain does not in any way detract from the quality of his genius or from the uniqueness of his writing. As one physical psychologist puts it, 'there is, and can be, no ... division between my brain and nervous system ... the self is not a neural object.'[36]

I recall that in the 1970s and 1980s, when computers were just beginning their astonishing technical progress, many computer scientists as well as members of the general public assumed that when computers reached a certain degree of complexity – roughly corresponding to that of the human brain – they would show a corresponding degree of consciousness. We have now, of course, created computers capable of vastly outstripping human powers of calculation and, useful as these are, they remain just that – machines. If desired, they can be programmed to show many superficially convincing imitations of human consciousness, including the ability to answer (predictable) questions, and even to learn from specific experiences, such as playing chess, but this is, nevertheless, precisely no more and no less than what they have been programmed to do. An increasing number of telephone enquiries are now dealt with by such computers. But, nevertheless, they are not *conscious* beings in the same sense that we – or even our pet dogs – are. They have no intelligence as we understand the term, no common sense. The result has been described

---

[35]Harari himself is seriously guilty of this cheap scientism: 'Scientists studying the inner workings of the human organism have found no soul there. They increasingly argue that human behavior is determined by hormones, genes and synapses rather than free will ..', *Sapiens*, p. 263. See also Raymond Tallis's review of Patricia Churchland's *Conscience: The Origin of Moral Intuition*, Times Literary Supplement, 26 June 2000.

[36]Denis Noble, (Oxford Professor of Cardiovascular Physiology), *The Music of Life: Biology Beyond Genes*, Oxford University Press, 2006, pp. 127–8.

as 'an artificial *idiot savant* that can excel at well-bounded tasks, but can get things very wrong if faced with unexpected input.'[37]

In a parallel movement to recent work on the brain, and its relation to cultural history, Iain McGilchrist's *The Master and His Emissary* offers a different and fascinating perspective on the history of Western culture.[38] While he does not directly discuss the role of religious belief or mysticism in that process, his ideas are entirely congruent with such an approach – and indeed even at times seem to require something approaching a version of Original Sin to describe the subversion of the right-hand lobe of the brain by the left. Certainly, the idea of tracing the development of Western culture in terms of an innate tension between the sides of the brain in our psychological development is both novel and revealing.

Nor is this cultural process confined to poetry or fiction. The very forces that seem to have created this long evolutionary development of consciousness seem to have been caught up, reflexively, in the process. As has been suggested, philosophy and even theology itself have progressively moved towards a recognition of inner space. The Reformation, with its emphasis on individual responsibility, was coupled with the invention of printing and a corresponding explosion of literacy,[39] but the Counter-Reformation bears witness to the fact that this trend did not remain peculiar to Protestantism – as the spiritual exercises of St Ignatius Loyola (1491–1556) show. No less significant is the Romantic development of the idea of the unconscious, and historical distance, with the appearance of new words, such as 'psychology', and 'hermeneutics' at the beginning of the nineteenth century. Even biblical criticism reveals similar tendencies. By the end of the eighteenth century biblical commentaries of all persuasions start to display an interest in the notion of 'character', and read biblical narratives less in traditional terms of typology, and more novelistically in terms of the inward motivation of individuals.[40]

---

[37]See 'Reality Check', *Economist*, June 13, 2020.

[38]Iain McGilchrist, *The Master and His Emissary: The Divided Brain and the Making of the Western World*, Yale University Press, 2009.

[39]Though Henry VIII's suppression of monastic schools may have actually *lowered* literacy in the immediate years after the English Reformation.

[40]See Stephen Prickett, *Origins of Narrative: The Romantic Appropriation of the Bible*, Cambridge University Press, 1996.

No culture, no religion, exists in isolation. Of the three great 'religions of the book', Judaism, Christianity and Islam, Christianity, by incorporating the Hebrew Bible into the Christian one, is the most open in admitting how much it has inherited from its parent. By the same token, it has also been the one that has most obviously changed in the course of its existence. Indeed, John Henry Newman (1801–90), the nineteenth-century convert from Anglicanism to the Roman Catholic Church, scandalized his critics by arguing that *change* was an essential 'sign of life' in an organization as much as in an individual, and the fact that Catholicism seemed *less* like the early Church than its Protestant rivals was actually itself a sign of its greater truth and vitality.[41]

What part religions have played in this growing self-consciousness is debatable, but in so far as they have promoted contemplation, self-examination and inner centredness, they have clearly pointed the way. By stressing its origins in the rejection of ideas of Jewish racial purity, codes of behaviour and dietary laws, Christianity has always been flexible, pragmatic and adaptable in a way that is much more difficult for Judaism and Islam, both of which are based on (relatively) inflexible and prescriptive legal codes.[42] For this very reason, it has (usually) been much more historically self-aware, both in its consciousness of change, and its efforts to understand and come to terms with those changes. Similarly, Christians have always recognized their scriptures as *translations*. Rather than adhering to the original languages of their Revelations, like Judaism and Islam (classical Hebrew and seventh-century Arabic respectively), Christianity has thus engaged in a kind of inward critical dialogue with itself, which has often been more difficult (though certainly never impossible) for the other two.

It is that story of growth and development of inner space and (no less significantly) the story of our growing consciousness of that inner world – what we feel makes us peculiarly *us*, and not someone else – that we shall try and pursue through the following pages.

---

[41] *The Development of Christian Doctrine* (1845).
[42] See *Interpreting Scriptures in Judaism, Christianity and Islam: Overlapping Inquiries*, eds. Adele Berlin and Mordechai Z. Cohen, Cambridge University Press, 2016.

1

Visions, dreams – and that which hath no bottom

Some two thousand eight hundred years ago a small boy was wakened from sleep by a voice calling his name. Not unreasonably, he first thought it was the voice of his master, a 98-year-old priest, to whom he was indentured. But after a quick check had resulted in equally quick denials, he replied to the mysterious voice in the customary third person of a servant to a superior, 'Speak; for thy servant heareth.'[1]

Thus, according to the Bible, the voice of God came personally to Samuel, but with public implications affecting a whole community: 'at which both the ears of every one that heareth it shall tingle ...'. The startling and unwelcome prophecy was that Eli, his master, was to be punished, 'because his sons made themselves vile, and he restrained them not' (1 Samuel 3.13). Both crime and punishment reflect the common assumption of that culture: that whatever individuality you may possess takes its form from your social context. Families were a single unit. Individuals had no real identity outside their extended family and tribe. Parents were responsible for their adult children; in this case misbehaviour by the latter resulted in the elimination of the entire line. And so, in the following chapter, we find both Eli's sons killed in battle with the Philistines. When the news is brought to him the old priest collapses and dies.

Though the episode that awakened the boy Samuel is actually described in the King James Bible as a 'vision' (1 Samuel 3.15), what is recorded in the

---

[1]King James Version, 1 Sam. 3.10.

passage quoted above is, of course, *not* a 'vision' at all in our modern sense of the word. The Hebrew word *ḥāzôn* covers visions in all our modern figurative meanings: from sights of things normally unseen to ecstatic states and even oracles and prophecies. But though, in retrospect, one might certainly describe what he experienced as some kind of supernatural event, Samuel himself is described as being quite sure he hears a *real* voice. The narrator of 1 Kings had no conception of any other form of communication. Our modern distinction between 'outer' and 'inner' experiences simply did not yet exist. As with the punishment for Eli's sons, this is a world of shame rather than guilt, where moments of inspiration are discovered as voices heard through the ears, rather than what we might nowadays describe, in a metaphor from twentieth-century technology, as 'light-bulb' moments of insight.[2] A 'vision', like any other discovery, is something experienced through the normal senses.

Fast-forward for perhaps another hundred years. The prophet Elijah is on the run from Ahab, the king. He has fled to Horeb, 'the mount of God'. He too is confronted with something like a vision. But this one is different.

> And behold, the Lord passed by, and a great and strong wind rent the mountains, and brake in pieces the rocks before the Lord; but the Lord was not in the wind; and after the wind an earthquake; but the Lord was not in the earthquake; and after the earthquake a fire; but the Lord was not in the fire; and after the fire a still small voice.[3]

Something had changed. Whereas what the infant Samuel heard sounded exactly like a human speech, this voice resembles nothing that has ever been heard before. The Hebrew tells us, literally, that it was 'a voice of thin silence'. What exactly is a 'silent voice'? It sounds more than a bit Zen. Is this some kind of 'inner' experience to be contrasted with earthquakes, winds and fires? It certainly has the modern translators in confusion. The Catholic *Jerusalem Bible* reads this as an entirely natural phenomenon, with no suggestion of speech, translating it as 'the sound of a gentle breeze' – which is a direct

---

[2]For a fuller discussion of this problem see Julian Jaynes, *The Origins of Consciousness in the Breakdown of the Bicameral Mind*, especially Book 2.
[3]1 Kings 19.11-12.

translation of the Vulgate's *sibilis aurae tenuis*: 'a thin whistling sound of the air'. The *New English Bible* also plumps for naturalism, giving us 'a low murmuring sound' – which unfortunately creates the impression that Elijah needs a hearing-aid, or that God is mumbling. For the *Good News Bible* it obviously means that God is indeed speaking in an undertone, with 'the soft whisper of a voice'. What marks out all these attempts to give a 'modern' rendering to an ancient oxymoron is their intolerance of the original ambiguity – and, even more important, a lack of historical understanding.[4]

For anyone steeped in an older way of thinking, the Vulgate's association of 'breeze' with the Holy Spirit would have been irresistible. The Hebrew word for 'wind' (or 'breeze') in this passage corresponds with the Greek word for 'spirit' in the Septuagint (the Greek translation of the Hebrew Bible) and the New Testament – making an easy link with the mighty 'rushing wind' of Pentecost. But that was still seven hundred years in the future. In this context the word 'wind' here has a quite different meaning – not to be associated with any voices, but to be lumped in with earthquakes and fires as noisy external phenomena which do *not* convey the Word of Lord. In its quietness, this 'voice' is in direct contrast with what has just gone before. What is described here is a vision so ambiguous, so oxymoronic, that, unlike the voice heard by the infant Samuel, we – and presumably Elijah also – simply do not know whether to interpret it as 'external' or 'internal'. If we had been standing beside Elijah at this point, would we have heard a voice as Samuel is reported to have done, or would the voice have been solely heard by the prophet – that is, as we would now say, *inside* his head?

We do not, of course, know who described this vision, or how it comes down to us. But even if it is simply an elaborated fiction – an event that some anonymous scribe imagined *ought* to have happened – what the unknown writer is struggling to describe is still immensely original. It is very possibly the first recorded moment in history when the language of the external world is used to describe something so odd and peculiar to the person that we cannot even tell if it is external or internal. All that we know is that this experience is intended to stand in direct contrast to the epiphanies of other pagan gods of

---

[4]For a more extensive discussion of this passage see Stephen Prickett, *Words and the Word*, Cambridge University Press, 1986, p. 12.

the surrounding cultures, for whose followers earthquakes, winds or fires were standard manifestations of divinity.[5] We cannot even know whether this 'voice of thin silence' represents the very first time in human history where what we must henceforth call 'internalization' is a possibility. But it may well be the first *recorded* moment. It makes sense, at least, for us to read it as a moment of transition – a moment when something hitherto exclusively *external* can be better understood (at least to us, with two and a half thousand years of hindsight) as something happening *inside* the head of the prophet.

But, of course, this is emphatically not (yet) a proper internalization. It is, as we have seen, a moment of transition, when something apparently new has appeared – something *so* new, in fact, that it cannot be effectively categorized at all. For much of the Hebrew Bible (or in Christian terminology, the Old Testament) such events remain ambiguous, though increasingly they tend to become more directly personal and less likely to be presented as something that might be overheard by others.

By the time of the New Testament, however, it is rare for angels to appear out of the blue – the most notable exception is the annunciation the birth of Jesus to the shepherds. This is, as it were, a very 'public' announcement, not a private revelation. We relish the stark realism of Rembrandt's famous illustration of the shepherds cringing, or running away, and the cattle scattering in panic all over the fields. But in New Testament terms, this is actually an old-fashioned intrusion. More usual is the delivery of divine messages in dreams or visions, such as the warning to Mary and Joseph to flee from Herod's murderous wrath, so tending to increase the distance between ordinary life and miraculous interventions.[6] Thus Peter, on the rooftop in Joppa, we are told, falls 'into a trance':

> And saw heaven opened, and a certain vessel descending unto him, as it had been a great sheet knit at the four corners, and let down to the earth: wherein were all manner of four-footed beasts of the earth, and wild beasts, and creeping things, and fowls of the air. And there came a voice to him, Rise, Peter, kill and eat . . .

---

[5] It is extraordinary how earthquakes, hurricanes and forest fires are still interpreted by the pundits of various religions from Iran to California in terms of the wrath of God.
[6] E.g. Matthew 1.20 vv 2, 13 and 19.

Now while Peter doubted in himself what this vision which he had seen should mean, behold the men which were sent from Cornelius ... stood before the gate.[7]

Here there is no ambiguity at least about the mode of transmission. The New Testament Greek word for 'vision' here is *'optasia'*, a reasonable equivalent of the Hebrew *ḥāzôn*. Even though he might be unsure of its meaning, Peter is left in no doubt at all that what he had experienced was both supernatural and peculiar to him alone.

Figure 1.1 *Rembrandt van Rijn,* The Angel Appearing to the Shepherds *(1634). The Sylmaris Collection, Gift of George Coe Graves, 1920.*

---

[7]Acts 10.10-17. For a more detailed exploration of this passage, see James Alison, *On Being Liked*, Darton Longman and Todd, 2003, pp. vii–xi.

Whether our modern sense of an inner world really started with the extraordinary experience of visions and dreams – and they are not confined to the Bible – is a moot point. What is clear from the Bible is that only slowly did people (or more properly, certain prophets) become aware of the division between their external senses and some kind of inner world of the spirit. But the problem then was who owned this inner world? For many, visions or dreams seemed to be controlled by someone or something else. Not merely did God or angels speak to you: so did demons and evil spirits. It sometimes took a smart prophet to distinguish one from the other.[8] Demon possession was a widely recognized phenomenon.[9] In the case of the Gadarene swine,[10] the so-called 'legion' of unclean spirits possessing the man pleaded, in this case with surprising success, to be given another 'home'. It was perhaps convenient that for Jews pigs were unclean animals, so that all two thousand of them rushing like lemmings down into the Sea of Galilee conveniently disposed of swine and demons alike.[11] But it is a reminder that modern theories of the unconscious are, in that sense a liberation, even a re-claiming, of what was at best neutral territory and at worst a kind of bridgehead, controlled if not by unfriendly powers then certainly by alien ones.

There are, of course, dreams and dreams. It was never in doubt that Martin Luther King's 'Dream' was to be understood as rhetoric. So is that of the so-called immigrant 'dreamers' in the USA, who are, presumably, dreaming of a better life. Rhetoric aside, if we are honest, most of our dreams are fragmentary junk. Only a few seem in retrospect to be coherent, and even fewer, significant. What we now call 'eidetic' dreams – those of peculiar vividness and intensity which stay in the memory afterwards[12] – are extremely rare for anybody, even the most psychic. The quotation from Etty Hillesum with which we began this

---

[8]See Matthew 24.4-5; 2 Peter 2.1.

[9]And, we must remember, to this day both the Church of England and the Catholic Church have trained exorcists.

[10]Mark 5.1-20.

[11]Presumably this was a financial catastrophe for whoever the non-Jew was who owned the herd.

[12]An eidetic image is a type of vivid mental image, not necessarily derived from an actual external event or memory. It was identified in the early twentieth century as a distinct phenomenon by psychologists including E. R. Jaensch, Heinrich Klüver, Gordon Allport and Frederic Bartlett. Some attempt has been made to distinguish eidetic dream images from actual memories.

book is an example of a twentieth-century eidetic dream that seems to have accompanied the doomed dreamer as a symbol of hope for the rest of her tragically short life.

Nevertheless, the belief in dreams or visions as sources of *divine* inspiration has never entirely gone away, though for non-believers the social context has become increasingly sceptical. Muslims believe that the Qur'an was dictated to Mohammed in some kind of trance by the angel Gabriel. The Mormons rely on the visionary testimony of their founder, Joseph Smith, who, we are told, was visited in 1823 by Moroni, son of Mormon, in the form of an angel, who revealed to him where the Book of Mormon, inscribed upon golden plates, was hidden in New York State. Because it was given to Smith *in writing*, the text, like that of the Qur'an, is believed by Mormons to be precise and unalterable, although to more historically critical eyes the stylistic debt to the King James 1611 version of the Bible seems fairly obvious.

More surprising, perhaps, is the testimony of Emanuel Swedenborg (1688–1772), a Swedish scientist and engineer, who described a series of visionary experiences of Heaven and Hell from the 1740s and 1750s in the same coolly rational style that he had previously used for reporting scientific experiments. Unlike Smith, Swedenborg never claimed to be founding a new religious movement, and even his followers, current members of the Swedenborg Society, are careful not to claim this. The poet and painter William Blake (1757–1827) was for a time a Swedenborgian. Unfortunately much of what Swedenborg reveals about Heaven and Hell can seem trivial and inconsequential to modern readers. The relationships between the various ranks of angels, for instance, rather than reflecting eternal truths, seem remarkably like contemporary eighteenth-century hierarchies.[13]

There are, of course, examples of what might be called 'secular dreams' where the dreamer is inspired with a problem-solving vision. Thomas Edison, who actually planned his life to include inspirational naps in his laboratory, is one significant example.[14] Nevertheless, the most famous is probably Kekulé's dream after dozing off on the top of a London horse-drawn omnibus. He

---

[13]See *Heaven & Hell* (original Latin 1758) English tr. Doris Harley, Swedenborg Society, 1989.
[14]See Matthew Walker, *Why We Sleep: The New Science of Sleep and Dreams*, Allen Lane, 2017, p. 232.

claimed that, after years of studying the nature of carbon–carbon bonds, he had discovered the elusive shape of the benzene molecule as a ring by dreaming of a snake seizing its own tail (an ancient symbol known as the Ouroboros).[15] There is no suggestion in his account that this was any kind of divine intervention. It seems, rather, to be an example of the familiar phenomenon of 'sleeping on a problem' – albeit in a slightly unusual place.

Other examples are not difficult to find, though in some quarters there is an understandable reluctance to turn scientific insight into unconscious inspiration. Anthony Stevens, a Jungian psychologist, records two striking examples, one from chemistry, the other from atomic physics:

> The nineteenth-century Russian chemist Dimitri Mendeleyev devoted immense conscious effort to an attempt to discover some ordering principle underlying the apparently random relationship between the basic chemical elements which make up the physical world. One afternoon he was dozing in a chair while his family played chamber music in the next room.[16]

Inspired by the music, 'I saw in a dream,' he wrote, 'a table, where all the elements fell into place as required. Awakening, I immediately wrote it down on a piece of paper.'

Fifty years later, the Danish physicist Niels Bohr carried Mendeleyev's insight a stage further. Bohr asked himself why the basic elements should exist in the first place. Why were they distinguished from one another and how did they maintain their stability? Why, for example, is there no transitional element between hydrogen and helium? After months of wrestling with this problem he had a dream in which he was at the races. The horses ran in lanes which were clearly marked with white dust. They were permitted to change lanes provided they maintained a distance between one another. If a horse ran along a white line and kicked up dust, however, it was immediately disqualified. When he awoke, Bohr realized that this 'rule of the track' symbolized the answer to his questions. As they orbit round the nucleus of an atom, electrons keep to their arbitrarily assigned course in the same manner as the horses kept

---

[15]See John Read, *From Alchemy to Chemistry*, London: Bell, 1957, pp. 179–80.
[16]Anthony Stevens, *Private Myths: Dreams and Dreaming*, Penguin, 1966, p. 282. See also Paul Strathern, *Mendeleyev's Dream: The Quest for the Elements*, Crux 2000.

to the lanes in which they ran. The paths followed by the orbiting electrons are determined by 'quanta' of energy and these simple facts account for the stability of the elements. It was on the basis of this experience that Bohr formulated his quantum theory, for which he was later awarded a Nobel Prize.[17]

Stranger even than these 'dreams', perhaps, is an example recorded by Arthur Koestler. Johannes Kepler (1571–1630), a German scientist, who was generally believed to be the finest mathematician of his day, was determined to solve the problem of the orbit of the planet Mars. But to do this, he needed more accurate observations of the planets than were then available. The one person who might have such data was the notoriously grouchy and difficult Danish astronomer, Tycho Brahe – who refused point-blank to cooperate. So Kepler went to Brahe anonymously and took on the job of what would now be called a 'lab assistant' and general factotum in order to gain access to Brahe's observations. Armed with this stolen data, he then encountered a further, even more daunting, mathematical problem, the extent of which is suggested by the fact that his manuscript calculations run to over nine hundred pages in small handwriting. What he had hit upon was a problem in the theory of gravity that would only be solved by Isaac Newton (1643–1727) years after Kepler's death in 1630. Kepler's 'solution', however, was startling. At the start of his calculation he 'absentmindedly' inserted three erroneous figures, and apparently went on without noticing what he had done. Towards the end of his calculations he made several more arithmetical mistakes – simple schoolchild howlers – which miraculously cancelled out his earlier errors and enabled him to come up with more or less the correct answer almost a century before the relevant mathematics were available. Such was his mathematical reputation, however, that this went unnoticed for centuries. In some peculiar way, he had, in Koestler's phrase, unconsciously 'sleepwalked' into the solution never knowing, and, apparently, without understanding, what he had done.[18] It was as if at some unconscious level he already knew the answer he was consciously striving for. But those nine hundred pages of futile calculations surely helped.

---

[17] Ibid., p. 282.

[18] Arthur Koestler, *The Sleepwalkers: A History of Man's Changing Vision of the Universe,* (1959) Pelican Books, 1964, pp. 325–6.

Yet if the Enlightenment turned minds towards scientific rather than supernatural explanations for dreams, the sheer variety and quantity, let alone the absence of any consensus in such modern so-called 'scientific' explanations, should give us pause. The 'unconscious' was not something discovered by Freud, 'but a hypothesis that emerged erratically between the seventeenth and nineteenth centuries'.[19] John Norris (1632–1704) maintained that 'there are infinitely more ideas impressed on our minds than we can possibly attend to or perceive'. Older theories have a remarkable way of re-emerging in modern clothes. The philosopher Gottfried Wilhelm Leibniz (1646–1716) compared what went on in the soul to the circulation of the blood, arguing that it sustains our conscious existence without our realizing it 'just as those who live near a water mill do not perceive the noise it makes'. Such notions were taken up enthusiastically by the Romantics.[20] Though editors of his work rarely recognize it in their indices, Freud was well-read in the English Romantics, and he clearly drew on them and other similar sources in his own writings. Nevertheless, his *Interpretation of Dreams* (1899) effectively aligned dreaming with the rest of his sexual psychoanalytical apparatus – given its most complete form in his theory of the Oedipus Complex. What is interesting is the way in which he attached to its creation something of the traditional certainty associated with dreams in a pre-scientific world. 'Do you suppose,' he wrote to a colleague in 1900, 'that some day a marble tablet will be placed on the house, inscribed with these words: "In this house on July 24, 1895, the secret of dreams was revealed to Dr. Sigm. Freud"? At the moment I see little prospect of it.'[21] Though he would, of course, have denied its vaguely supernatural connotations, the word 'revealed' is here significant. Given Freud's belief in a repressed libido which could discharge itself in inadvertent slips of the tongue, that word is doubly significant. Revealed *by whom*?

Needless to say, this theory of dreams is starkly different from that of his one-time associate, C.G. Jung, who, despite sharing similar ideas of the unconscious mind, held a theory of dreams which was in many ways a throw-

---

[19]Stevens, *Private Myths*, p. 29.
[20]See, for instance, Henri Ellenberger, *The Discovery of the Unconscious*, N.Y.: Basic Books, 1970 or L.L. Whyte, *The Unconscious Before Freud*, Palgrave Macmillan, 1979.
[21]Letter to Wilhelm Fliess, 12 June 1900.

back to a much older idea of inspiration, even though his idea of the Collective Unconscious, though clearly difficult to test experientially, gave it at least some kind of psychological underpinning.[22] A more thorough-going 'Jungian' approach to dreams comes from Anthony Stevens:

> In Jung's view our major difficulties, whether neurotic, psychotic, psychopathic, or political, come from losing contact with 'the age old unforgotten wisdom stored up in us'. If we wished to re-establish contact with this great reservoir of human potential then there was only one way open to us: we must pay close attention to our dreams.[23]

For the Jungian, dreams have a language of their own. 'There are symbols in dreams for the same reason that there are figures of speech in poetry and slang in everyday life.'[24]

After the First World War dreaming acquired a quite different 'scientific' explanation with J.W. Dunne's *Experiment with Time* (1927). Dunne, a qualified pilot and aeronautical engineer, starts with the arresting anecdote of how his engine failed when he was flying over Kent, and on looking for a safe place to land he recognized what turned out to be Lydd aerodrome from a dream he had had a few nights previously. He landed safely. From this experience, and from keeping a detailed diary of his dreams, he came up with a theory that he called 'Serialism', whereby he suggests, in a series of books throughout the 1930s, that dreams are in some way detached from our normal experience of time, able to reflect time past and time present in equal measure, giving a kind of bell curve of probability in relation to the present moment. From his research he argues that dreams most often refer to events that have just happened or are about to happen. Sometimes they re-run events in our waking life, but just as often they pre-figure them. Though Dunne does not explicitly say so, one notices that there is somewhere behind these apparently empirical experiments an updated version of a much older prophetic notion of the significance of dreams. Indeed, in his final and most autobiographical book,

---

[22]C.G. Jung, *Memories, Dreams and Reflections*, ed. Aniela Jaffé, tr. Richard and Clara Winston, Collins and Routledge & Kegan Paul, 1963.
[23]Ibid., p. 108.
[24]Calvin S. Hall, *The Meaning of Dreams*, (1953) Iconoclastic Books, 1966, p. 108.

Intrusions?, he cautiously describes himself as a Christian, and relates a number of meetings – the 'intrusions' of the title – with what he describes as an 'Angel'.[25] Though their content is very different, as befits a scientist, these encounters are reported with the same logic and mathematical precision that distinguished Swedenborg. Once again, attempts to create a 'science' of dreams seem to rest on something more than the vaguely metaphysical.

Other twentieth-century figures were fascinated by this same notion of 'intrusions' – from whatever presumed source. 'The shortest definition of religion: interruption' wrote Johann Baptist Metz in 1980.[26] In reply to the objection of the German theologian, Jürgen Moltmann, that this definition is inadequate, because, historically, a single interruption can always be deflected or absorbed, thereby allowing things to continue as usual,[27] Kevin Hart has suggested a 'second shortest definition of religion': 'absolute interruption.'[28] As he points out, the phrase comes originally from the French critic, Maurice Blanchot, though a similar concept is also to be found in the work of Blanchot's Jewish compatriot, the philosopher Emmanuel Levinas. Whatever modern sources one may select, however, as we have seen, narratives of absolute interruption abound in the Old Testament from the voice heard by the infant Samuel to Ezekiel's vision of the 'chariot' or Elijah on Horeb. But as both Blanchot and Levinas make clear, there is nothing exclusively or even intrinsically *religious* about such interruptions. The theoretical sciences, too, have interruptions – though, for instance, in the cases of both Swedenborg and Dunne, though not of Kekulé, one was to lead to the other.

Nevertheless, several thinkers have suggested the importance of such 'interruptions'. Hans Urs von Balthazar (1905–88), a Swiss Catholic theologian

---

[25]In his fourth and final encounter with the being he calls the 'Angel' he asks about the truth of Christianity. The Angel, enigmatic as ever, replies 'God lets it be true for those who want it to be true.' J.W. Dunne, *Intrusions*, Faber 1955, pp. 143–4.

[26]Johann Baptist Metz, *Faith in History and Society: Towards a Practical Fundamental Theology*, tr. David Smith, Burns and Oates, 1980, p. 171.

[27]Moltmann writes, 'Interruption is not an eschatological category. The eschatological category is conversion.' *The Coming of God: Christian Eschatology*, tr. Margaret Kohl, Minneapolis: Fortress Press, 1996, p. 22.

[28]Hart has successively held chairs in English Literature, Philosophy and Religious Studies. I owe this quotation, and much of what follows, to his essay, 'Absolute Interruption: On Faith' in *Questioning God*, ed. John D. Caputo, Indiana University Press, 2001.

best-known for his attempt to approach God by way of Kant's Third Critique (on Beauty),[29] was seen as startlingly unorthodox in the context of the conventional Catholic Thomism of his day, but has been hailed as prophetic by later generations. He writes that:

> Great works of art appear like inexplicable eruptions on the stage of history. Sociologists are as unable to calculate the precise day of their origin as they are to explain in retrospect why they appeared when they did ... [Art's] unique utterance becomes a universal language; and the greater the work of art, the more extensive the cultural sphere it dominates will be.[30]

From the little (the *very* little!) we know about the genesis of great art, connections with dreams and visions – let alone with theology – must remain highly speculative, but there is at least some evidence to suggest that many artists and writers have felt themselves in the grip of an alien, if not a higher, power in producing their most important work. Here one should certainly include some of the paintings of that extraordinary explorer of the unconscious, Hieronymus Bosch – of whom more later.[31] One of his most extraordinary pictures is of the ascent of the soul into Paradise in one of his last works, *Ascent of the Blessed and Hell* (see Pl. 1), dated somewhere between 1505 and 1515.[32] Here the saved soul is floating up a vast tube of light towards a distant figure, presumably of Christ, silhouetted in front of an even greater light – an experience more recently described in uncanny detail in many twentieth-century near-death experiences.

One of the strangest, and certainly most strangely documented, is that of John Milton (1608–74), the seventeenth-century poet and Puritan pamphleteer. By the time he came to write what is by far his best-known work, *Paradise Lost*, his political hopes for the republican Commonwealth and Cromwell's Protectorate had been dashed with the restoration of Charles II. He had been stripped of his family money, had lost two wives, had alienated his daughters

---

[29]See in particular his massive, seven volume work on theological aesthetics, *The Glory of the Lord*, ed. Joseph Fessio and John Riches, T&T Clark, 1982–9.

[30]Von Balthazar, *Two Say Why*, tr. John Griffiths, Search Press, 1973, pp. 20–1.

[31]See Chapter 3, p. 93.

[32]Hieronymus Bosch, *Ascent of the Blessed* (1505–15). Galleria dell'Accademia, Venice, Italy.

from his first and second marriages, and had gone blind. In 1663, at the age of 55, he married his third wife, Elizabeth, a yeoman's daughter some thirty years his junior. Under these distinctly unpromising conditions, in what would then have been old age, he received what he believed to be a divine visitation.

He called her Urania. This was the name of the classical Muse of astronomy, but for him, this was the 'heavenly muse', whom he invokes at the start of his great poem, and was clearly to be identified with the Holy Spirit itself rather than any member of the pagan pantheon.[33] Like St Paul, she had apparently guided him into the 'Heaven of Heavens'.[34] She was apparently sister to 'the eternal Wisdom' who, we are told in the Book of Proverbs, was with God before the creation of the world.[35] She was his

> ... Celestial Patroness, who deignes
> Her nightly visitation unimplor'd,
> And dictates to me slumbering, or inspires
> Easie my unpremeditated verse:[36]

Each night, he tells us, this female figure would come to him, and dictate up to 40 lines of verse, which he would then repeat in the morning, to an amanuensis, who would take the lines down and then read them back to him. He would then spend the rest of the morning chopping, changing and adapting them until he was satisfied with the result – often cutting them to half the length of the original. If the amanuensis was late, or there were other delays, he would chafe and complain, saying 'I want to be milked.' For him Urania was apparently no idle literary convention, but a dominating reality. That he believed in her existence was confirmed by others who knew him and by his wife, who also added that when he attempted to consciously compose outside his routine he was completely unsuccessful.[37]

Modern commentators are understandably cautious about accepting Milton's account of his muse. The literary critic John Carey writes:

---

[33] *Paradise Lost*, Bk. VII, 1–39.
[34] Ibid., 13.
[35] Proverbs 8. 25-27, 30.
[36] *Paradise Lost*, Bk IX, 21–4.
[37] One of the best accounts of this is by Stephen Greenblatt, *The Rise and Fall of Adam and Eve*, Bodley Head, 2017, pp. 201–3.

Whether or not we believe in Urania, the fact that the poem was initially composed during sleep suggests that it came from Milton's unconscious, though when he woke it was revised by his conscious mind. In this respect it could be seen almost as two poems in one. There is an official poem, articulating ideas that are endorsed by Milton's conscious intention. Intersecting with it there is an unofficial poem, releasing disruptive meanings that Milton would not have consciously endorsed.[38]

That there was a real conflict between Milton's 'official' theological beliefs and the much more disruptive opinions that bubble below the surface is certainly true – they range from Blake's opinion that Milton was 'of the Devil's party without knowing it' to the controversy over whether Adam's Fall was a case of uxoriousness or loyalty.[39] Whether Urania was an *external* figure, as Milton evidently believed, or *internal*, as Carey assumes, probably makes little difference from our point of view. This seems to be yet another example of the process by which what were once experienced as external and supernatural figures were progressively internalized over the centuries. In this case, however, what is more than a little astonishing – and astonishingly little commented upon – is the radical change in Milton's poetic construction introduced by Urania. What we now think of as the classic 'Miltonic' style – the long sentences, the heavily Latinate blank verse – belongs to this late period. Anyone who reads an early work of Milton's, such as *Comus*, the Masque, first presented at Ludlow Castle in 1634, without knowing the story of Milton's life, would be justified in assuming this was not written by Milton. The blank verse is quite different – in many ways more like that of Shakespeare – with shorter sentences, more colloquial language, and with little trace of the Latin inversions or verbs at the end of sentences common in Urania's dictations. Admittedly Milton was a colossally learned man, and much of his poetic output had been in Latin – mostly unread today. But if this new style was merely Milton's subconscious in action, some explanation might be appropriate as to why,

---

[38] *Times Literary Supplement,* 5 October 2017.
[39] See William Blake, '*The Marriage of Heaven and Hell*', 1790. For a revealing discussion of the latter point, see C.S. Lewis, *A Preface to Paradise Lost,* Oxford University Press, 1942, versus A.J.A. Waldock, *Paradise Lost and its Critics,* Cambridge University Press, 1961.

unlike in most other cases – Coleridge's for example – his subconscious was apparently much more formal than his conscious mind, and had its own distinctly different verse style.

Almost as striking is the example of the Nobel literary prizewinner, William Golding – of whom more below. Stephen Medcalf, a literary critic, always felt that the Golding he knew as a friend was simply not the same as the man who wrote the novels. The old Navy man was genial, humorous and convivial, whereas Golding the novelist was stark, humourless and worked in powerfully concentrated visual images – quite unlike his own conversational style.[40]

Medcalf went so far as to imagine that the novels were written by a 'daemon' or supernatural agent. Golding himself was half-prepared to countenance the idea. 'That is right,' he agreed, 'Sometimes I have felt it in myself and been astonished at what it accomplishes . . .' When writing in his journal he gave his 'real', everyday self, curious comic nicknames ('Pewter' and 'Bolonius') to distinguish the ordinary Golding from Golding the novelist, who remained, it seems, outside his knowledge or control.[41]

Though this sense of 'outside' inspiration was peculiarly strong in Golding, he was certainly not the only modern novelist to have recorded this feeling. Robert Louis Stevenson claimed that the plot of *Dr Jekyll and Mr Hyde* came to him in a dream. Even Rudyard Kipling threw out remarks to the same effect – and it is, of course, the theme of several of his stories. In *The Brushwood Boy*, for instance, the hero, an impossibly perfect but unimaginatively efficient young man in his waking life, has a vigorous and very different dream-life of a strange country beyond a pile of brushwood on a mysterious seashore. The total exclusion of fantasy from his waking life is matched by the peculiar vividness and intensity of this recurrent dream. Eventually, and quite by accident, he meets, literally, 'the girl of his dreams'. The story is not wholly successful – for the obvious reason that the waking hero might not suit the girl as much as his dreaming self – but as an exploration of a parallel inner world, apparently unconnected with the outer one, the story has astonishing power which overrides any weakness of characterization.[42]

---

[40]Also my own experience of Golding.
[41]John Carey, *William Golding: A Life*, Faber, 2009, p. 176.
[42]'The Brushwood Boy', *The Day's Work*, 1895. See Stephen Prickett, *Victorian Fantasy*, Harvester, 1979, p. 210.

Twenty-first-century studies, however, have played down, or ignored, the eidetic or prophetic significance of dreams and other recorded instances of interruptions, preferring to investigate dreams as an epiphenomenal by-product of brain studies, noting their recuperative and health-giving qualities – though precisely why the active brain needs such regular unconscious stimulation seems as yet to be unclear.[43] For Iain McGilchrist such an approach merges almost seamlessly into an interior geography all of its own. McGilchrist is perhaps the nearest thing to a polymath in a world of narrow-minded specialists. He is both a qualified psychiatrist and a brain surgeon, who has also taught English literature at Oxford. For him:

> ... the brain can be seen as something like a huge country: as a nested structure, of villages and towns, then districts, gathered into counties, regions and even partly autonomous states or lands – a conglomeration of nuclei and ganglia at one level, organizational foci and broader functional regions within specific gyri or sulci (the folds of the cortex) at another, these then forming lobes, and those lobes ultimately forming part of one or other cerebral hemisphere.[44]

Somehow the physical folds back into the metaphorical, into a space that might even be recognizable to the inhabitants of the Old Testament. But there is another characteristic that might be even more familiar. To the old question, 'Who owns this space?' McGilchrist adds a new and perplexing conflict. For him there is a fundamental and perpetual tension between the left- and right-hand hemispheres of the brain. If the right hemisphere (which, of course, controls the left-hand side of the body) is the 'master', the right hand (controlled by the left lobe) is the executor – with the power to over-rule or modify the commands of its twin. It is this basic potential conflict that lies at the heart of our very consciousness. In being human we inevitably buy into an unresolved tension that is an inevitable part of consciousness itself.

> ... the fundamental problem in explaining the experience of consciousness is that there is nothing else remotely like it to compare it with: it itself is the

---

[43]See Matthew Walker, *Why We Sleep.*
[44]Iain McGilchrist, *The Master and His Emissary,* p. 9.

ground of all experience. There is nothing else which has the 'inwardness' that consciousness has. Phenomenologically, and ontologically, it is unique.[45]

If he is right, then the evolution of our interior space is not so much a matter of scientific enlightenment, as one of learning to live with its perpetual contractions – or perhaps, as some would have it, its dialectic. Certainly, a blind faith in the progress of physical science might be the most dangerous illusion of all. McGilchrist quotes the philosopher Peter Hacker:

Scientism, the illicit extension of the methods and categories of science beyond their legitimate domain, is one such form, and the conception of the unity of the sciences and the methodological homogeneity of the natural sciences and of humanistic studies is one such myth. It is the task of philosophy to defend us against such illusions of reason.[46]

The ownership of inner space is, and it seems always will be, contested territory. I can recall highly lucid dreams in which I have carefully explained to others that this was *my* dream, and, for all their seeming reality, they were but figments of *my* imagination. (Unfortunately, I don't remember their responses!) A psychoanalyst once explained to me that we were at all times fully in control of our dreams and could always re-order nightmares. I can vouch for the fact that at least in my own case, this is simply untrue. Just as there are people with the most bizarre neurological disorders,[47] awake or asleep, there is an almost infinite variety of dreams, but very few of us, I suspect, can free ourselves with one bound from nightmares – or, what Jonathan Swift once graphically called 'the Hells beneath'!

If dreams – whether fictional, or real – are dangerous things, the distinction between the two is less clear than one might think. As we all know, whatever someone may *report* about a dream, there is no way of confirming their account. Though it is wildly possible (if most unlikely) that advances in brain research might change this, there is no category of what was '*really* dreamed'. Memories may be edited consciously or unconsciously. In other words, all

---

[45]Ibid., p. 19.
[46]Ibid., p. 157.
[47]See, for instance, Oliver Sacks, *The Man Who Mistook His Wife for a Hat*, Duckworth, 1985.

dreams may properly be described as 'fictional' – whether created as part of a story or ostensibly reported from memory. Moreover, we cannot even be sure of what constitutes a dream. As we have seen, the infant Samuel was (we are told) himself unsure what he was experiencing. Indeed, if Freud is correct, both kinds of account share what is in effect a similar associative symbolism.

Equally important, dreams are the ultimate form of solipsism. In our waking state, we are constantly interacting with other people who, in turn, have their own inner space. One thing that we can be certain of in dreams is that those we apparently encounter have no such independent existence. Hence the apparently common dreams of having tea with famous figures, such as the Queen, or those whom we know, on waking, to have been long dead.

It is perhaps no surprise therefore that dreaming should also have come to occupy a fictional convention, signalling a gateway into a world where the normal rules of realism do not apply. Yet there is more to dream literature than a lack of everyday realism. George MacDonald (1824–1905) one of the greatest and most prolific writers of fantasy literature in the nineteenth century reverses the normal connection by equating non-realistic stories with dreams.

If so much of our life is actually spent in dreaming, there must be some place in our literature for what corresponds to dreaming. Even in this region, we cannot step beyond the boundaries of our nature. I delight in reading Lord Bacon now; but one of Jean Paul's dreams will often give me more delight than one of Bacon's best paragraphs. It depends upon the mood. Some dreams like these, in poetry or in sleep, arouse individual states of consciousness altogether different from any of our waking moods, and not to be recalled by any mere effort of the will. All our being, for the moment, has a new and strange colouring. We have another kind of life. I think myself, our life would be much poorer without our dreams; a thousand rainbow tints and combinations would be gone; music and poetry would lose many an indescribable exquisiteness and tenderness. You see I like to take our dreams seriously, as I would even our fun. For I believe that those new mysterious feelings that come to us in sleep, if they be only from dreams of a richer grass and a softer wind than we have known awake, are indications of wells of feeling and delight which have not yet broken out of their hiding-places in our souls, and are only to be suspected from these rings of fairy green that spring up in the high places of our sleep.[48]

At what historical point the claim to be recounting a dream became a literary trope is a difficult question. As we have seen it has run parallel with claims of divine inspiration for hundreds if not thousands of years. As early as the fourteenth century – and perhaps much earlier – the announcement that the story being told was a 'dream' was a familiar way of telling the reader that what follows was not be taken literally. Such works include some of the best-known books in English, as well as many which are more obscure. Perhaps the earliest is the Anglo-Saxon *Dream of the Rood* – the cross on which Christ was crucified – which in the cross itself becomes a protagonist in dialogue with the unnamed dreamer. The anonymous fourteenth-century poem, *The Pearl*, is little known: whereas John Bunyan's seventeenth-century *Pilgrim's Progress* is one of the best-known works of all time; as are Lewis Carroll's *Alice* books in the nineteenth; while even C.S. Lewis's *The Great Divorce* from the twentieth has been in continuous print ever since it was first published in 1945. In all these cases the dream framework is explicitly a literary device.

In *The Dream of the Rood*, the symbolic and fictional nature of the dream is immediately clear in that the cross is now adorned with gems, and speaks to the narrator. In *The Pearl* a newly bereaved father sees his dead daughter crowned as 'Queen of Heaven'. When he expostulates, saying there can only be one Queen of Heaven, and that, as everyone knows, is the Virgin Mary, his daughter replies that though monarchy on Earth is, by its nature, exclusive, in Heaven, by *its* nature, what is *shared* is greater than what is exclusive: therefore 'we are all Queens in Heaven'. Despite the vivid setting, with the father separated from his daughter by a stream that he may not cross, we are not, I think, expected to read the story of the bereaved father's vision in the same light as Peter's vision in Joppa. Though it is a work of profoundly original vision, the structured poetic medium implies a work of fiction. Bunyan's full title is more openly explicit, telling us that Christian's journey is 'In the Similitude of a Dream'. Even without that, the very names, from Christian's

---

[48]George MacDonald, *Adela Cathcart*, 1864, pp. 226–7.

onwards, make it abundantly clear that his protagonist's adventures are an allegory. Alice's dream encounter with a white rabbit possessing a watch and chain, perpetually late for something, equally clearly belongs to a world of literary fantasy, not divine visions. Lewis's unnamed protagonist in *The Great Divorce* awakes from a Dantesque earthly paradise to a cold room with the air-raid siren howling overhead.

Certainly, by the time of Shakespeare the possibilities of dreams could be a vehicle of comedy. The most obvious 'dream' is, of course, *A Midsummer Night's Dream* – often referred to by Shakespeareans simply as *The Dream*. But that is yet another example of a title to warn a prospective audience that the normal rules of reality do not apply. This is a fairy tale. But the only real dream *within* the story concerns Bottom's enchantment where, complete with ass's head, he becomes the lover of Titania, the fairy Queen. In fact, she is the victim of a magic spell. Like the other lovers, Helena and Hermia, Demetrius and Lysander, she has the magic flower squeezed upon her eyelids by Puck, on Oberon's orders, to make her dote upon the first thing she sees on awakening. Apart from a little matter of an ass's head, and tastes in hay to match, Bottom is not really enchanted in this sense at all. He is certainly surprised and understandably delighted to find himself in such distinguished and magical company, but when he awakes alone in the forest it slowly dawns on him what has happened.

> I have had a most rare vision. I have had a dream, past the wit of man to say what dream it was. Man is but an ass, if he go about t'expound this dream. Methought I was – there is no man can tell what. Methought I was, and methought I had – but man is but a patch'd fool, if he will offer to say what methought I had. The eye of man hath not heard, the ear of man hath not seen, man's hand is not able to taste, his tongue to conceive, nor his heart to report, what my dream was. I will get to Peter Quince to write a ballet of this dream. It shall be call'd 'Bottom's Dream' because it hath no bottom . . .[49]

At one level this is pure comedy (and, well acted, very good comedy too). The synaesthia is pure Bottom. He is a born malopropist. But, as so often with

---

[49]*A Midsummer Night's Dream*, Act IV, sc. 1.

Shakespeare, there is more to this verbal confusion. Mixed images are the essence of dreams. The senses invoked, eye, ear, touch and taste, have all been invoked in the previous scene where he has been luxuriating with Titania and her attendant fairies. Yet behind the nonsense, and, at another level, there is an unnerving return to the old problem: who controls our dreams? Bottom was plainly not in charge – and knows it. The comedy floats unnervingly on the bottomless space opening up beneath consciousness.

The Taming of the Shrew uses a similar device, with an apparent dream that the audience knows is nothing of the kind. It opens with a drunken tramp, Christopher Sly, being fooled into believing that his previous existence was all a dream, and that he has now awakened to his 'real' life of idle luxury. The story of the bad-tempered Katherine and her subsequent 'taming' is then presented as an entertainment by a troop of strolling players. Whether or not this comes from an earlier play, re-worked by Shakespeare,[50] it shows not merely that he had seen some of the comic possibilities of a reverse-dream, but also that the device itself was probably familiar to much of his audience.

And yet … as always, there is more to Shakespeare's dreams than just a staged comedy. Hamlet's disquieting question, 'And in that sleep of death what dreams may come, when we have shuffled off this mortal coil?' is one that can still reverberate with the most stout-hearted atheist at 3.00 am – and is scarcely assuaged by Prospero's more apparently benign statement 'We are such stuff as dreams are made on, and our little life is rounded with a sleep.' A little unpacking of that may be in order. Usually it is assumed that this is another way of saying we are the 'stuff *of* dreams', but a more literal interpretation of that stubborn 'on' might mean that we are more like the base on which the pastry of dreams is fashioned. But 'stuff'? The original meaning of that word is simply 'material from which something can or may be made'. In other words, we are ourselves the raw material from which, and indeed *on* which, dreams are fabricated. As we have seen, we find our best hopes and our greatest fears within rather than without. And what of that 'little life'? An optimistic gloss, popular with some Romantics, including the German poet, Novalis (1772–

---

[50]See Anne Barton's Introduction to the play in *The Riverside Shakespeare*, Boston, MA: Houghton Mifflin, 1974, pp. 106–9.

1801), and the Scot, George MacDonald, might follow: along the lines that
Prospero means that when we die, we awake from the dream of life into true
reality—or at least into a truer dream. Certainly the master-magician is
projecting an image of the theatre as a place of unreality – a dream from which
we awake when we leave the unreality of the performance – but is that 'rounded'
a promise of comforting rest or the unspecified threat of being 'rounded up'?
The ambiguity is all.

By the time Henry Fielding (1707–54) published his eye-catchingly entitled
satirical novel, *A Journey from this World to the Next* (1743), the genre of the
dream was well-established.

> Whether the ensuing pages were really the dream or vision of some very
> pious and holy person; or whether they were really written in the other
> world, and sent back to this, which is the opinion of many (though I think
> too much inclining to superstition); or lastly, whether, as infinitely the
> greatest part imagine, they were really the production of some choice
> inhabitant of New Bethlehem,[51] is not necessary nor easy to determine.

However, perhaps one of the strangest and most extraordinary examples of
dream literature is Samuel Taylor Coleridge's poem *Kubla Khan*. The poem
itself makes no explicit reference to dreams, unless one reads the final couplet
as such:

> For he on honey-dew hath fed,
>   And drunk the milk of paradise.

But though it was probably composed in 1797, when it was finally published
almost twenty years later, in 1816, it was presented as an incoherent fragment
of a much longer lost poem, composed in an opium dream, and broken off by
the untimely arrival of 'a person from Porlock'. Coleridge writes how he had
been staying in a lonely farm house between Porlock and Linton, on Exmoor.

> In consequence of a slight indisposition, an anodyne had been prescribed,
> from the effects of which he fell asleep in his chair at the moment that he

---

[51]I.e. 'Bedlam'.

was reading the following sentence, or words of the same substance, in 'Purchas's Pilgrimes': 'Here the Khan Kubla commanded a palace to be built, and a stately garden thereunto: and thus ten miles of fertile ground were inclosed with a wall.'

The Author continued for about three hours in a profound sleep, at least of the external senses, during which time he has the most vivid confidence, that he could not have composed less than from two to three hundred lines; if that indeed can be called composition in which all the images rose up before him as things, with a parallel production of the correspondent expressions, without any sensation or consciousness of effort. On awakening he appeared to himself to have a distinct recollection of the whole, and taking his pen, ink, and paper, instantly and eagerly wrote down the lines that are here preserved. At this moment he was unfortunately called out by a person on business from Porlock, and detained by him above an hour, and on his return to his room, found, to his no small surprise and mortification, that though he still retained some vague and dim recollection of the general purport of the vision, yet, with the exception of some eight or ten scattered lines and images, all the rest had passed away like the images on the surface of a stream into which a stone had been cast, but, alas! without the after restoration of the latter.

Whereas other examples of dream literature normally signal their non-realistic status as part of a literary convention in the text, *Kubla Khan* is probably unique in so far as only its author apparently questions its realism, by his own account quite unnecessarily, nineteen years later. Ironically many critics have regarded both the dream and the unnamed 'person' as themselves convenient fictions to distance the reader from the poem. It is unlikely that we shall ever know the truth about this event. Presumably the only way it could be verified would be a diary entry from someone who lived in Porlock at the period saying he had called on the poet and wakened him from a dream. Needless to say, numerous fictions have already been created about this possibility.[52] Be that as it may, so

---

[52]See, for instance, Vincent Starrett, *Persons from Porlock & Other Interruptions* (1938); Louis MacNeice, *Persons from Porlock, and Other Plays for Radio* (1969); Douglas Adams', *Dirk Gently's Holistic Detective Agency* (1987); A.N. Wilson, *Penfriends from Porlock* (1988); and Stevie Smith, 'Thoughts About the Person from Porlock'.

far from authenticating an experience, let alone recording a divine vision, with a strange perversity the claim is here being used to 'de-authenticate' Coleridge's source of inspiration by attributing it to a state of drug-induced sleep.

Though the claim to dream status has a long and rich history as a recognized genre of fiction, it does not offer any solutions to the basic problem noted with real dreams: that of ownership or control of those depths of the psyche beneath conscious control. This is important in what must be the most popular dream novel of the nineteenth century: Dickens's *Christmas Carol*. While Scrooge's experiences with the three ghosts are never specifically described as 'dreams', they have all of the standard features of dreams, sliding imperceptibly from one scene to the next, and even apparently overlapping in time. The visit of the first spirit – that of Christmas Past – is, in effect, a piece of regression therapy. Scrooge is shown significant moments from his own childhood and youth, reminding him how he used to be – and, from the mouth of his former fiancée, how he had altered and become more money-grubbing. The second spirit – that of Christmas Present – shows him how he is now seen by others. The third spirit – that of Christmas Yet to Come – shows shadows of the future: the death of Tiny Tim, and finally, his own death. It is important to see that throughout these visions Scrooge's own character *does not change*. As a miser, he is at great pains to be seen as the *most* mean skinflint of his kind, with his 'Bah Humbugs', the almost sadistic persecution of his clerk, Bob Cratchit, and his Malthusian opinion that the death of paupers would conveniently 'reduce the surplus population'. As a convert to the Christmas spirit, he is equally concerned to be the *most* generous benefactor around, sending the very *biggest* turkey available to the Cratchits, and showering praise and plenty upon everyone he meets.

In short, the whole narrative is an extended and, indeed, brilliant exploration of Scrooge's psyche, revealing an inner world made up of childhood reminiscences, current hopes and future fears. But once again we are faced with the question of the origins of these ghosts.

'You don't believe in me,' observed the Ghost.

'I don't,' said Scrooge.

'What evidence would you have of my reality, beyond that of your senses?'

'Because,' said Scrooge, 'a little thing affects them. A slight disorder of the stomach makes them cheats. You may be an undigested bit of beef, a blot of mustard, a crumb of cheese, a fragment of an underdone potato. There's more of gravy than of grave about you, whatever you are!'[53]

Partly this is sheer bravado. Scrooge is, not unreasonably, terrified and even if Victorian beliefs about the psychedelic effects of bad diet do not sound very convincing to the modern ear, the question: 'is this really an external visitation, or some apparition from the depths of my own psyche?' remains relevant. Nor is Marley's response, to shake his chains 'with a dismal and appalling noise', really a satisfactory answer. More to the point, perhaps, there *is* no satisfactory answer. One can read *Christmas Carol* as a straight story of a miser strangely converted by spirits, or one can indeed read it as an internal psychodrama. Is Scrooge ultimately saved by his own subconscious?

This is a question replayed in one of the most extraordinary novels of the twentieth century. There is no hint at the beginning of William Golding's novel, *Pincher Martin*, that this is anything but a grimly realistic story of the Second World War.[54] The eponymous hero's real first name is Christopher. 'Pincher' is the not very flattering nickname applied to him by those who have known his ruthless selfishness. Martin has fallen overboard from his ship in some unspecified naval engagement, and rather to his surprise eventually finds himself washed up on a mid-Atlantic rock – perhaps a bit like Rockall. The rest of the story is about his struggles to stay alive in this inhospitable environment – punctuated by flashbacks to particular moments in his past. Finally, he is confronted by what he believes is a hallucination: a man in fisherman's dress and seaboots seated on the rock above him. Martin looks at him dismissively: 'You are a projection of my mind.' Then the man speaks: 'Have you had enough, Christopher?'

'Enough of what?'
'Surviving. Hanging on ...'
'I hadn't considered.'

---

[53]Charles Dickens, *The Christmas Books*, Vol. 1: *Christmas Carol & The Chimes*, Penguin, 1971, p. 59.
[54]The title and the bare bones of the plot appear to have been taken from a novel by Henry Taprell Dorling ('Taffrail'). As so often, Golding seems, perhaps unconsciously, to have re-worked that story with a much darker ending. See Carey, pp. 194–5.

'Consider now?'

'What's the good? I'm mad.'

'Even that crevice will crumble.'

He tried to laugh up at the bloodshot eye but heard barking noises. He threw words in the face. 'On the sixth day he created God. Therefore I permit you to use nothing but my own vocabulary. In his own image created he Him.'

'Consider now.'

'. . . I will not consider! I have created you and I can create my own heaven.'

'You have created it.'[55]

The apparition, Martin insists, is nothing but a hallucination; a creation of his own diseased psyche. But the apparition has disturbing qualities that are outside his control. Whatever he is, the man seated above him on the rock continues relentlessly to probe Martin. He simply ignores Martin's protestation that he is mad anyway, and that his mysterious interrogator is a creation of his subconscious, that there is nothing outside himself. Then that becomes true.

The sea stopped moving, froze, became paper, painted paper that was torn by a black line. The rock was painted on the same paper. The whole of the painted sea was tilted but nothing ran downhill into the black crack which had opened in it. The crack was utter, was absolute, was three times real.[56]

Patiently and relentlessly Martin's entire world is removed. His body follows, so that he can no longer even speak. All that is left of Martin is his 'centre'.

Still the centre resisted. It made the lightning do its work according to the laws of this heaven. It perceived in some mode of sight without eyes that pieces of the sky between the branches of black lightning were replaced by pits of nothing. This made the fear of the centre, the rage of the centre vomit in a mode that required no mouth. It screamed into the pit of nothing voicelessly, wordlessly.

'I shit on your heaven!'

---

[55]William Golding, *Pincher Martin*, Faber, 1965, pp. 195–6.

[56]Ibid., p. 200.

Now there are only claws left, clinging only to each other. Nothing else exists.

> The lightning crept in. The centre was unaware of anything but the claws and the threat . . . The lightning came forward. Some of the lines pointed to the centre, waiting for the moment when they could pierce it. Others lay against the claws, playing over them, prying for a weakness, wearing them away in a compassion that was timeless and without mercy.

In the final chapter two men have found Martin's body washed up on the shore of a Hebridean island. One of them wonders aloud whether he could have suffered in drowning. The other replies '. . . don't worry about him. You saw the body. He didn't even have time to kick off his seaboots.'

The reader will recognize that scene on the rock as a Last Judgement – one of the most powerful evocations of such in the last half millennium. But what is significant is the way in which an apparent totally naturalistic story is suddenly, and without warning, re-calibrated as totally metaphysical – though one might hesitate to call it visionary in the usual sense. Moreover, the now-familiar counters have been re-shuffled. It is Martin himself who insists that he really is a solipsist; that what he is experiencing is from his own subconscious – for him that would be better than the alternative, a *real* outside 'intrusion'. Even while knowing it is untrue, he continues to pretend the whole scene is his own invention – and, therefore, by implication, in some way invalid. This is, of course, exactly Scrooge's manoeuvre when faced with Marley's ghost. Marley simply terrifies him into submission with a terrible cry and clanking of chains – a very corny Gothic touch, and perhaps the weakest bit of the whole novel. Here the figure on the rock is not interested in defining or defending his own identity. Whether he is 'internal' or 'external' is of no significance. He is totally in control. And he is totally relentless. What is significant is his complete power to remove the sea, the sky, rock, and eventually every bit of Martin himself except the claws which, finally, have only themselves to cling on to. Thus even the name 'Pincher' is progressively re-defined as Martin loses anything else to seize or hold. Finally he can only *pinch* himself. His own consciousness – the well-named 'centre' of his lifelong self-centredness – is all that is left.

Golding was once asked by a student at Sussex University, 'How long does it take Pincher Martin to die?' He replied 'Eternity'. 'But', she persisted, 'how long does it take in real time?' Golding paused, and then said 'Eternity'.[57]

There speaks the daemon.

We shall never know whether our sense of inner worlds began with dreams and visions, but from what written records we have, it is clear that such irrational perceptions played a large part in their creation. But the three-thousand-year-old question of *who* controls such experiences remains unanswered. Few of us have ever encountered the kind of significant and life-changing 'intrusions' recorded in the Bible, and at intervals, by the most unlikely people, ever since. But they are sufficiently unnerving and disturbing to constitute a kind of constant background noise to the more domestic kind of inner spaces we all in some sense possess and enjoy.[58]

---

[57] As reported by Stephen Medcalf. See Carey, p. 196.

[58] My image is, of course, that of the constant hiss from the Cosmic Microwave Background Radiation from outer space, now omnipresent throughout the entire universe – the remnants from the original Big Bang – discovered by Arno Penzias and Robert Wilson.

2

Space on all three floors: Dante to MacDonald

When I first started teaching at the University of Sussex in the 1960s, one of the most interesting interdisciplinary courses on offer was one on 'Paul, Augustine and Dante'. Coming from the more watertight confines of Cambridge, when I first came across it I was astonished that such a course could be considered academically viable. But my colleague, the late and much-lamented Stephen Medcalf, who had created the course, gave me his rationale. All three figures, he pointed out, whatever their previous personal struggles towards knowledge of God, were mystics, with a strong personal inner sense of having been *chosen* by Him. The first two, in their very different ways, would from their own experience, endorse some version of Predestination, even if not with the ferocious legal finality introduced by Calvin. In contrast, the third, Dante, would turn out to be the great champion of free will, and therefore of choice. What he could have added was that all three were pioneers in the extension of inner space. With them the imagined universe became a multi-storey one.

Paul's conversion on the road to Damascus is famous – celebrated in art and literature almost to the point of cliché (see Pl. 2). After such an experience, it is hardly surprising that he should have felt in some way marked out by God. Perhaps less well known, but as significant in his own life, is his later admission of being 'caught up to the third heaven'.

('Whether in the body, I cannot tell; or whether out of the body I cannot tell: God knoweth;) such an one caught up to the third heaven ... How that he was caught up into paradise, and heard unspeakable words, which it is not lawful for a man to utter.[1]

That last sentence seems to suggest unequivocally that Paul is here writing of himself. Whatever Paul meant by 'the third heaven' must forever remain a source of speculation – in Jewish mythology it is the dwelling-place of God – but it is clear that Paul is here acknowledging (in his own phrase, 'boasting') other mystical experiences perhaps even more significant to him than his dramatic conversion. In retrospect, at least, that number three has been of more lasting importance than any specific content which may, or may not, have influenced the development of his theology.

If, as we have seen, many figures were troubled by the sense that their psyche was a battleground of outside forces, whether good or bad, Augustine had no such fears – or, more precisely, he had them, and had a way of dealing with them. He specifically *invites* God into his psyche. The main document of evidence, his autobiographical *Confessions*, is, in effect, an extended interior dialogue with God. Whether or not God was there to start with – and Augustine certainly came to believe He had been – it is the internalized presence of God afterwards that provides the driving-force of his subsequent career. Augustine's conversion is perhaps less dramatic than Paul's, but the event, recorded in Book 8 of his *Confessions*, was still seen by him as the decisive turning point in his life, when he finally shook off the Manichaeism of his youth, and accepted the Catholicism of his mother, Monica. He was, he tells us, in the garden of a house in Milan where he, his mother, and a friend were staying. Torn between his sexually active past – he had a child by his (unnamed) mistress – and the chastity demanded by his Catholicism, he had thrown himself down under a fig tree in tears. Suddenly he heard a child's voice from a neighbouring house repeating over and over again *tolle lege, tolle lege* ('take and read').[2] Opening his bible at random[3] he was confronted with the word from St Paul's Epistle to the Romans:

---

[1]King James Version, 2 Corinthians 12.2-4.
[2]*Confessions*, tr., Albert C. Oulter, 1955. Book 8, XII, 29.
[3]A surprisingly common practice for those seeking guidance down to the present.

Not in rioting and drunkenness, not in rioting and drunkenness, not in chambering and wantonness, not in strife and envying. But put ye on the Lord Jesus Christ, and make not provision for the flesh, to fulfil the lusts thereof.[4]

This conversion was followed shortly afterwards by a mystical experience. Augustine and his mother were standing talking in a window at Ostia, the seaport of Rome, about to embark on the voyage back to their home in Africa, when they seem together to have entered a trance-like state.

> And when our conversation had brought us to the point where the very highest of physical sense and the most intense illumination of physical light seemed, in comparison with the sweetness of that life to come, not worthy of comparison, nor even of mention, we lifted ourselves with a more ardent love ... and we gradually passed through all the levels of bodily objects, and even through the heaven itself, where the sun and moon and stars shine on the earth. Indeed, we soared higher yet by an inner musing, speaking and marveling at thy works.[5]

Then, perhaps most mysterious of all, Augustine records that 'we came at last to our own minds and went beyond them', to encounter something – or someone – he calls 'Wisdom'. If he heard a voice, it was one quite unlike that heard by Samuel, or even Elijah.

> If he alone spoke, not through them but by himself, that we might hear his word, not in fleshly tongue or angelic voice, nor sound of thunder, nor the obscurity of a parable, but might hear him – him for whose sake we love these things – if we could hear him without these, as we two now strained ourselves to do, we then with rapid thought might touch on that Eternal Wisdom which abides over all.[6]

This encounter was experienced as something outside both time and place: in eternity. One biographer comments that this was the most intense experience

---

[4]Romans 13.13-14.
[5]*Confessions*, Book 9, X, 24.
[6]Ibid., Book 9, X, 25.

of his life, even, perhaps, 'the most intense ever commemorated'.[7] Like many
such spiritual climaxes, it lasted but a moment – or, perhaps, without time, an
eternity – and then with a sigh 'we returned to the sounds of our own tongue,
where the spoken word had both beginning and end.'[8]

The whole event left an indelible mark upon him – the more so because his
mother died only a few days later without ever returning to Africa. Augustine
was left with an almost inexpressible certainty that they had encountered a
higher reality against which the apparent reality of this world counted for
nothing. How far this guiding recollection of his life was comparable with
Paul's vision of the Third Heaven is, of course, an impossible question. Mystical
experiences are, by definition, incommensurable, as well as unknowable to
outsiders. The common characteristic of all such accounts is that they were
'indescribable'. But it was to leave him with an overwhelming sense of the
vastness of the interior space encompassed by his own mind. Having soared
through the solar system, he writes 'we came at last to our own minds' – as if
everything that had happened so far was *within* him – as indeed, in some sense
it had to be. Whether coming to 'their own minds' was thus a part of that inner
spatial movement, or a recovery of external consciousness is not clear – and it
is, of course, perfectly possible that he was not clear himself. But what this did
do was to lead him into further reflections on that sense of illimitable inner
space.

Part of that space might involve eternity itself. Since at least the
mid-seventeenth century the word has housed two very different meanings in
constant tension with one another. The most popular meaning is, of course,
'world without end' – an extension of time into infinity. Trying seriously to
imagine real infinity is difficult enough, but the other meaning – already
present in Augustine, not to mention Golding's *Pincher Martin* – is perhaps
even more difficult. That is the total *absence* of time. No time whatsoever. Try
to imagine an instantaneous flash – infinite space of absolutely no temporal
duration – in which past, present and future are all fully present simultaneously

---

[7]Rebecca West, *St Augustine*, Peter Davies, 1933, p. 91, quoted by Stephen Greenblatt, *The Rise and Fall of Adam and Eve*, Bodley Head, 2017, p. 96.
[8]Though perhaps one of the earliest descriptions of such experiences, it follows what is now seen as a classic form. See David Hay, *Exploring Inner Space*, Pelican, 1982.

down to the finest detail.[9] It may indeed be possible that this is what those who think of the eternal bliss of Heaven – or even Hell – will actually discover at the point of death: not endless time, but a singularity outside time. Perhaps the best way to approach (if not to grasp) what Augustine might have experienced would be in the words of Henry Vaughan's mystical poem:

> I saw Eternity the other night,
> Like a great ring of pure and endless light,
> All calm, as it was bright;
> And round beneath it, Time in hours, days, years,
> Driv'n by the spheres
> Like a vast shadow mov'd;

Who knows if this is what Augustine also 'saw'?

At a more mundane level, Augustine turns with a conscious nod to Plato, towards 'the vast cave of the memory' – making it not merely the storehouse of memory, but a complete world in itself. But in his 'Cave Myth' Plato was not thinking of different metaphysical levels – or at least not here. His is still in theory a one-storey world, where we are looking in the *wrong* direction, so that all we see are shadows cast by the light behind us. In effect, of course, the two 'directions' amount to something more like a contrast between the practical everyday world versus a more mystical world of truth, a world of ideal 'forms' and greater reality. Augustine knew Plato well – he was at one stage a Neo-Platonist[10] – and the greater reality, of which this world was but a shadow, was not, of course, anything in pagan philosophy, but the ineffable illumination of Christianity, whose Wisdom he had once so movingly encountered.

---

[9] One of the most arresting accounts of such a vision is, surprisingly, from a children's book: 'Everything changes. Or, rather, everything is revealed. There are no more secrets. The plan of the world seems plain, like an easy sum that one writes in big figures on a child's slate. One wonders how one can ever have wondered about anything. Space is not; every place that one has seen or dreamed of is here. Time is not; into this instant is crowded all that one has ever done or dreamed of doing. It is a moment and it is eternity. It is the centre of the universe and it is the universe itself. The eternal light rests on and illuminates the eternal heart of things.' *The Enchanted Castle*, by E. Nesbit (1907) p. 347.

[10] *Confessions*, Book 7.

But there is something beyond even memory. What that 'something' might be, Augustine is not sure. In the immortal words of Donald Rumsfeld, this is a case of an 'unknown unknown'. Augustine muses introspectively:

> I do not myself grasp all that I am. Thus the mind is far too narrow to contain itself. But where can that part of it be which it does not contain? Is it outside and not in itself? How can it be, then, that the mind cannot grasp itself?[11]

Whether this represents a reaching out towards a theory of the unconscious fifteen hundred years before Freud must remain a matter of conjecture. But it is certainly close. What Augustine calls 'memory' embraces a huge range of experiences, many of which he cannot at any moment recall, but will come to the surface with the appropriate stimuli. He is constantly aware that his mind is multi-layered, and that there is more to it than his consciousness can locate or control. Here, if anywhere, is Augustine's most revolutionary contribution to human thought. Whereas Plato had urged his followers to make a spiritual *turn*, to face away from appearances towards what he believed was the reality of ideal forms, it was still expressed physically in terms of the *exterior* world. Augustine urges us to turn *inward*. 'Do not go outward; return within yourself. In the inward man dwells truth.'[12] The light of God is not just 'out there', illuminating the order of being, as it is for Plato; it is also the 'inner' light – a point echoed fourteen hundred years later by the Quakers and the Romantics.

But it is, above all, to Dante, some eight hundred years later, that we owe the lasting sense of living in a three-storied world (see Pl. 3). He did not, of course, invent the notion of heaven, purgatory and hell as three contiguous layers of the after-life, but he gave a popular belief such a lasting form and imaginative substance that no subsequent writer on the mind could ignore them[13] – even, as we have seen, Freud, the non-believing Jew, whose 'superego', 'ego' and 'id' occupy much the same three-storey space in his psychology.

---

[11]Ibid., Book 10, VII, 15.

[12]*Noli foras ire, in te ipsum redi; in interiore homine habitat veritas. De Vera Religione*, XXXIX, 72.

[13]See Jacques Le Goff, *The Birth of Purgatory*, (1981), tr. Arthur Goldhammer, University of Chicago Press, 1986.

If Dante had undergone any kind of conversion experience, he does not tell us about it. The poem for which he is primarily remembered, the *Divine Comedy*, belongs to the category of self-confessed fiction which we looked at in the last chapter – and though it is manifestly symbolic in almost every respect, it makes no claim to be a dream. Indeed, he tells us at the very beginning, in the first canto, that he had apparently just 'awakened'; and during the narrative (which lasts for the whole of Easter week) he mentions sleeping on a number of occasions. Like almost everything else in the *Comedy*, this 'awakening' is as much a spiritual or allegorical statement as it is a literal one.

Nevertheless, despite this, even during his lifetime at least some of his contemporaries took it literally. In his *Life of Dante*, Giovanni Boccaccio (1313–75) tells the story that once, when Dante was in Verona:

> ... when the fame of his works was already widely spread, and especially that part of his *Comedy* which he calls the *Inferno*, and when he was known by many, both men and women – that, passing before a door where many women were sitting, one of them said softly to the others (but not so softly that she was not heard by him and his companion), 'Do you see the man who goes to hell, and returns when he pleases, and brings back news of those who are below?' To this one of the others responded naively, 'Indeed, you must be speaking the truth. Don't you see how his beard is crisped and his complexion browned by the heat and smoke that is below?' Hearing these words said behind him, and knowing that they came from the women's simple belief, he was pleased, and passed on ...[14]

Dante was not, however, always so pleased with what he overheard concerning his great life's work. Franco Sacchetti, another Florentine poet, tells the story of Dante before his exile, attacking a blacksmith in Florence because the man was singing bits of the *Divine Comedy*, mixing the lines up, leaving bits out, and adding material of his own.[15]

The women's very literal view of Dante was, however, correct in one respect. His three-storey world is given a very specific geographical location – at least for Hell and Purgatory. Hell is entered by a cave in the ground apparently

[14]Giovanni Boccaccio, *Life of Dante*, tr. J.G. Nichols, London: Hesperus Press, 2002, pp. 40–1.
[15]Franco Sacchetti, *Il trecentonvovelle*. Cited by Nichols, above, p. xii.

beneath Jerusalem – but since it has a lengthy inscription over its ominous portal, concluding with the notorious words 'Abandon Hope, All Ye That Enter Here', it is already clear that that this is a one-off entry, open only to still-living poets who are accompanied by the shade of Virgil, and definitely not available to local tourists. From there Hell opens up into a vast series of concentric rings descending in a huge spiral down to the centre of the earth. The outer rings (home to the virtuous pagans) are temperate enough, but as we descend there are tempests (for the lustful) and appropriate fires and tortures enough for all the deserving sinners. Beyond this, right at the centre of the earth, is a lake of ice, where Satan himself, the ultimate traitor, is forever frozen in. There follows a wonderful description of Dante and his guide and mentor, Virgil, continuing their descent, clinging to his fur (yes, he is *very* hairy) until they suddenly find themselves *climbing* as they pass the centre of the earth and begin the long ascent to daylight at the other side of the world. Here they find the island mountain of Purgatory, towering up into the sky.

The second book of the trilogy, the *Purgatorio*, is fundamentally different from both the first and the last in that, unlike them, it is totally dominated by time. Though both Hell and Paradise receive constant new recruits (the former presumably more than the latter . . .) both are essentially *outside* earthly time. They are eternal. Whether we interpret that as an endless temporal sequence, or, as freed from time, existing in a single everlasting moment, is, literally as well as metaphorically, immaterial. Neither can readily be imagined. In Purgatory, however, time is all-important. The souls of the dead, whose sins are purged as they ascend, press forward up the mountain in constant hope. Their future will be in Paradise, and, however long is their allotted purgatorial span, nevertheless every hour brings them nearer their desired goal.

The mountain itself, though steepest at the base, and progressively more gentle as Dante and Virgil slowly ascend by a narrowing spiral path (the opposite to the downward spiral of Hell), is also increasingly beautiful – itself remarkable in a society which saw mountains as dreadful and usually to be avoided[16] – and full of music: sometimes sung by angels, but more often by the repentant souls

---

[16]See Marjorie Hope Nicholson, *Mountain Gloom and Mountain Glory: the Development of the Aesthetics of the Infinite*, Weyerhaeuser Environmental Classics, 2009.

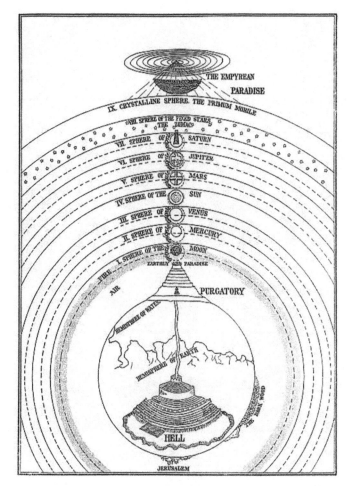

Figure 2.1 *Map of Dante's Comedy.*

themselves. Music, of course, is the art form of time. A picture is a frozen instant, always eternally static; music is always a *sequence* of notes. It cannot exist outside time.

At the summit they enter the Earthly Paradise – what Eden should have been – and here Dante, who has now lost Virgil, his earthly guide, and has been joined by Beatrice, his heavenly one,[17] passes upwards, again, into Paradise itself.

---

[17]See Stephen Prickett, *Words and the Word*, Cambridge University Press, 1976. Chapter 4, pp. 149–73. 'Elijah and Dante: The Word and the "Voice"'.

Figure 2.2 *Dante's Purgatorio.*

In the Ptolemaic universe, Paradise is presumably in or even beyond the realm of the fixed stars, the outermost sphere of the universe, but Dante knows perfectly well that no earthly mountain could stretch so far. Whereas the first two, the *Inferno* and *Purgatorio*, are very definitely presented as a part of our material world, with a precise geographical location, here we have for the first time moved from Earth to another dimension altogether, a strictly non-material sphere of existence. Yet, as one might expect, there are further peculiarities to this structure that immediately undermine this apparent materiality. From the very first lines of the *Inferno* we are left in no doubt that this is a highly symbolic narrative, not some kind of spiritual geography lesson. As any educated medieval reader would be well aware, such a story, like those of the Bible itself, would be multivalent, packed with layer upon layer of symbolic meaning. In this case, as Dante explained in a letter to his patron, Can Grande della Scala, the literal narrative is to be seen as complemented by three further layers: the allegorical, the anagogical and the mystical. We must not lose sight of the fact that Hell and Purgatory are chasms and mountains of the imagination.

Moreover if, as we are told, Dante begins his supernatural journey in Jerusalem, within the poem he is given no way back to his native Tuscany. He awakes from sleep at the beginning, not the end. The *Paradiso* finishes not with any return to Earth, but in a different dimension, with a sublime vision of the Trinity.

> All'alta fantasia qui mancò possa;
> Ma già volgeva il mio disio e 'l velle,
> Sì come rota ch' igualmente è mossa,
> L'amor che move il sole e l'altre stelle.

> [*Here power failed the high phantasy; but now my desire and will, like a wheel that spins with even motion, were revolved by the Love that moves the sun and other stars.*][18]

Sinclair, whose translation this is, was careful not to translate the Italian *fantasia* by the English word 'fantasy', but to use the less common 'phantasy'. *Fantasia* is a difficult word to find an equivalent of in English, especially since Dante, in another work, the *Convivio*, had given it his own personal twist, defining it as 'the power by which the intellect represents what it sees'. It is the essence of poetry. This is much closer to Coleridge's use of 'imagination' than to the normal English 'fantasy' (which Coleridge despised), and even seems to offer something closer to a visionary quality, although less a vision imposed from outside than one internally generated.

However, there is one story connected with the ending of the *Divine Comedy* that does include a dream. Boccaccio, in his biography of Dante, tells us that after Dante's death the final thirteen cantos of the *Paradiso* – including the lines above – were found to be missing. Then his son, Iacopo, had a dream in which his father appeared to him 'dressed in spotless clothes, and with an

---

[18]*Paradiso*, Canto xxxiii, 142–5, tr. J.D. Sinclair, Oxford University Press, 1939.

unusual light shining in his face'. In reply to his son's question as to whether he
still lived, he replied that he was, 'but in the true life, not ours.'

> And then it seemed that his father took him by the hand, and led him to the
> room where he was accustomed to sleep when he lived in this life, and
> touched a spot there, and said, 'That which you have so much sought after
> is here.' ... So, with much of the night still remaining, [he and a friend]
> went to the place mentioned, and there found a mat fixed to a wall. Gently
> lifting this, they saw a little opening, which neither of them had seen before
> or knew was there, and in it they found some writings, all mildewed by the
> dampness of the wall, and near to rotting had they stayed there only a little
> longer. Carefully cleaning the mildew from them, they read them, and saw
> that they contained the thirteen cantos which they had so much sought.[19]

Whether it is true, as Boccaccio also claimed, that previous accounts of Hell
were all written by pagans and that Dante's was the first Christian account, it is
certainly true that, as we have seen, the *Divine Comedy* was already so famous
by the time that Dante died, in 1321, that the three-storey universe of Hell,
Purgatory and Heaven was firmly established for all time in his image. Despite
some opposition – astonishingly, from the Catholic Church itself – Dante's
three-storey geography provided a convenient template for further divine
judgements.

Why should a narrative so firmly grounded for two-thirds of its length in
terrestrial geography have such an impact on the interior mental worlds not
merely of its readers – in a world of manuscripts, a fairly small group until the
invention of printing nearly quarter of a millennium later – but of those who
had listened to public recitations of the whole work or who (like the women in
Boccaccio's anecdote) had merely heard something about it? One obvious
answer is that this is a psychodrama projected on to the real world. Virgil is the
spirit of ancient poetry, who, in turn, is the successor to Homer and the antique
epic. Dante, by implication, is their successor as epic poet in the European
Christian world. Before Virgil finally leaves him in the earthly paradise (Canto
XXVII), he gives Dante a blessing: having ascended purgatory for the first time

---

[19]Boccaccio, *Life of Dante*, pp. 65–6.

in his life his hitherto corrupted human will is genuinely free. The gifts that have brought him so far, Virgil tells him, are *ingenio* and *arte*, usually translated as '*understanding*' and '*skill*' – the intellectual insight and the necessary technical craft to give that insight effective expression:[20] terms that, as we have seen, are closely allied in Dante's vocabulary with *phantasia*, the power of the intellect to represent what it sees. However apparently anchored on this terrestrial globe, the *Divine Comedy* is, of course, totally imaginary. In the end, the poetry is not about the geography of the physical world; it is about the geography of the human mind. And – as Augustine had already seen – the world is contained by the mind. There is, in this sense, no world without mind.

And so it was to prove. Dante's 'high phantasy' was to change the way in which people imagined the world, and therefore imagined themselves. In many cases, the vastness of the imagined three-storey universe was long to outlast any literal belief in a Dantean Hell, Purgatory and Heaven. In one obvious development, the middle section, Purgatory, was replaced by the earth – or just mundane life. In another, what we might call the geography of inner space expanded to embrace the whole known universe. Astonishingly, given that this was three hundred years before Ferdinand Magellan first sailed around the world (1519–22), Dante seems to have had – or at least seen – a map of the Southern hemisphere stars. Augustine's mystical journey out through the solar system until he came 'at last to his own mind', was augmented and extended by Dante's no less mystical journey through the earth, up through Purgatory and into Paradise. In this new mystico-cosmology, inner space now *includes* outer space.

Similarly, at the end of Chaucer's poem, *Troilus and Criseyde*, probably written around 1385, when Troilus dies his spirit drifts outward through space in what we would now call the 'solar system' – though then, of course, it was still a pre-Copernican earth-centred universe with the sun rotating around it. Looking back Troilus sees 'this little spot of earth, that with the sea/Embraced is' and contrasts his unhappy life with the 'plain felicity/That is in heaven above.' That line about the sea surrounding the land seems eerily to anticipate the photographs of our blue planet taken by NASA from beyond the moon.

---

[20]See Prickett, *Words and the Word*, pp. 150–1.

Troilus's spirit, however, has a more curious fate. As a good pagan from the pre-Christian dispensation, he is placed in the realm of the stars by the pagan god Mercury. But then, in an astonishing turn-around, Chaucer suddenly dispenses with the entire pagan metaphysical machinery of his narrative – gods such as Mars and Venus intervening in human affairs to alter the fates of those they favour or dislike – and points out that these all belong to the pre-Christian world, and that *readers* should remember that they are privileged to live under the new dispensation of Christ. Critics seem still divided as to whether this is some kind of conventional genuflection to received norms; irony; or an apology for using a pre-Christian narrative at all: none of which options makes much sense. Throughout the Middle Ages and, indeed, much of the Renaissance, we see a kind of invisible glass wall between the pagan gods of the classical world and the Christian world-picture. The two co-exist without mixing – which makes Chaucer's intervention even more unusual. Part of the disjuncture is that 'religion' simply has a different meaning within the two worlds. 'Mars', 'Venus' etc. are used more as psychological counters than as divine beings. Mars makes people warlike. Venus makes people fall in love. Moreover, any 'religious' system that makes Augustus – and later, Caligula – 'gods' is not operating in any system recognizable to a biblical monotheist.

What is interesting for us, however, is Troilus's journey outwards through the cosmos so that he can look back at that tiny spot of earth. We cannot know if Chaucer had actually read Augustine's *Confessions*, with its mystical movement out from the earth to reach 'his own mind', but Chaucer was a highly educated man, and it seems more than likely.[21] He certainly mentions Augustine by name, which is not so surprising, and also Dante, which is much more surprising, even though we also know that Chaucer did read Italian.

If St Paul felt that he was 'not permitted to tell' of his mystical experiences, John of Patmos, the author of the biblical book of Revelation, had shown no such inhibitions. It contains one of the most extensive and extraordinary descriptions of the last things ever written, which has inspired a long tradition

---

[21] See J.M. Ganim, 'Identity and Subjecthood', in *The Oxford Handbook of Mediaeval Literature in English*, eds. Elaine Treharne, Greg Walker and William Green, Oxford University Press, 2010, p. 227.

of artists and commentators ever since – including such diverse figures as Dante himself, Hildegard of Bingen, St John of the Cross, St Teresa, Ignatius Loyola, Albrecht Dürer, Isaac Newton, Immanuel Swedenborg and William Blake, to name but a few. Though it has been responsible for innumerable works of art through the ages – more, we are told, than any other book in history[22] – one of its strangest features is that though it is presented in a series of dramatic images, when looked at more closely what distinguishes so many of these images is their sheer *resistance* to normal visualization.

Individual fragments – the Whore of Babylon astride the seven headed Beast, the Four Horsemen of the Apocalypse, or particular warrior angels – have been the subject of many pictures, but how does one set about representing the Woman Clothed with the Sun, or the opening of a Seal? Though the reader is given a series of vivid and exotic descriptions, with a spiritual geography vast and vague in the extreme, there are already visions of Hell and Paradise with all the elements that would later be brought together in a more explicitly stratified form in the medieval three-storey universe.

While there is a long tradition of paintings and prints of images from the Apocalypse, as we shall see in the next chapter, there is circumstantial evidence that sometime during the fifteenth century painters and artists in the Low Countries began to see biblical images in a quite new, and newly realistic, way that was to lead on to the Reformation itself.[23] For them, in contrast with the symbolism of medieval painting, realism was the path to a new kind of internal awareness. This was partly driven by things as simple and material as changes in the economic and banking structure of the area, partly even by changes in paint technology – both in finer brushes and the introduction of oil paint – and, above all, by changes in theology, religious practice and spirituality. As one art historian writes, 'Realism was not so much an objective in itself, as a means of shaping a new spirituality . . . It was not a renouncement of mediaeval transcendence, but a new form of religious experience.'[24]

---

[22]See Anthony and Natasha O'Hear, *Picturing the Apocalypse: The Book of Revelation in the Arts over Two Millennia*, Oxford University Press, 2017.

[23]See the Introduction to Christopher Herbert, *Foreshadowing the Reformation: Art and Religion in the Fifteenth Century Burgundian Netherlands*, Routledge, 2017.

[24]See Dirk de Vos, *The Flemish Primitives*, Princeton University Press, 2002, p. 10.

Of the many paintings and prints of images from the Apocalypse produced in the Netherlands at this period, one in particular stands out in its implications. It is Hans Memling's *St John Altarpiece*, a triptych commissioned for St John's Hospital in Bruges (1474–9), where it still is (see Pl. 4). The right-hand panel shows a thoughtful John of Patmos seated on a rock with a book and a pen (in his left hand). Above him are scenes from the Apocalypse: God, enthroned within an elliptical rainbow, surrounded by the four-and-twenty elders, including figures from the first thirteen chapters of Revelation, while on the right are other horsemen and the handing over of power from the Dragon to the Sea Beast (see Pl. 5).

The right-hand panel is one of the first known attempts to portray the images of the Apocalypse in one piece, and, though these secondary images are painted with exquisite care and skill, most are so small that it is difficult to make them out even in good reproductions. They would certainly have been invisible to the original inhabitants of the hospital themselves.

Natasha and Anthony O'Hear, in *Picturing the Apocalypse*, suggest that this is not an accident.[25] This panel is, in short, an early attempt– perhaps *the* earliest attempt – actually to *picture* internalization. We are even meant to see John himself, in the foreground, as visionary, while the contents of his vision, spread out above and behind him, are not so much entities in themselves as the contents of his mind.

Milton was, of course, one of those inspired by the Reformation. But he had also read Dante, and, indeed, explicitly saw *Paradise Lost* as a work to rival the *Divine Comedy*. He, too, writes of a cosmos that enfolds heaven, earth and hell all within a single vast space. After the war in Heaven, Satan with all his rebel angels is thrown out of Paradise and come to rest in Hell, which – as many readers have noticed – bears an uncanny resemblance to the republican Parliament. From there Satan sets out for a journey in search of Adam and Eve who are to be found in Eden, as the first inhabitants of the newly-created Earth. It is usually argued that Milton's purpose in writing his great epic is to give the whole story such intense poetic realism as to 'justify the ways of God to man'.[26]

---

[25]Natasha and Anthony O'Hear, *Picturing the Apocalypse*, pp. 34–5; 78–9; etc.
[26]This is the main thesis of the Milton chapters of Stephen Greenblatt's *Rise and Fall of Adam and Eve*.

This involves, of course, an intensely realistic cosmos – even more essential if such 'realism' includes not merely Earth, but Heaven and Hell as well. Yet despite the fact that Milton's universe, in a post-Copernican world, is vastly bigger than Dante's, the planetary system in which Satan discovers our first unfallen ancestors is not the modern solar system, but the pre-Copernican Ptolemaic system, with the earth, not the sun, at its centre. Why did Milton deliberately choose what he well knew to be an antiquated and obsolete model of the cosmos? He had even met Galileo, whose observations with his newly invented telescope had given extra weight to the Copernican hypothesis.

One obvious answer is that if, like Dante, he needed to mix physical earthly geography and metaphysical entities such as heaven and hell, the older system, which allowed for a heaven beyond the sphere of the fixed stars, was symbolically more convenient. In the Ptolemaic system the outermost sphere was that of the Prime Mover – ultimately God himself. So presumably here was also at least the possibility of a physical location for heaven. But this is a two-edged sword. If the older system made it easier to integrate incompatible realms (as indeed it might well do) then it also undermines the very 'realism' which he was trying to create in his narrative. Though Raphael tries to hedge his bets and allow for various possibilities in his mini-lectures to Adam on science and the general nature of things in books Seven and Eight of *Paradise Lost*, the problem is that we have already seen Satan in earlier books entering what seems unmistakably a geocentric universe. The possibility that Raphael is a modern Copernican, while Satan is scientifically ignorant and out-of-date, seems just a little far-fetched even for such a world of extraordinary events.

Once one begins seriously to search out the geography of *Paradise Lost*, of course, the problems come thick and fast. Nor is there any effective solution to such an attempt to fuse what are totally incompatible entities, and we should rather be amazed by the way in which Milton very nearly gets away with the impossible. In the process, he has created a cosmos vastly bigger than anything revealed by Galileo's telescope. This is simply the biggest interior space yet envisaged by any writer in the world. Not merely do we have the Earth, whether in a geocentric or solar system: we have both Heaven and Hell, not to mention another realm more or less invented by Milton called Chaos, which even has its own ruler – or rather, since ruling is, by definition, impossible, its supreme

Anarch. From the description this is, in itself, unbelievably vast – so much so that even Satan himself is daunted by the need to cross it. Not least of the problems he encounters is that since, again more or less by definition, Chaos has no dimensions at all, 'crossing' it is to say the least, problematic. It is

> . . . a dark
> Illimitable Ocean without bound,
> Without dimension, where length, breadth, and highth,
> And time and place are lost;[27]

Though Heaven is clearly 'up', and Hell is 'down' – in 'bottomless perdition', to be precise – this is undoubtedly a three-storey universe of a kind to be unequalled for centuries to come. Not until Einstein and the twentieth century's visual and radio telescopes enlarged our ideas of deep space, has anything on an even remotely comparable scale even been imagined.

Given the infinity of Milton's epic imagination, the next developments were not so much of size, but concerned the psychological implications of such spatial imagination. The so-called 'Romantics'[28] were fascinated both by Milton and by the developing ideas of human consciousness. In almost the first use of the word, Percy Shelley (1792–1822) was to call William Wordsworth the 'subtle-souled Psychologist' – and not without reason. Wordsworth's most famous poem about the development of the human mind, only named after his death as *The Prelude*, climaxes with an ascent of Snowdon, which he treats as a metaphor for human consciousness. Climbing the mountain in the dark, he and his unnamed companions suddenly break through a layer of cloud into bright moonlight. Below them, the lower part of the mountain is covered by mist, but from where they are standing, the rest of the ascent to the summit is brightly illuminated.

> I looked about, and lo,   40
> The moon stood naked in the heavens at height
> Immense above my head, and on the shore

---

[27]*Paradise Lost*, Book II, lines 891–3.
[28]The term, of course, was never used by the English Romantics, but was applied to them by analogy from the German Romantics, by Hippolyte Taine, the French literary critic.

I found myself of a huge sea of mist,

Which meek and silent rested at my feet.

A hundred hills their dusky backs upheaved   45

All over this still ocean, and beyond,

Far, far beyond, the vapours shot themselves

In headlands, tongues, and promontory shapes,

Into the sea, the real sea, that seemed

To dwindle and give up its majesty,   50

Usurped upon as far as sight could reach.

Meanwhile, the moon looked down upon this shew

In single glory, and we stood, the mist

Touching our very feet; and from the shore

At distance not the third part of a mile   55

Was a blue chasm, a fracture in the vapour,

A deep and gloomy breathing-place, through which

Mounted the roar of waters, torrents, streams

Innumerable, roaring with one voice.

The universal spectacle throughout   60

Was shaped for admiration and delight,

Grand in itself alone, but in that breach

Through which the homeless voice of waters rose,

That dark deep thoroughfare, had Nature lodged

The soul, the imagination of the whole.[29]

Wordsworth goes on to suggest that this is 'the perfect image of a mighty mind' that is 'exalted' by what he calls an 'underpresence' – or what, within a few years, would come to be called the unconscious. Consciousness is but the tiny illuminated summit above the vastness of the unconscious mind below. Yet, we note, even that 'illumination', moonlight, is actually reflected light from a further concealed source: the sun. All around him streams of water are plunging down the mountain from light into darkness, suggesting how the unconscious might be fed from above by the conscious mind. Their noise is

---

[29]William Wordsworth, *The Prelude* (1805), Book XIII, lines 40–65.

returning back into the upper world through that rent in the clouds, which he fixes on as an image of the poetic imagination – the place where the conscious and the unconscious minds meet.[30] Inspiration comes of being able to tap into what is unseen beneath the clouds.

For avid Jungians there is a further twist. Though the clouds appear to the observers like 'a sea', beyond them is the Menai Strait – 'the real sea' – providing a kind of second layer to the unconscious, akin perhaps to Jung's concept of a racial or 'collective unconscious'. Though this is not quite the metaphysical three-storey universe of his medieval predecessors, in its secularized structure it is astonishingly close to them. Wordsworth was a self-declared Nature mystic, and, for those with eyes to see, the 1805 version of *The Prelude* showed clear traces of its earlier roots. The poem has thirteen books, precisely the same as in Augustine's *Confessions*, and thirteen is a prime number that also reflects the number of Christ and his twelve apostles – which in turn harks back to the twelve tribes of Israel. His 'conversion' to Nature, if it may be so called, rescuing him from his despair at the failure of his love affair with Annette Vallon and his ideals for the French Revolution, occurs in Book IX, at the same position as Augustine's conversion. *The Prelude*, at least in its original form,[31] is the story of Wordsworth's own spiritual and psychological journey, which parallels that of Augustine's devout self-exploration, but whereas Augustine's is a story of supernatural election, Wordsworth's story, explicitly 'the growth of a poet's mind', is one of natural psychology.

But Wordsworth is not the only early nineteenth-century figure to make use of the three-storey universe for psychological purposes. George MacDonald, the displaced Scottish Congregational Minister, is now best remembered not so much as the author of his many realistic novels, but as one of the great originators of Victorian fantasy. His first published work was entitled *Within and Without* (1855), a dramatic poem about the contrast between our inner and outer worlds. He was a friend of both Charles Dodgson – better known as Lewis Carroll, the author of the *Alice* books – and of Charles Kingsley (1819–75), author of *The Water Babies*. It was to MacDonald that Carroll sent the

---

[30]See Stephen Prickett, *Coleridge and Wordsworth: The Poetry of Growth*, Cambridge University Press, 1970.

[31]The 1850 text, a longer version unpublished at the time of his death, has fourteen books.

original manuscript of *Alice in Wonderland* to get his opinion as to whether it should be published. MacDonald read it aloud to his children who enthusiastically reported in favour.

MacDonald's own children's books, *The Princess and the Goblin* (1872), and *The Princess and Curdie* (1883), have demonstrated their continued popularity by staying in print continuously ever since their first publication, albeit mostly under the radar of critical attention. The former, in particular, has long been a favourite. G.K. Chesterton (1874–1936), himself a brilliant fantasy writer, and one of the few to write about MacDonald, declared it was his masterwork: all his other fairy stories were 'illustrations and disguises of that one'.

Figure 2.3 *Princess's Castle. From George MacDonald,* The Princess and the Goblin, *illustrated by Arthur Hughes, Puffin, 1964, p. 11.*

The coexistence of different worlds is set out very cleverly in *The Princess and the Goblin*. The princess Irene is sent away to the Mountains because her mother is not strong, and is brought up by her nurse 'in a large house, half castle, half farmhouse, on the side of a mountain, about halfway between its base and its peak.'[32] Suggestions of an allegorical middle-ground are rapidly, if unobtrusively, amplified as the story unfolds. Not merely is the castle halfway up the mountain, but Irene herself holds a halfway position in the house. In the attics, up a strangely elusive stairway – sometimes to be found, at other times not at all – she finds a very old but beautiful lady whose name is *also* Irene.

Figure 2.4 *Great-great-grandmother. From George MacDonald,* The Princess and the Goblin, *illustrated by Arthur Hughes, Puffin, 1964, p. 8.*

---

[32]*Princess and the Goblin*, illustrated by Arthur Hughes, Puffin, 1964, p. 11.

She claims to be her great-great-grandmother – and is getting on for two thousand years old. She lives off the eggs of her flock of white doves, and seems to spend most of her time spinning in her room. Not surprisingly the princess's nurse, who is the epitome of materialist common sense, doesn't believe a word of this improbable story, and Irene discovers that her old lady is not always so accessible. On her next trip up to the attics she is nowhere to be found. This elusiveness even extends to the grandmother's possessions. On a later, successful, visit, Irene is shown her grandmother's bedroom, where there is an enormous moon-like light that never goes out. Sometimes, especially in crises, this light can be seen outside the castle miles away; at other times it seems to be invisible.

Figure 2.5 *Stairway. From George MacDonald,* The Princess and the Goblin, *illustrated by Arthur Hughes, Puffin, 1964, p. 8.*

One curious property is that it is often more visible from a distance than close up. The old lady tells the princess a 'secret' – that 'if that light were to go out you would fancy yourself lying in a bare garret, on a heap of old straw.'[33] This is subsequently confirmed by the miner's son, Curdie, who cannot at first see either the grandmother or her wonderful possessions.

All he can see is 'a big, bare, garret room . . . a tub, and a heap of musty straw, and a withered apple, and a ray of sunlight coming through a hole in the middle of the roof and shining on your head, and making the whole place look a curious dusky brown.'[34] Only after a series of tests that involve trusting

Figure 2.6 *Goblins. From George MacDonald,* The Princess and the Goblin, *illustrated by Arthur Hughes, Puffin, 1964, p. 155.*

[33]Ibid., p. 8.
[34]Ibid., p. 155.

Irene's word is he able (or, perhaps, permitted) to see the grandmother and her world.

Just as the princess has her elusive grandmother, and namesake, living above her, so there are also creepy things below – goblins burrowing into the mountainside and even into the cellars of the castle itself. These goblins, although they are horrible and misshapen, shunning the light of day, were once 'very like other people'. Their ancestors had chosen to go underground because the then king had imposed too many taxes, and 'required observances they did not like'. As a result, they had been repressed and became ever more degenerate and foul – the more dangerous for being invisible. Most dangerous of all is their queen, who, unlike her subjects, with soft and flabby feet, is armoured with *stone* shoes.

Clearly, we have here the makings of the familiar three-storey universe. The grandmother's attributes, such as her age ('getting on for two thousand years') her name (Irene, meaning 'peace'), and her sustenance by the doves, all suggest an allegory of the Church. Her spinning suggests a more classical activity as one of the Fates. Her role as guardian and seer support this. Seeing her involves an act of faith: not just belief, or even acceptance, but here a *moral* principle that involves, among other things, acting on trust. Partly as a result, however, she is accessible to remarkably few people – and even those to whom she chooses to reveal herself often have difficulty in finding her. Even more embarrassing, she is totally invisible to such servants as the nurse. Her marked preference for royalty is reinforced when, much later, we learn that even Curdie (whose father's name, significantly, is 'Peter') is really of royal lineage himself. Some of this no doubt reflected MacDonald's own practical experience of the Church. He had been expelled from his Congregational Church in Arundel for what was deemed heresy by the elders,[35] and thenceforth had made his living as a professional writer.

With a magical grandmother above her, and goblins in the cellars, the princess is poised – like Dante – if not in mid-life, certainly in the middle of this world. The queen of the goblins is here clearly a foil to the grandmother herself. But this being the nineteenth century, and in a post-Romantic world,

---

[35]Criticisms included an over-familiarity with German theology, and a remark in one of his sermons that, for all he knew, animals had souls.

there is another possibility more easily expressed in Freudian terms of *superego*, *ego* and *id*. The goblins were once surface-dwellers and have chosen to go underground. They are evil primarily in their desire to go their own way at all costs. They hate the light and the people of the surface – especially miners like Curdie and his father who tunnel into their world – but they also want to kidnap the princess and drag her underground to be the wife of their own hideous prince, Harelip. There are clearly shades here also of the Pluto and Persephone myth, with similar psychological undertones. Above all, they cannot bear to be laughed at, or hear poetry of any kind – a point that Dante and Milton would surely have appreciated. On several occasions Curdie effectively routs them simply with mocking and insulting doggerel rhymes. Eventually the goblins divert streams within the mountain with the intention of flooding the castle and drowning its inhabitants: but this, also, is thwarted by Curdie, who, from the mine, had overheard their plotting and so had been able to block their channels, and ensure that nearly all of them are drowned in their own inundation.

Given that this comes so soon before Freud's and Jung's three-storey psychological models, it would be easy to argue that *The Princess and the Goblin* is a transitional late Romantic work in which the internalized religious model gives way to a rather different psychological internalization: one which in the twentieth century was eventually to replace the older one. This is an idea which Freud would surely have embraced. He had, after all, carefully placed himself in the great tradition of thinkers who had displaced humanity from centre stage: Copernicus, who had displaced the geocentric universe; Darwin, who had displaced the idea of humanity as a special creation; and then Freud, himself, who displaced the idea that we are 'masters in our own house'.[36] But

---

[36]'Humanity has in the course of time had to endure from the hands of science two great outrages upon its naive self-love. The first was when it realized that our earth was not the centre of the universe, but only a tiny speck in a world-system of a magnitude hardly conceivable; this is associated in our minds with the name of Copernicus, although Alexandrian doctrines taught something very similar. The second was when biological research robbed man of his peculiar privilege of having been specially created, and relegated him to a descent from the animal world, implying an ineradicable animal nature in him: this transvaluation has been accomplished in our own time upon the instigation of Charles Darwin, Wallace, and their predecessors, and not without the most violent opposition from their contemporaries. But man's craving for grandiosity is now suffering the third and most bitter blow from present-day psychological research which is endeavouring to prove to the "ego" of each one of us that

this raises problems. As we have seen, Augustine's *Confessions* is as much a work of self-analysis as it is a description of his religious experience – indeed, in his case the two are more or less inseparable. And if we read him carefully, the same might be said of Dante. Their psychological languages might be different, but in fact just as the apparently external religious model is always also internal, so the avowedly secular psychoanalytic one seems to have a three-storey structure remarkably similar to the older one.

In fact, this was not even the last fictional gasp of the religious three-floor model. As we have mentioned, C.S. Lewis's *The Great Divorce*, first published in 1945, is a piece of classic dream fiction. It opens in what turns out to be perpetual dusk in a vast and dreary city which is apparently empty, apart from a somewhat cantankerous queue for a bus. This, it turns out, will take them, if not quite to Heaven, to a place that (apart from the bus service) explicitly resembles Dante's earthly paradise. This is a daily service, with room for everyone who wishes to board it, and the passengers are free to stay in the earthly paradise if they so wish. The problem, it turns out, once they move from the dreary city into the brilliant light of eternity, is that all these people are shades: semi-transparent ghosts of what they used to be. And the earthly paradise in which they find themselves is correspondingly solid – so solid, in fact, that grass is painful to walk on, blown leaves are dangerous, and golden apples almost impossible to lift. The parallels with Dante become even more explicit, when the unnamed 'I' of the story is met by George MacDonald himself, who takes the place of Beatrice for Dante, and explains what is going on. He emphasises that this is not *true* Heaven – which is still unimaginable to humans – but, like Dante's earthly paradise, the gateway to heaven from purgatory, for souls going that way.

For all but one of the passengers on the bus, who are overwhelmingly preoccupied with themselves and their own petty selfish concerns, the place is quite unbearable, and they choose, of their own free will, to return to the dreary city. For them, it will now be Hell in the permanent isolation they have

he is not even master in his own house, but that he must remain content with the veriest scraps of information about what is going on unconsciously in his own mind. We psychoanalysts were neither the first nor the only ones to propose to mankind that they should look inward; but it appears to be our lot to advocate it most insistently and to support it by empirical evidence which touches every man closely.' S. Freud, *A General Introduction to Psychoanalysis* (1943), p. 252.

chosen; for those who make the searing choice to drop all their previous obsessions, and to try to survive in this super-solid existence, it will turn out to have been Purgatory, and they will eventually themselves become solid 'real' people. When the narrator asks where the immense cliff was which the bus had to scale to reach this place, MacDonald goes down on his knees to point to a crack in the soil.

> 'I cannot be certain,' he said, 'that this *is* the crack ye came up through. But through a crack no bigger than that ye certainly came.'
>
> 'But – but,' I gasped with a feeling of bewilderment not unlike terror. 'I saw an infinite abyss. And cliffs towering up and up. And then this country on top of the cliffs.'
>
> 'Aye. But the voyage was not mere locomotion. That bus, and all you inside it, were increasing in size.'
>
> 'Do you mean then that Hell – all that infinite empty town – is down some little crack like this?'
>
> 'Yes. All Hell is smaller than one pebble of your earthly world; but it is smaller than one atom of this world, the Real World.'[37]

In a passage that seems to anticipate Golding's last judgement in *Pincher Martin*, MacDonald proceeds to explain that though the inhabitants of this Purgatory or Hell, can visit at least the earthly paradise, those in Heaven cannot visit Hell, just because they are too large.

> For a damned soul is nearly nothing: it is shrunk, shut up in itself. Good beats upon the damned incessantly as sound waves beat upon the ears of the deaf, but they cannot receive it. Their fists are clenched, their teeth are clenched, their eyes fast shut. First they will not, in the end they cannot, open their hands for gifts, or their mouth for food, or their eyes to see.[38]

Hell and Purgatory have been conflated into a single (if infinite) place; Dante's vast mountain has been reduced to a crack in the soil; the arduous ascent can now be overcome in a free scheduled bus ride: but the three-story universe

---

[37]C.S. Lewis, *The Great Divorce*, HarperCollins, 2002, pp. 137–8.
[38]Ibid., p. 139.

remains. The biggest difference between Dante's universe and Lewis's is simply scale. Whereas Hell and Purgatory were vast terrestrial structures, and Paradise an immaterial if theoretically infinite topping, here the greatest concrete reality is Paradise itself, solid and even painful to the touch, and the rest is – literally – *immaterial.* Inner space has been made infinite, and, at the same time, shrunk to molecular size.

Lewis was, of course, well aware of the parallel models of the late nineteenth and earlier twentieth-century psychoanalysts, Freud and Jung; but in a strange way he is more theoretically optimistic than either. What concerns him particularly is the paradox of free will. We may not be in control of our destinies, but just as ill-health can result from unhealthy lifestyle rather than bad genes, there was once real choice for these figures, even if it is the nature of choice eventually to eliminate choice altogether. Freud, however, parallels the older religious models of Augustine or Calvin in his belief that we are *not* – and never were – masters in our own houses. But whereas belief in original sin was part of a system that also offered at least (conditional) salvation, all psychoanalysis could offer was greater personal insight, with the unspoken assumption that this was all that we needed to achieve whatever 'salvation' we desired in the here and now – if, of course, we could pay the requisite fees.[39] Both Freud and Jung emphasize how much that is going on beneath the surface is also somehow beyond our control. Nor has the work of subsequent psychoanalysts done much to change this assumption. One mid-century analyst comments that

> Freud's contribution to the spiritual malaise of our century is not to be overlooked. Squinting through his narrow theoretical keyhole at our hidden lechery, he encouraged us to believe that it was always the worst possible explanation of our behaviour that came nearest to the truth.[40]

Some of the more perceptive of Freud's disciples have been prepared to face the question of their complicity in this denigration. Erik Erikson writes:

---

[39]One recalls the Harry Belafonte song about 'The set of circumstances/ Which enhances the finances/ Of the followers of Doctor Sigmund Freud.'

[40]Anthony Stevens, *Private Myths*, p. 336.

... we were dismayed, when we saw our purpose of enlightenment perverted into a widespread fatalism, according to which man is nothing but a multiplication of his parents' faults and an accumulation of his own earlier selves. We must grudgingly admit that even as we were trying to devise, with scientific determinism, a therapy for the few, we were led to promote an ethical disease among the many.[41]

Secularization has not freed us from the haunting sense of impotence and loss of control of our inner worlds. No change here, then. But the comforts of religion – such as they were – have now been removed. Where once the great-great-grandmother sat spinning, and sending out her light, all that is left now in the garret loft is dust and straw.

---

[41]Erik Erikson, *Young Man Luther: A Study in Psychoanalysis and History*, 1962.

3

The mind has mountains:
Landscape into psyche

In 1925 Carl Gustav Jung (1875–1961) visited East Africa for the first time. He recorded his impressions on first seeing what he took to be a natural landscape untouched by humans.

> From a low hill in this broad savanna a magnificent prospect opened out to us. To the very brink of the horizon we saw gigantic herds of animals: gazelle, antelope, gnu, zebra, warthog, and so on. Grazing, heads nodding, the herds moved forward like slow rivers. There was scarcely any sound save the melancholy cry of a bird of prey. This was the stillness of the eternal beginning, the world as it always had been, in the state of non-being; for until then no one had been present to know that it was this world. I walked away from my companions until I had put them out of sight, and savoured the feeling of being entirely alone. There I was now, the first human being to recognise that this was the world, but who did not know that in this moment he had really created it.

After billions of years of blind evolution, Jung realized, consciousness had finally created objective existence. Not merely did the outer world exist, but with the coming of humanity, we could see and think about it as an objective entity outside and separated from ourselves. He continues:

> Now I knew what it was, and knew even more: that man is indispensable for the completion of creation: that, in fact, he himself is the second creator of

the world, who alone has given to the world its objective existence – without which, unheard, unseen, silently eating, giving birth, dying, heads nodding through hundreds of millions of years, it would have gone on in the profoundest night of non-being down to its unknown end. Human consciousness created objective existence and meaning, and man found his indispensable place in the great process of being.[1]

Though it seems to have come with the force of revelation to Jung, he was, of course, by no means the first person to have realized that, in this sense, consciousness creates our world. As so often, Augustine had struggled to articulate much the same idea fifteen hundred years earlier:

Men go forth to marvel at the heights of mountains and the huge waves of the sea, the broad flow of the rivers, the vastness of the ocean, the orbits of the stars, and yet they neglect to marvel at themselves. Nor do they wonder how it is that, when I spoke of all these things, I was not looking at them with my eyes – and yet I could not have spoken about them had it not been that I was actually seeing within, in my memory, those mountains and waves and rivers and stars which I have seen, and that ocean which I believe in – and with the same vast spaces between them as when I saw them outside me. But when I saw them outside me, I did not take them into me by seeing them; and the things themselves are not inside me, but only their images. And yet I knew through which physical sense each experience had made an impression on me.[2]

What the two have in common is what I earlier called a 'double consciousness'. Jung is awestruck both by this view of nature in the raw, undisturbed by humanity, and at the same time by his own consciousness of himself looking at it. In fact, as he was well aware, that first impression was an illusion. This was a game reserve. So far from being a natural environment, it was one created by humans to allow wild animals to continue, as far as possible, in what humans imagined was a state of nature. In recent years such an idyll – if that is what it

---

[1]C.G. Jung, *Memories, Dreams, Reflections*, ed. Aniela Jaffé, tr. Richard and Clara Winston, Collins and Routledge & Kegan Paul, 1963, p. 240–1.
[2]*Confessions*, 9, VII, 15.

was – has been rudely shattered by the increasing slaughter of elephants and rhinos for their tusks and horns to satisfy the rapacious illusions of Chinese folk medicine. But nonetheless Jung's *feeling* of the conscious mind looking at the vast and varied fecundity of unconscious life, and bringing it to consciousness, as it were, for the first time, is as we shall see an expression of a key modern idea of our relationship with nature.[3]

Augustine's double consciousness is essentially similar, though since he stubbornly believed in the literal truth of the Creation story in Genesis, he was less concerned with the historical feeling of the animate world coming to consciousness for the first time. Adam and Eve were there in the first week or so – and, anyway, since God was there as Creator, there was never any question of a blind evolution slowly coming to consciousness. What interests Augustine is the way in which his own mind embraces all the vastness of external space and allows him to think about it when it is no longer present in front of him.

Neither thinker, profound as both were, lived to see the latest twist in the story of consciousness. As I mentioned in the Introduction, as a young man in the 1960s and 1970s I knew computer experts who took it for granted that when computers reached the same processing power as the human brain – then an almost unimaginable feat in the future – consciousness would follow as a matter of course. Consciousness was for them an inherent quality of complexity. Now, of course, we have super-computers capable of calculations unimaginable to us.[4] The surprise – to some at any rate – is that such machines remain just that: machines. They may perform incredible feats of calculation; they can apparently answer intelligently on the phone to a range of pre-determined questions put to them by members of the public who may believe they are speaking to a real person; they can even improve their chess from learning by experience of thousands of games to out-manoeuvre any human player; but they are not 'conscious' in that way that even a pet cat or dog is. What we mean by 'mind' has been unexpectedly proved to be profoundly different from 'brain' in ways that we still do not, and, – who knows? – may

---

[3]See, for instance, Owen Barfield, *Saving the Appearances*.
[4]A recent one in China can, apparently, do 92,000 calculations per second. By the time this book appears, this figure will doubtless be obsolete.

never understand.[5] But the kind of double consciousness of a person looking at a landscape and being simultaneously aware of themselves looking at the landscape, as experienced by both Augustine and Jung, seems still to be fundamentally different from any computerized complexity. It would, presumably, be possible to programme a computer to take account of its own activities, but this would still not be consciousness in the human sense. Similarly, a camera set to photograph a view of Jung's plain in East Africa, however high the quality of its definition, would not be bringing that view to consciousness until the picture was looked at by a human – a paradox strangely echoing that of 'Schrödinger's cat', the proverbial imaginary animal in quantum theory who is neither alive nor dead until it is observed.[6]

Jung's feeling that the human observer is in a very real sense the 'second creator of the world' reflects a long tradition of philosophical idealism which, though rarely absent from debate over the last few centuries, has equally rarely been dominant. Keith Ward, a contemporary scientist/theologian, follows in this tradition by insisting that Mind is prior to matter – both logically, and (more problematic) historically.[7] Consciousness, he argues, is 'a basic feature of reality' and strict materialism is, therefore, ultimately self-refuting. For him what makes Bishop Berkeley's position, argued with such brilliance in his *Three Dialogues*,[8] suddenly relevant again, is modern quantum physics, where such classical but mysterious phenomena as the two-slit experiment suggest that the material activity of particles actually seems (against all common sense) to be ultimately dependent on our observation.

Such an inversion of common sense is not unique in the history of science – one only has to think of Copernicus's discovery that the Earth, against all appearances, revolves around the Sun, rather than vice versa. But since idealism puts mind before matter, the mental state of Jung or Ward in making this leap is central to any such inversion itself. This comes back to what the

---

[5]For some of the most recent thinking on this topic, see Brian Cantwell Smith, *The Promise of Artificial Intelligence*, MIT Press, 2020.
[6]For a more detailed discussion of computers and consciousness see Keith Ward, *The Christian Idea of God*, Cambridge University Press, 2017, pp. 86–91.
[7]Ibid., p. 38.
[8]George Berkeley, *Three Dialogues between Hylas and Philonous*, 1713.

Romantics, following Coleridge, called 'imagination'. As so often, George MacDonald is one of the most articulate in formulating the definition:

> The imagination is that faculty which gives form to thought – not necessarily uttered form, but form capable of being uttered in shape or in sound, or in any mode upon which the senses can lay hold.[9]

The innate connexion between inner and outer worlds can be seen even in the words we use to describe a scene.

> For the world is – allow us the homely figure – the human being turned inside out. All that moves in the mind is symbolized in Nature. Or, to use another more philosophical, and certainly not less poetic figure, the world is a sensuous analysis of humanity, and hence an inexhaustible wardrobe for the clothing of human thought. Take any word expressive of emotion – take the word *emotion* itself – and you will find that its primary meaning is of the outer world. In the swaying of the woods, in the unrest of the 'wavy plain,' the imagination saw the picture of a well-known condition of the human mind; and hence the word *emotion*.[10]

To be reminded of the connection between 'emotion' and its root, 'motion', is also a reminder that perception is not a fixity, but a fluid and ever-changing *process*.

What lies at the base of both writers' perceptions is language itself. Double consciousness is a product of the act of description. It *creates* our internal space. As Rowan Williams has put it, language allows us 'to make us strangers to ourselves and then recognize our world afresh.'[11] This is precisely what Jung is doing. But there is an important caveat. Williams adds:

> Notice that I am not talking about the relation of 'language' with 'the world': . . . this begs a question, assuming that there is somewhere a straightforward catalogue of neutral phenomena to be isolated as what is basically *there*, and

---

[9]George MacDonald, 'The Imagination: Its Functions and its Culture', *A Dish of Orts*, Sampson Lowe, 1882, p. 2.

[10]Ibid., pp. 9–10.

[11]Rowan Williams, *The Edge of Words*, Bloomsbury, 2014, p. 19.

that anything else is what we choose to say, or at best what we vaguely and intuitively decide to add to the iron rations of description … such a distinction is unworkable; and the instability or uncertain 'fit' of what we say to the environment we inhabit and with which we negotiate is not a mark of its arbitrariness. We test our schema, we criticize and enlarge and rework our representation structures, transforming both our relationships with each other and our capacity to negotiate with the environment.[12]

In other words, the creation of 'objectivity' hailed by Jung, and his state of double consciousness, is not so much a product of any neutral observation as of an extreme *subjectivity*. The idea of things 'as they really are' is always a chimera – a product of our imaginations, receding like a rainbow as we try to close in on it. But, of course, this is not a denial of external reality, rather that language must be seen as the natural integrating factor in the evolving material universe. 'We look to language to show us what matter is,' Williams continues:

That is, language exhibits a pattern of cooperative agency in which the structure of life or action in one medium is rendered afresh (translated) in another. The material universe appears as an essentially symbolic process.[13]

Just as every language and culture surveys the world differently, so that there is very rarely a one-for-one correspondence between words in different languages, there is very rarely a one-for-one correspondence between words and things. The French words *chez moi* do not really correspond to 'home' in English; the Italian word *furbo*, literally translated, means 'cunning, crafty or shrewd' – in a streetwise sense – but whereas in English that carries distinctly dodgy connotations, in Italian there is usually a wry admiration implied for anyone who is so described by this trait.[14] Perhaps more surprising, an apparently simple descriptive word like 'mountain' carries different connotations not merely in different languages in different parts of the world, but also in different historical periods. What for us, in our post-Romantic state, is a thing of beauty, sublimity and awe, was for inhabitants of the

---

[12]Ibid., p. 44.
[13]Ibid., p. 102.
[14]A word frequently used in Boccaccio's *Decameron* – always with admiration.

early medieval world a thing of fear and horror to be avoided whenever possible.[15]

As if to illustrate the symbolic nature of perceptions of the material world, Kenneth Clark begins his seminal book, *Landscape into Art* (1949), with the following statement:

> Facts become art through love, which unifies them and lifts them to a higher plain of reality; and, in landscape, this all-embracing love is expressed by light. It is no accident that this sense of saturating light grew out of a school of manuscript illuminations, and first appears in miniatures.[16]

This suggestion of emotional involvement as integral to perception is echoed by Julian Barnes:

> (Love) gives clarity of vision: it's a windscreen wiper across the eyeball. Have you ever seen things so clearly as when you were first in love?[17]

For Clark an astonishing revolution begins in the Netherlands in the first half of the fifteenth century with the work of Hubert van Eyck and his brother Jan. 'Hubert van Eyck has, at one bound,' writes Clark, 'covered a space in the evolution of art which a prudent historian would have expected to stretch over several centuries ...'[18] Discussing one of the surviving fragments of a manuscript tragically damaged by fire in 1904, he continues: 'It is a pure landscape; for Hubert van Eyck is so much in love with the effects of light that the figures are entirely subordinate and the legend depicted is the slightest possible pretext.'[19] In fact, some of the landscapes described are background to scenes from the Bible or extra-biblical religious traditions, but others exist at the bottom of the pages as landscapes in their own right without figures – 'pure landscape' in the most literal sense – and they are, indeed, extraordinary.

Clark was not, of course, focusing on the kind of double consciousness that we have been discussing, where the painter, both as viewer and as the imaginative creator, is thinking about himself thinking about the scene before

---

[15]See Marjorie Hope Nicholson, *Mountain Gloom and Mountain Glory*.
[16]Kenneth Clark, *Landscape into Art* (1949), Harmondsworth: Pelican, Penguin Books, 1956, p. 31.
[17]Julian Barnes, *A History of the World in 10½ Chapters*, Cape, 1989.
[18]Clark, p. 31.
[19]Ibid., p. 32.

him. Yet that is what van Eyck – and his younger brother, Jan – are actually doing. We recall Augustine's words quoted earlier:

> I was not looking at them with my eyes – and yet I could not have spoken about them had it not been that I was actually seeing within, in my memory, those mountains and waves and rivers and stars which I have seen, and that ocean which I believe in – and with the same vast spaces between them as when I saw them outside me. But when I saw them outside me, I did not take them into me by seeing them; and the things themselves are not inside me, but only their images.

Though such images, both in the *Turin Hours* and in the later and more famous *Ghent Altarpiece*, also probably by the van Eyck brothers, are benign landscapes, even holy ones, irradiated by this new sense of light, that does not mean that here and elsewhere in contemporary Flemish painting such illumination cannot be set against the most gruesome scenes of torture and martyrdom – the most obvious example being the Crucifixion itself.

What is important from the perspective of inner space is the degree of self-consciousness creeping into the construction of such landscapes. Whether or not we accept Clark's particular selection, at some point during the fifteenth century landscape backgrounds to paintings ceased to be just background and began to take on an added symbolic significance. One interesting feature of so many Flemish paintings of this period is a background panorama of jagged mountains and steep river valleys quite unlike anything in the flat Netherlands in which they were painted. Clearly for many of the artists these mountainous views provided an exotic escape from the level fields and canals of their homelands.

It has been suggested that these landscapes often resemble the rugged terrain of northern Spain, Castile and Leon, through which many painters would have to have passed on their way to Madrid, capital of the sixteenth century Spanish rulers of the Netherlands. But, in fact, the Netherlands in the fifteenth century were still largely under the control of the Dukes of Burgundy. Only after a series of political and dynastic marriages were they acquired by the Spanish to become part of the Hapsburg Empire in the sixteenth century.[20]

---

[20]Philip, the son of Mary of Burgundy (daughter of Charles the Bold) who had married Maximilian. He later became Holy Roman Emperor and married Joanna of Castile.

The change in culture so imposed by the less tolerant Catholicism of the Spanish Crown was, of course, a major factor in the Dutch revolt and eventual independence of the Netherlands. Be that as it may, by the late fifteenth century backgrounds had acquired symbolic significances that could almost rival the official subject of the painting.

One art historian, Christopher Herbert, to whom we referred in the last chapter, has dramatically extended Clark's thesis by claiming that these changes in northern painting at precisely this period can be seen as foreshadowing the Reformation itself.[21] He opens with the argument that 'Paintings are the history of ideas in visual form' – taking his specific examples from the Burgundian Netherlands in the works of Robert Campin, the van Eyck brothers, Roger van der Weyden and Hans Memling. Behind these, and other contemporary artists, lay not merely new materials, and a popular system of lay patronage, but also a new kind of spiritually charged 'realism' that sharply influenced the way that the world was seen and portrayed. He quotes Dirk de Vos:

> Realism was not an objective in itself, but a means of shaping a new spirituality. In this way the divine was brought closer to humankind, so that meditation passed via the real, and evangelistic events were projected into one's own familiar environment. This was recommended by the new religious practice known as the *Devotio Moderna*. I cannot help but wonder if it was not thanks to the new realism that painting started to play an active role in the interaction between the human and the divine. It was not a renouncement of mediaeval transcendence, but rather a new form of religious experience. By the way it was arranged, the real was also the clarification, the embodiment of the symbol.[22]

Herbert's prime example of the new realism is Campin's *Dijon Nativity*. It is unusual in that it is not a triptych, but instead of the conventional three panels, it incorporates the nativity, the midwives, and the adoration of the shepherds all in a single 'realistic' visual image (see Pl. 6). Herbert writes:

---

[21]Herbert, *Foreshadowing the Reformation*, p. 1.
[22]Dirk de Vos, *The Flemish Primitives*, Princeton University Press, 2002, p. 10.

Until the early years of the fifteenth century in Europe, paintings of the nativity would have been set either against a golden background to indicate timelessness and the eternal verities, or in a rocky geological setting; think, for example, of Giotto's nativity fresco in the Lower Basilica of Assisi. But here in Campin's *Nativity*, most Italo-Byzantine influences have been abandoned. The scene is pastoral; 'real' people are going about their daily lives. The eternal is firmly located amongst farms, meadows and trees that have been pollarded.[23]

The background, Herbert suggests, might just be part of the Netherland enthusiasm for mountains, mentioned above, but could also be an implicit reference to the Messianic interpretation of Psalm 72. Verse 3 reads: *May hills and mountains provide your people with prosperity in righteousness.* He continues:

There is a walled city in the background in which is set, anachronistically, a spired church. The walls of the city stretch down to a lake on which a boat is sailing. Slightly nearer the stable scene, small figures are involved in their daily occupations: one of them seems to be carrying a basket of eggs on her head. It is as though the world carries on its way, oblivious of the miracle which is taking place close by. And then running away from the stable scene is a road which snakes its way to the city. Is this a reference to 'The Way' or is it simply a visual device to ensure that our eyes not only take in the nearby nativity scene but are taken imaginatively towards other worlds, our sight having been 'informed' by the foreground events.[24]

This landscape, he argues, involves allusions to both a 'real' and a metaphysical one.

What Campin has done is to fuse the two, and in doing so, he has developed the tradition which derives from illustrations in Books of Hours ... Yet one can sense that the world as it really is, is increasingly brought to the attention of the viewer ... But something else is happening. The 'real' is seen as the setting of the metaphysical.[25]

---

[23]Ibid., p. 21.
[24]Ibid., pp. 20–1.
[25]Ibid., p. 22.

Though I do, one does not have to agree with all the details of this analysis to recognize the quite new kind of landscape realism that becomes an integral part of this Burgundian vision inspired by the *Devotio Moderna*. Landscape has moved from being a semi-invisible background to being (at this stage) an essential part of the whole picture – without it, the meaning of the design is incomplete. Or, to put it another way, landscape has taken on a new reality because of the artist's mind contemplating it and re-creating it in the new work. We return to the idea of the double consciousness with which we began this chapter. Realism, however symbolic, shades into a different idealized landscape in what is often seen as the van Eycks' masterpiece, the *Ghent Altarpiece* (see Pl. 7).

Herbert describes the centre panel as 'a kind of heavenly parkland where the only vertical movement is provided by urban spires and exotic trees.' Moving towards the Lamb of God on the altar are four processions: bishops and confessors; virgins and martyrs; popes, deacons and martyrs, including Stephen the first martyr; patriarchs, apostles and major prophets.[26] It is hard not to imagine that this 'symbolic parkland', with its flowers and laden fruit trees, with ecclesiastical processions closing in on the ever-flowing fountain of the water of life and the redeeming Lamb, owes much to the final cantos of Dante's *Purgatorio* – already so famous throughout Europe that vernacular translations were subsequently published in Antwerp in 1482, and 's-Hertogenbosch in 1484. Where it differs, of course, is in the distant background of the domes and spires of many churches, making the point – in case we had missed it – that the way into this magic sunlit upland is by way of the Church.

But this is not the only kind of landscape to emerge from the fifteenth-century Netherlands. Hieronymus Bosch's *Garden of Earthly Delights* (see Pl. 8) has been given a variety of dates from 1480 to 1503. Like the *Ghent Altarpiece* it is a triptych, but, unlike the former, probably not meant for a church but for a private chapel, to celebrate a marriage.[27] Though the left and

---

[26]Ibid., p. 97.
[27]Opinions as to whose marriage seem varied. Some have put it as early as 1490, but Stefan Fischer argues for that of Henry III of Nassau, 1503. *Hieronymus Bosch*, Taschen, 2016, p. 101.

central panels seem to show a continuous park-like landscape very much in the tradition of the *Ghent Altarpiece*, their content is, of course, strikingly different – as is the right-hand panel which shows a peculiarly bizarre version of Hell. Moreover, even the left-hand panel representing Eden, the creation of Adam and Eve, and Christ blessing this first marriage, is markedly un-idyllic in detail (see Pl. 9). In the background a lion has killed a deer, while in the foreground a cat has caught and is making off with its rat-like prey, while some very nasty creepy-crawlies are emerging from a lake in the middle distance.

The huge centre panel (87 × 77 in) is assumed to represent the state of humankind before the Flood and, following a tradition of the period that interpreted the unspecified 'wickedness of man' in Genesis as largely sexual,[28] is taken up with an extraordinary variety of lascivious misdemeanours and depravities, sometimes visually explicit, but more often represented by the elaborate symbolism of the day. All are naked. In the foreground a huge variety of figures express lust in its many various forms – including figures eating from fruit trees remarkably like those portrayed in the *Ghent Altarpiece*. At its centre, in the middle distance, is a circular pool containing a number of women; around them circles a much larger number of men mounted on a variety of animals, birds and other creatures.

Even if we understood them all, which we do not, this is hardly the place even to try and list the range of sexual activities in what is clearly one of the most extraordinary pictures ever painted. What concerns us, once again, is the self-consciousness of the landscape itself. Poised between Eden and Hell, the centre panel of this triptych would normally represent some kind of a middle state – but here this is one of exuberant, if somewhat strange and distasteful, eroticism. At one level the scene seems to be biblical, showing the four rivers of Paradise; at another it seems like a deliberate parody of the *Ghent Altarpiece*. One of the most conspicuous features of the van Eyck painting is a solitary palm tree, standing up well above the other trees around it. In Medieval Mediterranean Europe, palms were common enough.

Nevertheless, despite what one would suppose to be the well-known uselessness of the palm trunk (it is, after all, an overgrown 'grass', a

---

[28] Gen. 6.6.

monocotyledon in biological terms, not a 'tree', a dicotyledon) some authorities declared it to be the tree of life in the Garden of Eden, and therefore also the tree from which Christ's cross was made.[29] Any carpenter – including presumably the one crucified – could have put them right. Nevertheless the single palm makes its appearance again in the Bosch picture, but this time on the left panel in Eden, standing directly up above a strange and slightly sinister rock, looking weirdly like the face of Salvador Dali – who, it is claimed, with his usual showmanship, actually tried to model his own face and moustache on this picture.

The right-hand panel of Hell presumably shows the punishment awaiting these sinners in due course. But this is no conventional Hell. It is, in fact, yet another earthly landscape, but in contrast with the other two, one of war and desolation. In the background is a burning city, populated not by raging devils, but by equally malign humans (see Pl. 10). Unlike the naked figures in the other two panels, this is an army, helmeted and in full armour, crossing a bridge over a river or lake, with bodies struggling or floating in it. Here is contemporary warfare: a hell created by *humans*.

A similar background of a burning city occurs in the centre panel of another triptych by Bosch: *The Temptation of St Anthony* (see Pl. 12), painted shortly before, in 1502. Given the savagery and destruction that was to follow the Reformation – especially in the Thirty Years' War – there is something distinctly ironic in Bosch's move to humanize what had previously been a supernatural preserve, and therefore to suggest increased human responsibility. The devils and their victims in the foreground are not torturing their victims at random, but mostly re-creating the sins that have brought their victims there – drinking in an alehouse, gambling and prostitution.[30] Inside the famous 'tree man' – so called because his legs seem to turn into decaying tree stumps – is what appears to be an alehouse scene (see Pl. 11). The barmaid is pouring beer from a cask, and the patrons, seated at a table, seem unusually comfortable for a pub in Hell – except perhaps for the odd fact that they are sitting on a giant toad.

Nor is Bosch unique in such symbolism. In Roger van der Weyden's *Beaune altarpiece*, the sins of those being driven towards Hell (see Pl. 13) are also

---

[29]See sermon by Jan Brugman: Fischer, p. 105.
[30]Ibid., p. 116.

indicated. The man with his hand in his mouth, for example, has been interpreted as symbolizing gluttony. If Bosch had shown that the new landscape realism had its darker side, as well as divine promise, that was a polarity that was to persist in later centuries.

As usual, Shakespeare got in on the act. When the old Scottish King Duncan reaches Macbeth's castle as an honoured guest, he remarks with genial innocence

> This castle hath a pleasant seat, the air
> Nimbly and sweetly recommends itself
> Unto our gentle senses.

Macbeth's fellow general, Banquo, follows this up with his own elaborate ornithological observations:

> This guest of summer,
> The temple-haunting martlet, does approve,
> By his loved mansionary, that the heaven's breath
> Smells wooingly here; no jutty, frieze,
> Buttress, nor coign of vantage, but this bird
> Hath made his pendant bed and procreant cradle.
> Where they most breed and haunt, I have observ'd
> The air is delicate.[31]

Yet we, the audience, have just heard Lady Macbeth's response to the news of Duncan's imminent arrival, with the ominous words:

> The raven himself is hoarse
> That croaks the fatal entrance of Duncan
> Under my battlements . . .[32]

Two landscapes – or, rather, perhaps birdscapes – of the mind collide, and the inevitable result will be Duncan's assassination, followed shortly afterwards by that of Banquo, who has himself so disastrously misread the scene in front of him.

---

[31] *Macbeth*, Act I, vi.
[32] Ibid., Sc. v.

By the eighteenth century the internalization of space was less a matter of drama, and more one of financial and cultural status. Arthur Devis's portrait of the Bacon Family (1742/3) represents a precisely defined moment in both time and space (see Pl. 14). But the huge red curtain top right continues to suggest that, in some sense, this is still also theatre. This is show and tell. In the far room are two pictures, one of a scene with classical architecture; the other a portrait of a Protestant clergyman with Geneva bands on his collar. This, it is implied, is the family background: ancient, aristocratic and pious. The timing of the current moment is made precise by the family grouping, in particular by the ages of the four children in 1742. The eldest – clearly the heir – appears to be around ten years old. His cultural achievements are musical: he holds a flute and a sheet of music. The next child, a daughter at her mother's knee, is apparently just learning to read: she holds a sheet of paper with both pictures and writing. Of the two remaining children, the boy demonstrates his (considerable) manual dexterity by building a house of cards. His little sister – whose card house has just collapsed on the floor around her – is demonstrating her helpfulness by handing him another card. The largest and most colourful object in the room is, of course, the oriental carpet on which the whole family is seated – perhaps demonstrating their wealth as well as their break with the seventeenth-century custom of treating their carpets as too valuable to go on floors, and displaying them on tables. What is remarkable – and we are, of course, meant to remark on it – is that this is the *modern* four-suit 52 card pack, so new in the eighteenth century that it was not even patented until 1799. Even the oriental carpet, the biggest object in the room, may well signify that whereas an earlier generation would have preserved it on a table, the family is now prosperous and fashionable enough to place it underfoot.

The positioning in space is even more remarkable. On the billiard table in the far room is a contemporary vacuum pump. In front of it is a naturalist's microscope, in its open case, designed to be portable in the countryside where the larger instrument would be impossible. Under the table are two globes: one is a terrestrial globe. In the light of the astronomical equipment in the foreground, it would be a fair guess that, the other, only partially visible, showing the stars and constellations, is a celestial globe. On the right in the front room is an astronomical telescope: this, it is clear, is not merely a musical family, it is also a *scientific* one. More remarkable, however, is the large instrument behind the telescope. This is a quadrant – an instrument in astronomy used to measure the angle of elevation of bodies in the solar system. Again, the message is there to read. This is serious professional equipment: John Bacon is no gentleman amateur astronomer. He is actively engaged in scientific research – and, since he was the only Bacon elected at this period, we must assume that it was he who became a member of Royal Society in 1751.

This is hardly a celebration of personal identity – the whole family have curiously wooden, almost blank expressions – but few pictures have ever linked time and space so explicitly. However, 'space' here is no longer a matter of any mere terrestrial landscape. Indeed, it is possible that the second, half-hidden globe in the back room symbolizes the current ignorance of the extra-terrestrial universe, something, of course, that John Bacon wishes to change. His imagination no longer embraces the Earth, but the entire solar system. This picture is, not least, a record of that ambition.

Some twenty years later, in 1781, the alliteratively named Brooke Boothby (1744–1824) chose to immortalize not so much his wealth as his aesthetic sensibility, with another portrait in a landscape, this time by Joseph Wright of Derby (1734–97). A cynic might well assume from his elegant position that he was actually painted on a sofa and then by a piece of eighteenth-century photo-shopping, transferred in spotless condition into what could be quite a muddy rural environment (see Pl. 15). Note the brook in the foreground – implying the obvious pun on the sitter's name. The dual lighting, bringing out both the fields and hills in the background but also falling on Boothby in the foreground, frames the scene, and highlights the important clue to what he wants recorded; the book in his hand, carefully held so folded that one can read the author's name on the spine – Rousseau. In other words, this is a visual and public declaration of Romantic sensibility. Whether or not Boothby owns this wooded rural landscape is now not so important. What we are meant to infer is that he is enjoying – or indeed, *part* of – nature in a Romantic, highly contrived (and literary) solitude.

But of course it was William Wordsworth a generation later who was really to complete our internalization of landscape. Ever since 'Tintern Abbey' was first published as a last-minute addition to the 1798 edition of the *Lyrical*

Ballads, readers and critics alike have been unsure whether what he is describing with such obvious intensity is some kind of mystical experience – possibly of the kind we have looked at in the first chapter – or whether Wordsworth, writing of what he 'half-creates' and perceives, is more concerned to describe the imagination and processes of perception which were later to be laid out in prose by such avid Wordsworthians as George MacDonald. The most famous passage links perceiver and perceived in a kind of indissoluble bond at once aesthetic, psychological and moral.

> For I have learned
> To look on nature, not as in the hour
> Of thoughtless youth; but hearing oftentimes
> The still sad music of humanity,
> Nor harsh nor grating, though of ample power
> To chasten and subdue. – And I have felt
> A presence that disturbs me with the joy
> Of elevated thoughts; a sense sublime
> Of something far more deeply interfused,
> Whose dwelling is the light of setting suns,
> And the round ocean and the living air,
> And the blue sky, and in the mind of man:
> A motion and a spirit, that impels
> All thinking things, all objects of all thought,
> And rolls through all things. Therefore am I still
> A lover of the meadows and the woods
> And mountains; and of all that we behold
> From this green earth; of all the mighty world
> Of eye, and ear, – both what they half create,
> And what perceive; well pleased to recognise
> In nature and the language of the sense
> The anchor of my purest thoughts, the nurse,
> The guide, the guardian of my heart, and soul
> Of all my moral being.

'Tintern Abbey', l. 77–113

This was actually written at a time when Wordsworth and his friend Samuel Taylor Coleridge were at their closest, and when the latter described himself in some notes to another poem, 'This Lime-Tree Bower my Prison', (1797) as a 'Berkleian'. This, in effect, buys into one of the longest and most complex of eighteenth-century debates over the nature of reality itself. In an essay entitled 'The Pleasures of the Imagination', in *The Spectator* for 1712, Joseph Addison (1672–1719) had meditated on the apparent paradox of sense-perception.

> Things would make but a poor Appearance to the Eye, if we saw them only in their proper Figures and Motions ... We are every where entertained with pleasing Shows and Apparitions, we discover Imaginary Glories in the Heavens, and in the Earth, and see some of this Visionary Beauty poured out upon the whole Creation; but what a rough and unsightly Sketch of Nature should we be entertained with, did all her Colouring disappear, and the several Distinctions of Light and Shade vanish? In short, our Souls are at present delightfully lost in a pleasing Delusion, and we walk about like the inchanted Hero of a Romance, who sees beautiful Castles, Woods, and Meadows; at the same time hears the warbling of Birds, and the purling of Streams; but upon the finishing of some secret Spell, the fantastick scene breaks up, and the disconsolate Knight finds himself on a barren Heath, or in a solitary Desart.[33]

The Spectator was one of the most widely read journals of the early eighteenth century, and, in itself, there was nothing particularly new in this conclusion. It was one obvious way of reading Sir Isaac Newton's *Opticks,* which had been published in 1704, only eight years before, and presented a startlingly new understanding of light. For Addison, Newton (1643–1727) seemed to confirm John Locke's rather grim portrayal of the true nature of things in his *Essay Concerning Human Understanding* (1690). According to this view we are sealed off from the world of 'real' objects, which are cold, hard and colourless. The rest is pleasing illusion. Colour is, after all, just a trick of light, not a property of objects themselves; sound is merely a matter of vibrations in the air. We are insulated from the true barrenness of reality only by the

---

[33]Joseph Addison, 'The Pleasures of the Imagination', (1712) *Spectator*, p. 413.

demonstrable unreliability of our senses which, as it were, adds emotional ribbons, bells and whistles.

The idealism of Bishop George Berkeley (1685–1753) was a bold attempt to refute such an interpretation of Newton. For him, 'reality' lay not in any mysterious quality of 'things in themselves', but on the contrary, in what we actually *see*. In other words, light and colour, our basic means of visual perception, are the *only* reality we can ever know. In three brilliant and wittily entertaining dialogues he argues that even the familiar objects that surround us can only exist in so far as they are perceived.[34] His philosophic common-sense fall-guy, called Hylas (i.e. 'matter' or the materialist), is overwhelmed by the arguments of Philonous (i.e. 'lover of mind'). But this counter-intuitive truth is a recipe not for universal scepticism but for a reality based on the ultimate observer: God himself, who alone, by definition, 'sees' everything, and is the ultimate guarantor of the world.[35] So far from the human mind being the climax of aeons of evolutionary development and consciously creating the observed scene for the first time, as Jung concluded, Berkeley – like Augustine – believes in more or less the same process, but the creating (in both senses) by God – who, as the limerick has it – 'is always about in the quad'.[36]

It was left to Wordsworth and the Romantics to take up this refutation of Locke's apparent impasse, and to show that this Lockean world of 'things in themselves' was itself an illusion – and in so doing, bring in a quite new meaning of 'imagination'. 'Reality' is not something invisible; it is what we see – what our senses affirm. It is the rest that is an illusion of half-baked scientism. Light, colour and sound are among the given premises of the world. We cannot consider them in detachment, nor can we (in the proper sense of the word) be 'deceived' by them because they are part of the very framework of our experience – part of the 'givenness' of things.

---

[34]Berkeley, *Three Dialogues*, 1713.

[35]See Stephen Prickett, *Coleridge and Wordsworth: The Poetry of Growth*, Cambridge University Press, 1970, p. 96.

[36]There was a young man who said: 'God   Dear Sir, your astonishment's odd
  Must find it exceedingly odd   *I* am always about in the Quad.
  When he sees that this tree continues to be   And that's why this tree continues to be
  Though there's no one about in the quad.'   Since observed by
                                                 Yours faithfully, God.

It is also possible that Wordsworth was influenced – as ever, via Coleridge
– by the German philosopher Immanuel Kant (1724–1804), who argued like
Berkeley, if rather more obscurely, that 'things in themselves' were *essentially*
unknowable, and all that we could ever know was our *impressions* of them. It
was he, probably unwittingly, who laid down what is in effect the philosophic
basis for our modern theory of perception: that, as we have seen, we perceive
by another process of projecting schemata and accommodating these, by a
process of mix-and-match, to the sense-data received.

Whatever the philosophic substructure, and whether or not we assume that
Wordsworth's 'sense sublime of something far more deeply interfused' includes
both a description of the role of imagination in perception *and* possibly a
Berkleian or Kantian idealist view of any world so perceived, it is clear that
Wordsworth is here describing the same double consciousness that we have
seen in Jung and Augustine. He internalizes by using language to distance
himself (in Williams' sense) *from* the experience in order to *see and write about
himself* experiencing nature.

By and large, however, many in the nineteenth century chose to ignore the
subtleties of Wordsworth (and MacDonald) for the more simple-minded
formulations of Matthew Arnold, who continued to write about the existence
of 'things in themselves'. As with his forays into theology, Arnold's common-
sense approach ended in some spectacularly muddled thinking.[37]

One poet who did understand Wordsworth, however, was the Jesuit priest,
Gerard Manley Hopkins (1844–89) who in his relatively short life realized
and explored the complex relationship between nature and the perceiving
mind more profoundly than perhaps any other writer of his age. Since his
earliest ambition had been to be a painter he retained a strong visual sense of
nature in all his writing. One of his early poems directly echoes Wordsworth's
sonnet beginning, 'My heart leaps up when I behold/A rainbow in the sky.' But
this sonnet, written in 1864, when Hopkins was only 20 years old, confronts
the relationship of mind to perception even more directly:

It was a hard thing to undo this knot.
The rainbow shines, but only in the thought

---

[37]See Stephen Prickett, *Romanticism and Religion*, pp. 211–48.

Of him that looks. Yet not in that alone,
For who makes rainbows by invention?
And many standing round a waterfall
See one bow each, yet not the same to all,
But each a hand's breadth further than the next.
The sun on falling waters writes the text
Which yet is in the eye or in the thought.
It was a hard thing to undo this knot.

Neither Berkeley nor Jung could have put it better.

Nor does Hopkins give up on the problem as he turns from outward nature to inward being. In his sonnet 'As kingfishers catch fire . . .' (written probably in 1881 or 1882) he tackles the theology of what he called 'inscape' – a word formed from the internalizing of 'landscape' – his word, in effect, for inner space:

As kingfishers catch fire, dragonflies draw flame;
As tumbled over rim in roundy wells
Stones ring; like each tucked string tells, each hung bell's
Bow swung finds tongue to fling out broad its name;
Each mortal thing does one thing and the same:
Deals out that being indoors each one dwells;
Selves – goes itself; *myself* it speaks and spells,
Crying *Whát I dó is me: for that I came.*
I say móre: the just man justices;
Keeps grace: thát keeps all his goings graces;
Acts in God's eye what in God's eye he is –
Chríst – for Christ plays in ten thousand places,
Lovely in limbs, and lovely in eyes not his
To the Father through the features of men's faces.

In the first section, the octet, each thing listed, from the flash of dragonflies in sunlight to the noise of stones falling in a well, is experienced *externally*. What each thing *does* reveals its particular 'being indoors'. As with Berkeley and Kant, and in a bold reversal of traditional Catholic Thomist philosophy, which divided the material world between 'substance' (the thing in itself) and 'accidents' (how it appears to us), Hopkins suggests that the way we know a thing, that is by its accidents, is the true reality. In particular, we, like inanimate objects, are *also* to be known by what we do, rather than what we are. But there is a twist in the tail.

The keyword here is Hopkins' made-up word 'Selves' – taken from the Anglo Saxon and used to mean roughly the same as our Latinate 'to individuate'. Part of the intense vigour and freshness of Hopkins' nature poetry is that, as we have seen, it was not really until the nineteenth century that the separation between nature and the human observer could be said to be complete. It was, in this sense, speaking and spelling *myself* almost for the first time in Hopkins' generation. One thinks, for instance, of Ruskin's endless detailed drawings of rocks and plants, or Constable's sketches of clouds. The 'fire' of the kingfisher's flight or the dragonfly's wing is deliberately and self-consciously subjective – as it were, *made real* by observation.

When we come to the last six lines (the sestet) this externality of nature is paralleled by the corresponding internality of humanity. What distinguishes us is not outward appearance but inwardness – for Hopkins the priest – as a vessel of God's grace. The depth and complexity of this inwardness of Christ is emphasized by a series of what is probably the most massive series of puns anywhere in English literature. The key phrase is 'Christ plays in ten thousand places ...'. Both sections are ultimately about *playing*. Thus if Christ 'plays' on mankind as a musician might, this takes up the theme of the musical harmony of Creation from the octet: 'each tucked string tells, each hung bell's/Bow swung finds tongue to swing out broad its name ...'. If Christ 'plays' as an actor, it is to 'act' the just man's part – 'that keeps all his goings graces'. If Christ 'plays' as a child might play in a game, it is to express the joy of Creation as a great dance in which the kingfisher and the dragonfly play their unwitting parts. Hence, too, the 'deals', as when a card player deals from a deck of cards. Seen from the back, generically, all are identical; but from the front, all are different, individuated and unique. If Christ is taken as 'playing', as a fountain of water, we are reminded of the well wherein stones ring, the fountain in the midst of the garden, and the river of life – not to mention the older Catholic metaphor, invoked by Marlowe's Dr Faustus, where he sees 'Christ's blood streams in the universe'. Behind this is a hydraulic image linking the water level in the bottom of a well with the entire catchment area and the underground water table. Christ is thus seen as the invisible pressure system underlying the whole landscape.[38] If Christ 'plays' across the face of nature like the subtle play of light and shade, he is the Light of the World that plays on the kingfisher and the dragonfly alike to reveal their individual inscape. If Christ is to be found in the free 'play' of the mind over its subject, and thus the mind of the poet himself, we are brought back to the poem itself as artefact. If Christ is thus seen to be as at 'play' within the words of language itself, and is thus present in this outrageous seven-fold pun, it is only a minute example of the ten thousand places where he is to be glimpsed fleetingly as the flash of sunlight on a bird's wing, and in the creation of new meaning.

Yet this was to be one of Hopkins' last flashes of sunlight. Within a few years depression, which had always lurked beneath the surface of his manic-depressive temperament, seems to have overcome him, at least for much of the time. Overwhelmed by feelings of guilt, grief, loss of poetic power, even loss of faith in God's presence – perhaps all of these things together – he embarked on a series of sonnets portraying breakdown almost as never before. There is much that we do not know. But what we have in these last so-called 'terrible sonnets' is one of the finest written expressions of the internalization of landscape. Here is the ending of the untitled sonnet of (probably) 1885, known by its ominous first line, 'No worst, there is none . . .':

> O the mind, mind has mountains; cliffs of fall
> Frightful, sheer, no-man fathomed. Hold them cheap
> Who ne'er hung there. Nor does long our small
> Durance deal with that steep or deep. Here! creep,
> Wretch, under a comfort serves in a whirlwind: all
> Life death does end and each day dies with sleep.

---

[38]See stanza 4 of *The Wreck of the Deutschland*:
I steady as water in a well, to a poise, to a pane,
But roped with, always, all the way down from the tall
Fells or flanks of the voel [hill], a vein
Of the gospel proffer, a pressure, a principle, Christ's gift.

4

From China to Peru: Global imaginations

In an attempt to beat the stultifying boredom of his twenty-year sentence in Spandau Prison for deploying forced labour, Albert Speer (1905–81), Hitler's architect and later general organizer of the Nazi war-machine, set out to walk in his imagination around the world. First he made 2,000 laps around the prison garden to simulate a journey from Berlin to Heidelberg. When he had done that, Speer decided to set off on his imaginary journey towards Asia. He ordered guidebooks, maps and other materials about the countries through which he imagined that he was passing so as to be able to create as accurate a picture as possible. He meticulously calculated every metre he travelled and mapped distances to the real-world geography. He began in northern Germany and then, to avoid the Communist countries, which he thought might give him trouble, he made his way across the Middle East. 'A long hot tramp,' Speer wrote. 'I hope I find oases.' He passed through Asia by a southern route before entering Siberia, then crossed the Bering Strait, entering the USA, and continued southwards, finally ending his imaginary journey in Mexico. When he was eventually released from jail in Berlin he sent a message to a friend: 'Please pick me up 35 km south of Guadalajara.'[1]

Though there is more than a certain irony in one of the leading engineers of the Nazi war effort, who had helped to deprive millions of their freedom, consciously trying to create in his own confined circumstances something of

---

[1]Report in the *Times*, Tuesday, 24 April 2018, p. 13.

the same inner space that Etty Hillesum had dreamed of as she was on her way to the Nazi gas chambers, both were articulating in their very different ways a sense of space which, though not peculiar to the twentieth century, was increasingly a part of that century's consciousness. Speer was in many ways as unusual as his highly imaginative project, but the fact that it was possible for him to make such a 'journey' in his mind illustrates the extraordinary spread of modern geographical knowledge. Unlike our forebears, we all know a vast amount about countries and places we have never visited – and, if we are honest, are unlikely ever to visit. This is not a case of 'need to know'. More perhaps one of 'prefer to imagine' – though not always under the same pressure as the imprisoned Speer. Moreover, like much of the content of inner space, this is probably a fairly recent extension of our imaginative life – coinciding, for obvious reasons, with exploration of the real geographical world.

The great *Mappa Mundi* in Hereford Cathedral (usually dated to around 1300) is the largest and most detailed surviving medieval world map. Despite the fact that it seems to represent the world as round, it would not be any help to anyone actually trying to travel – and would certainly have been no help to Speer: unless, of course, he had decided to add time travel to his adventures and traverse the world in 1300. On the *Mappa Mundi* (see Pl. 16) Jerusalem is at the centre of the world. East is at the top of the map, because that is where the sun rises and where medieval Christians believed Christ would appear at his second coming. However, it you had wanted to take a ship to the Holy Land, as many had already done during the Crusades, it is unlikely that your captain would have wasted any time with this map.

Though some kind of world-picture was in the possession of educated people at least as far back as the Graeco-Roman era, the mixture of fact and fiction would have been impossible to disentangle. The world-picture of the Vikings would have been very different, and presumably a little more accurate, at least on the existence of North America. Similarly, medieval people may have cherished the idea of the kingdom of Prester John, the great Christian empire believed initially to be somewhere in Asia and eventually in Africa south of Egypt; but though it was sometimes invoked during the Crusades, this did not amount to any kind of detailed geographical knowledge. Far from it, in fact. A more detailed knowledge of contemporary Ethiopia would have been enough to dispel the myth.[2] Thus though there *were* a few examples of deliberate exploration in classical times, not until we get to Columbus's very public discovery of America,[3] and Magellan's circumnavigation of the world, do we get geographical exploration as open recorded knowledge, with the corresponding creation of new descriptions and new maps.

It is no accident that both the Reformation and the great voyages of discovery occurred at the end of the fifteenth and the beginning of the sixteenth century. Both rode on the back of the printing press. New ideas, new discoveries, new theories: all flourished in a world where knowledge and debate could, for almost the first time, circulate freely across national boundaries and attract hitherto undreamed-of audiences. Map makers – especially in the Netherlands – flourished. Voyages of discovery became best sellers. In England Richard Hakluyt (1553–1616), a clergyman, published *The Principal Navigations, Voyages, Traffiques and Discoveries of the English Nation, Made by Sea or Overland to the Remote and Farthest Distant Quarters of the Earth at Any Time Within the Compasse of these 1600 Yeares* – more commonly known as the *Voyages* – which appeared in three volumes between 1589 and 1600. It was a major source for Shakespeare. Material for a fourth volume was gathered after Hakluyt's death by Samuel Purchas (1575–1626), who used the volumes in abridged form in his *Pilgrimes* (1624–5) – a source, in turn, for Coleridge's *Rime of the Ancient Mariner* (1798).

This was a world in which it was always difficult to distinguish fact from fiction, and in many cases they were inextricably entwined. Voyages of exploration were at once valuable sources of information and equally valuable platforms for wild invention.[4] *Robinson Crusoe* (1719) by Daniel Defoe (1660–1731) is a case in point. Ostensibly based on the adventures of Alexander Selkirk (1676–1721), a Scottish naval officer who was marooned on an uninhabited island for four years, it was an instant success, and was translated so often that it is said to be second only to the Bible in number of translations.

---

[2]See Keagan Brewer, *Prester John: The Legend and its Sources,* Farnham: Ashgate, 2015.

[3]The Viking discovery of America was not public, in the sense that it was not generally known outside immediate Viking circles.

[4]See, for instance, Chet Van Duzer, *Sea Monsters on Mediaeval and Renaissance Maps*, British Library, 2013.

Nevertheless in spite of the book's claims to historical accuracy part of it is clearly fiction, and a number of different islands have been confidently identified, and in one case even named, as 'Crusoe's Island'.

Meanwhile a whole range of other subsequent fictional works have traded on the 'Robinson' title, including the entirely fictitious *Swiss Family Robinson* (1812) by the Swiss pastor, Johann David Wyss (1743–1818), which underwent numerous English translations and even adaptations throughout the nineteenth century. Unlike Defoe's novel, however, this was intended from the start as a work for the moral improvement of children. The improbably eclectic selection of animals they encounter are, in this sense, background material, even though for children they are now the main excitement in reading the book. The same theme of fictionally exotic islands is continued in Muriel Spark's novel, *Robinson* (1958). Each 'Robinson', in turn, plays on the readers' recognition of the name, if not the content, each moving further and further into imaginary islands: or indeed galaxies. The Robinson family have even been re-imagined for the future: in the 1960s TV series *Lost in Space*; a 1998 film; and a Netflix TV series in 2018. The trope seems inexhaustible.

Just how difficult it is to distinguish fact from fiction – or in Truman Capote's portmanteau word 'faction' – can be seen from another travel book from this same period. *The Surprising Adventures of Mr Robert Drury During Fifteen Years Captivity on the Island of Madagascar* appeared in 1729. It tells the story of how Drury (1687–1743/50?) was shipwrecked on the coast of Madagascar in 1701 and enslaved for some fifteen years, before escaping and returning to England. He then turns slaver himself and, by his own account, continues the career of pillage and murder he had previously been forced to carry out for his masters. He may also have been a pirate. However he does not seem to have been very successful in any of these roles, since he apparently ended up as a porter at East India House – when he was not to be found at Old Tom's Coffee House in Birchin Lane telling anyone who would listen about his adventures in Madagascar. What is perhaps more surprising is that, with no satiric intent at all, he praises the moral qualities of the Madagascans as being far superior to the 'white Christians'. This did not, of course, stop him enslaving or killing them when the opportunity occurred. Though not a 'journal' in any recognizable sense – it was later more accurately re-named *Adventures in Madagascar* – it proved very popular, went through seven editions up to the end of the nineteenth century, and is now available in paperback. The paperback, however, is to be found under not Drury's name but the more familiar one of 'Daniel Defoe'. Though it shows a detailed knowledge of certain parts of Madagascar, this might well be explained by very extensive paraphrases from a *History of Madagascar* by the French writer and Governor of Madagascar, Etienne de Flacourt (1607–60), published in English in 1658. Moreover Drury had the same publisher as Defoe, and what looks like a remarkably similar literary style. In short, Defoe could well have been Drury's ghost-writer. On the other hand, he may not have been. Equally, the whole book may be a fiction by Defoe based on conversations with Drury supported by information from Flacourt's book – with no royalties going to Drury. This would make sense. Defoe had been so frequently in debt that he was sometimes referred to as 'the Sunday gentleman', because that was the only day of the week when he could venture outside without fear of being arrested by the bailiffs. Certainly the modern re-publication under Defoe's name in the effort to sell more copies may only be the latest in a series of dubious attributions. It is unlikely that we shall ever know for certain, but ironically it seems that in this case the information about Madagascar in the book was considerably more accurate than the attributed authorship.

As so often, however, eighteenth-century fictional islands were more bizarre than any later ones, in terms of both content *and* authorship. *Gulliver's Travels* (1726), a satire on the already flourishing genre of outlandish adventures from outlandish places, is, of course, by Jonathan Swift (1667–1745), Dean of St Patrick's Cathedral in Dublin. I say, 'of course' since no one ever seems to have doubted it, then or now. In this case there is literally no evidence for his authorship at all. Because it was (rightly) seen as an incendiary satire on the politics of the day, and because its author might have been liable for prosecution, the entire manuscript was copied out by a clerk, so that no trace of Swift's handwriting could be discovered in the text, and then delivered anonymously to its London publisher. He, in turn, made what are believed to have been further changes and placed different parts of the book with different printers, to make it more difficult for it to be suppressed before publication. The original manuscript was probably destroyed, but for those who believe it may have survived, finding it has become a kind of Holy Grail for literary detectives.

As this was a work of satire no attempt at realism was involved. The first and second parts, the voyages to Lilliput (the island of little people) and Brobdingnag (the island of giants), are clearly enough satires on the politics of Queen Anne's reign. Making your politicians no more than six inches high is always a useful device, and the reverse, making us tiny by comparison with the benevolent giants, no less so. The latter also allowed Swift's disgust at the human body free play, since it involved close-ups of otherwise attractive female anatomy – as when, at one point, Gulliver is almost smothered by being clutched to his protector's enormous breast. But these transformations in scale are as nothing to Laputa, the flying island, filled by mad intellectuals; or, finally, to the Land of the Houyhnhnms, the super-rational intelligent horses. Again, trading on the inversion of norms, the horses are the 'masters', displaying all the Enlightenment virtues, and the humans – or 'Yahoos' – are filthy and degenerate creatures naturally despised by every right-thinking horse.

While using the current vogue for travel writing to satirize contemporary politics, Swift of course achieved something else that was probably quite unintended. The progress from wildly possible fact, typified by *Robinson Crusoe*, into the wildly impossible fictions of Gulliver, moved travel literature itself into a new fictional form: fantasy. This was not the first travel fantasy, but by not even pretending to possibility, it caught the imagination of the age in a way that nothing before had achieved, and added, in effect, a whole new dimension to interior space. It is not accidental that Swift's imaginary islands soon became standard children's reading. Indeed as with the progress of the 'Robinson' trope, the Lilliput trope passed into the language, with many illustrated editions and later films; and in turn gave rise to such works as *Mistress Masham's Repose* (1946) by T.H. White (1906–64), in which Maria, a 10-year-old girl, discovers a colony of exiled Lilliputians living on an overgrown island in a lake in an English country house park. Their back-story is carefully rooted in Swift's own narrative, and the Lilliputians themselves speak in a wonderfully accurate version of early eighteenth-century English.

But there is a darker side to Swift's narratives. What had begun as a satire on the trivialities of Queen Anne's government gradually morphs into a collective hatred of the entire human race. To the physical repulsion of the Brobdingnagian close-ups is added a growing contempt for the intellectual life of his contemporaries, and finally a visceral horror of humanity as a whole. Gulliver ends his days avoiding his neighbours, his wife and his family as much as he can, and spending hours a day in the stables with his horses. How much this represents Swift's own view has been a matter of debate, but Gulliver's progress, followed through, is one that passes from disinterested observation of human folly to fully-fledged misanthropism.

It is against the background of this ambiguous interest in world exploration, not to mention its possible downside, that Samuel Johnson (1709–84) began his poem 'The Vanity of Human Wishes' (1749):

> Let observation with extensive view
> Survey mankind, from China to Peru.

Though such a geographical sweep may seem commonplace today, this moment in the mid-eighteenth century was one of the earliest when such a survey could be deemed possible. In retrospect – and despite some problems with scansion – a better opening line might have been 'Let *imagination*, with extensive view ...' Any 'extensive view' on this scale would still have been more a matter of imagination than information, even in the eighteenth century. In the seventeenth century it would have included just too many blank or conjectural spaces to offer the same kind of unanimity about the universal misery of the human condition that Johnson wanted to invoke. Moreover, the *direction* of the view is also important. Most of us, I suspect, would in our mind's eye take the shortest route from China to Peru: that is, across the Pacific Ocean. But Johnson wanted to be as inclusive as possible, and to achieve that he had mentally to travel *west* from China, across the landmass of Eurasia, North Africa, the Atlantic and the Americas. Magellan may have crossed the Pacific more than two hundred years earlier, but much of that vast ocean space was still unknown. Though Dutch and Portuguese ships had traversed some of the area, and given names to the various lands, it was not until the time of Captain James Cook (1728–89) that the exact positions of the Great South Continent – to be named at first New Holland, and then Australia – and New Zealand were finally established.

A place did not, of course, have to be imaginary, or even far away, to be a prop for satire. After all, Voltaire had gained much satiric effect with his thoroughly European *Candide*, and Johnson had made similar use of a much more sketchily conceived Abyssinia in his novel *Rasselas: Prince of Abyssinia* (1759). Even closer to home, *Tom Thumb the Great* (1730), a play by Henry Fielding (1707–54), is set in a farcical version of King Arthur's England, and with the diminutive size of its hero (who is later eaten by a cow) is clearly trading on the success of *Gulliver*, published only four years before. Tom Thumb himself was widely seen as a caricature of Robert Walpole[5] – who had already effectively created what became the new political role of Prime Minister. It was an instant success. When Swift himself went to see it, it was reported that he laughed out loud – an event apparently so rare as to be noted with incredulity by witnesses.

Nevertheless in general the less well known a place, and the further away it was, the better it could be used for satire. Here China fitted the bill well. In 1757 Horace Walpole (1717–97), unlikely brother of the politician,[6] published his *Letter from Xo Ho*, which went through five editions that year. His acid comments on the British political system are astonishingly relevant even today.

> ... an Englishman has no fixed ideas; his Prejudices are not of his country, but against some particular Parts or Maxims of his Country; his Caprices are his own; they are the essential Proofs of his Liberty ... An Englishman loves or hates his King once or twice in a Winter, and that for no Reason, but because he loves or hates the Ministry in being.[7]

The formula – confronting a naïve foreigner from another unrelated society with the peculiarities of our own – has stood the test of time well. It is, with variations, the same as that of Johnson's *Rasselas*[8] and, with the addition of time travel to add further distance, also that of Robert Southey's *Colloquies on Society*, where he interviews characters from the past;[9] of William Morris's

---

[5]Pat Rogers, *Henry Fielding: A Biography*, Paul Elek, 1979, p. 49.

[6]He was so unlike his brother that many sceptics, then and now, raised doubts about their parentage.

[7]*Letter from Xo Ho, a Chinese Philosopher at London, to his Friend Lien Chi at Peking*, 1757.

[8]*The History of Rasselas, Prince of Abyssinia*. 1759.

[9]*Sir Thomas More; or, Colloquies on the Progress and Prospects of Society*, by Robert Southey, Esq., LL.D., Poet Laureate. 2 vols. 8vo. London: 1829. See Chapter 6.

novel of the future, *News from Nowhere*;[10] and of Edith Nesbit's children's journeys into the past in *The Story of the Amulet*.[11]

However *The Citizen of the World* (1760) by Oliver Goldsmith (1730–44) is not *just* satire. Though Goldsmith borrows the name of Walpole's imaginary Chinese recipient, Lien Chi, now as his visitor to London, and many of his letters follow the standard pattern, with descriptions of local politics, wars with the French, codes of dress etc., there is also the much more serious suggestion of the superiority of Chinese civilization over that of Europe. Comic interludes remain morally ambiguous – as when a woman that we recognize (but he does not) as a prostitute offers to take away his watch for repair, assuring him that it will cost her nothing.[12] Is such innocence that of a fool, deserving to be exploited, or that of someone whose society has always been safely based on mutual trust?

Not only does poor Lien recoil in tasteful horror from the excesses of London *chinoiserie* – which he notes might as well be called Egyptian as Chinese[13] – but also he is made to show consistent moral and intellectual superiority over his British hosts. His Chineseness is much more than a mere satiric device. Goldsmith had consulted some of the best sources then available to him.[14] Though he goes to some trouble not merely to establish the character of Lien as an 'outsider', but to give him a specifically Chinese viewpoint, his judgements are consistently liberal and humane in tone. Goldsmith even has him retell, with approval, the story of the Chinese Emperor who instead of giving his subjects the usual pageant and fireworks at the Feast of the Lanterns gave clothes and money to the blind, the maimed and the strangers in the city. Lien Chi concludes:

> The people were at first amazed, but soon perceived the wisdom of their king, who taught them, that to make one man happy was more truly great than having ten thousand captives groaning at the wheels of his chariot.[15]

---

[10]*News from Nowhere*, Kelmscott Press, 1890.

[11]First published by T. Fisher Unwin, 1906.

[12]'A Citizen of the World', *Collected Works of Oliver Goldsmith*, ed. Arthur Friedman, Oxford, 1966, II, p. 43.

[13]Ibid., p. 64.

[14]These included the third edition of Louis le Comte's *Noveaux mémoires sur l'état present de la Chine* (1697), and English translation of Du Halde's *Description of the Empire of China* (1738–41) and the 1755 edition of the Marquis d'Argens' *Lettres Chinoises*.

[15]Goldsmith in *Collected Works*, p. 101.

Though one might justify this optimistic portrait of China on the grounds that this is meant to be satire anyway – and who would believe it of China? – the fact remains that neither Walpole nor Goldsmith had been forced to choose the Far East. Unlike Arthurian Britain, China was a real place; and real civic virtue there, however unlikely, was at least always possible.

There were, however, two other reasons why Johnson might have chosen two countries on opposite sides of the world for his survey of human futility and delusion. Both China and Peru represented ancient civilizations – known to be much older than Johnson's own English society. In other words, the vanity of human wishes was an age-old phenomenon and, despite Goldsmith's chink of optimism, part of the eternal human condition. Johnson has been described as a 'cosmic Tory'. But there was a third reason that might – just *might* – have threatened this pessimism.

As Neil Rennie has shown in his hugely entertaining book *Far Fetched Facts*,[16] Europe had long clung to the hope that somewhere, somehow, there would be found an idyllic society of simple happy people living in peaceful community without wars, injustice or civil strife. To this, the more optimistic (or more frustrated) visionaries added the fantasy of free love and complete sexual freedom. To begin with the realm of Prester John in Ethiopia seemed a possible candidate, but a growing acquaintance with East Africa made this less and less attractive. For a while, as we have seen, China and even Australia provided backgrounds for speculative European projections;[17] but by Johnson's time the only places where there was sufficient blank space for such hopes were the famed but as yet mostly unknown 'South Sea Islands' of the Pacific.[18] The idea of Tahiti as just such an idyll of free love was even reinforced by Cook's first voyage. Many of his crew had found themselves Polynesian women for short, and occasionally longer, liaisons. Even Joseph Banks, one of Cook's passengers and later to be President of the Royal Society, had experienced

---

[16]Neil Rennie, *Far-Fetched Facts: The Literature of Travel and the Idea of the South Seas*, Oxford: Clarendon Press, 1998.

[17]For instance *Parjumouf: A Tale from New Holland*, by the Swedish author, C.J.L. Almqvist (1817). This is the first work of fiction to have an Australian setting.

[18]Margaret Mead's *Coming of Age in Samoa* (1928) was perhaps the last in a long line of such attempts to present the Pacific islands as home to such sexually uninhibited societies.

something of this attractive southern comfort when in Tahiti as a young man.[19] His initial delight in this uninhibited 'innocent' society was, however, shattered when he discovered that infanticide was a common and accepted practice. It was this reputation for free love that had persuaded the mutineers on the *Bounty* to stop off at Tahiti, where they collected a number of native women, on their way to the then uninhabited Pitcairn Island as a refuge. For Johnson's panoramic survey of human misery, the Pacific was possibly a disturbingly optimistic gap, and was therefore best left out of his imaginative, if consequently not quite so extensive, view.

In much the same spirit of disinterested enquiry and mild titillation, it was a standard procedure for maps of the sixteenth and seventeenth centuries to include alongside the ships and strange sea monsters a mass of marginal illustrations around the edges to show something of the people who inhabited these places (see Pl. 17): their looks, their dress, (if any): together with any other relevant material.[20]

As we have seen, some kinds of information were more accurate than others, and, once again, it is difficult to separate plausible fact from plausible invention, or plausible invention from deliberate fiction, as geographers found themselves torn between the desire to assert European supremacy and the genuine hope that somewhere there might be a society that had solved the manifest problems that plagued their own.

An eighteenth-century Italian map of the southern hemisphere follows this tradition by showing a bare-breasted woman holding a feathered arrow and sitting on a crocodile (see Pl. 18). Whether this represents an everyday story of country folk in Australia, New Zealand, South America or unspecified South Sea Islands is unclear, but it certainly suggests how exotic and wonderful such places might be.

It also illustrates how an interest in exploration was not confined just to the exploring countries – Britain, Denmark, France, Netherlands, Portugal, Spain, Sweden – but was Europe-wide. Germany, for instance, like Italy, was still a

---

[19]See Richard Holmes, *The Age of Wonder: How the Romantic Generation Discovered the Beauty and Terror of Science*, Harper, 2008, pp. 1–59 'Joseph Banks in Paradise'.
[20]For a detailed examination of these marginalia in the sixteenth century see John Gillies, *Shakespeare and the Geography of Difference*, Cambridge University Press, 1994.

collection of independent states in the eighteenth century, with almost no naval presence. But it had a large and literate population, with more journals and magazines than anywhere else in Europe. As a result, it had long maintained a keen interest in overseas exploration.

It is, for example, not widely known that the great German theologian and philosopher Friedrich Schleiermacher (1768–1834) also wrote a history of the English Colony of New South Wales in 1798. Only in 1988 were Schleiermacher's papers from his Berlin period first published. Almost unnoticed by theologians and philosophers, among the notebooks, letters and work on Plato, Shakespeare, the Schlegel brothers, Fichte etc. was a collection of papers dating from 1799–1800 on the British settlement of New Holland – or New South Wales, as it is now better known.[21]

It seems that Schleiermacher had been approached in 1798 or early 1799 by the Berlin publisher, Karl Philipp Spener (1749–1827), who since 1784 had been producing a series of annuals entitled *The Historical Genealogical Calendar or Yearbook of the Most Remarkable Events of the New World*. The idea was for Schleiermacher to translate *Account of the English Colony of New South Wales* (1798) by David Collins (1756–1810) for the 1800 Yearbook. Such was Schleiermacher's enthusiasm for this project that he started to read everything he could lay his hands on about the colony. Not surprisingly, deadlines slipped, and the quantity of information so outgrew Spener's original projected space, that in 1802, when Schleiermacher moved to his new post at Stolpe, he was finally forced to abandon the scheme.

Since only a few pages of what was a monumental two-volume effort seem to have survived, much of our information has to come from Collins' description – and this in itself would have been quite enough to show that Australia, at least, was no home to any idyllic primitive society.[22] Collins was at some pains to dismiss the Enlightenment version of the noble savage. Without reverting to the alternative and older view – still argued at that period by some

---

[21]*Materialien zur Siedlungsgesichte Neuhollands 1799–1800. Schriften aus der Berliner Zeit, 1800-1802*, ed. Gunter Meckenstock (Berlin: de Gruyter, 1988), pp. 249–79. Much of the following material is drawn from the same source, particularly from the 'Historical Introduction', pp. lxxxii–xciii.

[22]See Stephen Prickett, 'Coleridge, Schlegel and Schleiermacher: England, Germany (and Australia) in 1798', *1798: The Year of the Lyrical Ballads*, ed. Richard Cronin, Macmillan, 1998.

defenders of slavery – that negroes (and/or Aborigines) belonged to a different biological species from Europeans, he takes it for granted that, though utterly different in all observable respects, these are people like ourselves. What he records is a classic encounter with the 'other' in its most extreme and most uncompromising form. For all his scholarly caution and reminders of the uncertainty and sketchiness of our knowledge, his picture of aboriginal life is truly grim – even apparently by the standards of the eighteenth-century penal colony of Sydney Cove. Not merely, he tells us, do they have no religion at all, but the plight of their womenfolk, ravished from other tribes, is pitiable.

> The condition of these women is so wretched, that it is scarcely possible for a thinking mind to forbear, on seeing a female infant, from anticipating its future miseries, and feeling regret that the Almighty disposer had permitted it to enter a world where its only portion was to be suffering.[23]

This is not quite the case of advanced Enlightenment sympathy for the disadvantaged and oppressed that it might appear, since the tribe in question, on the south shore of Sydney harbour, was later effectively exterminated by disease (not to mention more brutal means) by the settlers themselves. As a result, we have no means of knowing whether or not this sympathy for women was well placed, or part of a much wider case of cultural misunderstanding. It also strikes at the heart of the original description of Australia as *terra nullius* – a land totally uninhabited, and therefore open to settlement. What matters to us is the portrait of Australia that was being added to a growing European awareness of the known world. Whether or not this was Collins' intention, conscious or unconscious, it also helped to justify the colonization of yet another far-off part of the earth.

While we should not discount the obvious fact that Schleiermacher, at this stage of his career, was short of money, his over-enthusiasm for the whole project resulted in its having to be abandoned, suggesting that his interest was much more than merely commercial. During this same period he was also working on another book that was to give him lasting fame – and controversy. This was entitled *On Religion: Speeches to its Cultured Despisers* (1799), which was his attempt to defend his own religious beliefs against his circle of Romantic

---

[23]David Collins, *An Account of the English Colony of New South Wales*, 2nd edn, London, 1804, p. 375.

friends, centred mostly at the University of Jena, for whom religion was an obvious anachronism. For a man who was working on a definition of religion that had to be simultaneously universal enough to satisfy these most 'cultured despisers' and powerful enough to point towards what he believed to be the basic truth of Christianity, Collins' account of the Australian aborigines had to be the ultimate challenge – and Schleiermacher was always a man who thrived on challenges. Setting aside any doctrines, metaphysical beliefs or even, indeed, any overt belief in a God, Schleiermacher grounds his idea of religion in what he calls an 'intuition of the infinite' (*Anschauung des Unendlichen*).

This is, by definition, a deeply personal and even essentially incommunicable experience. 'Intuition is and always remains something individual, set apart, the immediate perception, nothing more ... Others may stand right behind you, right alongside you, and everything can appear differently to them.'[24] Such an 'intuition of the infinite', in this sense of a highly subjective apprehension of the wholeness of things, is a familiar feature of Romantic thought. Following Schleiermacher's friend F.W. Schelling (1755–1854) – another of the 'cultured despisers' – Coleridge was later to find in it his idea of the 'primary imagination', which he calls the 'prime act of all human perception'. Here at least, in the first response of the senses, in this primary awareness could, be found not merely a basis for a common humanity, but also a foundation for a primary *religious* impulse. I perceive, therefore I believe. The logic is not as immediately transparent as Descartes' more famous formulation, but given the premises of the Kantian notion of the imagination – central to the thinking of the Jena Romantics – nonetheless it follows.

> The universe exists in uninterrupted activity and reveals itself to us in every moment. Every form that it brings forth, every being to which it gives separate existence according to the fullness of life, every occurrence that spills forth from its rich, ever-fruitful womb, is an action of the same upon us. Thus to accept everything individual as part of the whole and everything limited as a representation of the infinite is religion.[25]

---

[24]Friedrich Schleiermacher, *On Religion: Speeches to its Cultured Despisers*, tr. Richard Crouter, Cambridge University Press, 1996, pp. 105–6.
[25]Ibid., p. 105.

Schleiermacher has, in effect, now grounded religion not in any of the higher faculties, nor even in an articulated sense of God, but in the primal act of sense perception itself. That, at least, must be common to all humanity. If this is phrased more in the language of aesthetics and of a Romanticism common alike to Hölderlin and Wordsworth than in theology or philosophy, its long-term effects on both ways of thinking were to prove profound. From Schleiermacher springs the work of Dilthey, Heidegger, Gadamer and Ricoeur – in a very real sense the roots of modern European philosophy lie in that first unpromising meeting of cultures in Sydney Cove.

From our point of view, Schleiermacher has effectively interiorized the debate about religion, so that henceforth it becomes an essential and necessary part of our inner space. For him sense perception cannot be separated from our entire collective environmental and cultural background. As John Henry Newman (who in old age improbably denied ever having read any Coleridge or German philosophy)[26] once wrote: 'we are what we are, and we use, not trust our faculties ... We do not confront or bargain with ourselves.'[27] How we perceive is part of our total personality. Our sense of space, knowledge of geography, great or small, and where we suppose ourselves to be, is all part of us. In the same essay Newman comments that he, like almost all the rest of us, takes on trust that Great Britain is an island (or islands), without feeling any need to check up on this. But to discover this was wrong would entail a quite radical re-think of his entire universe – not just physical, but mental as well.

Nowadays we could extend this sense of geographical space to include the terrestrial globe on which we live, the position of the Earth in our Solar System, and our place in our home Milky Way galaxy – amid, we are told, billions of other such galaxies. Most of us have no way to check on these facts, and, unlike Newman, our little lives would not change radically if (as they probably will) these figures are modified at some time in the future. Dark energy and dark matter somehow symbolize our massive ignorance of the universe where we live – which in some ways gives us more in common with the geographical

---

[26]Taken by many of his contemporaries more as a sign of failing memory than a statement of ignorance.
[27]John Henry Newman, *A Grammar of Assent*, ed. I.T. Ker, Oxford: Clarendon, 1985, p. 323.

ignorance of the seventeenth and eighteenth centuries than it does with the relative geographical confidence of the nineteenth.

But – and this is a very large 'but' – this is to ignore the fact that the greatest spatio-temporal transformation of all was happening in the middle of the nineteenth century – something to which Newman makes no reference at all. This is the discovery of Deep Time – in many ways a far more disturbing change than the subsequent discovery of Deep Space.

In 1812 Baron Georges Cuvier (1769–1832), Europe's most eminent anatomist, startled the scientific world by announcing that a pair of jaws over four feet long dug up in a mine in Maastricht in 1770 had belonged to an extinct creature of gigantic proportions. The remains of similar vast monsters, apparently dating from before the Flood, were coming to light elsewhere. In 1822 Gideon Mantell (1790–1852), a doctor in Lewes, Sussex, had his attention drawn by his wife to some fossil teeth in a pile of chalk by the roadside and realized from their size that they did not belong to any known animal. Following the chalk fragments back to the quarry whence they had come, he retrieved enough of the skeleton to be able to publish a description of the animal by 1825. From the similarity of its teeth to the modern iguana, he named it an 'Iguanadon'.

The year before, the Rev. William Buckland (1784–1836), the Oxford Professor of Geology, had published an account of another huge skeleton from a local quarry, which he called simply a 'Megalosaurus'.

Figure 4.1 *Nineteenth-century reconstruction of Iguanodon.*

Though the term was not coined until 1841, the great age of dinosaur discovery had arrived. Monsters, more vast and variegated than the most fantastic imagination could dream of, were now suddenly turning up literally underfoot. Within a very few years they were to transform the whole picture of the world.

When in 1845 the Victorian poet John Burgon (1813–88) described Petra, the newly discovered city of the Nabateans in what is now Jordan, as a 'Rose-red city, half as old as time', he meant it not as a metaphor, but *literally*. From studying the Bible, the seventeenth-century Archbishop James Ussher (1581–1656) had, with improbable precision, discovered that the world had been created at 10.00 am on 23 October 4004 B C,[28] which would, indeed, have made Petra half the age of the world. On Tuesday, 11 April 1848, the Cambridge Theological Examiners asked the question: 'Give the date of the deluge.' The correct answer, as candidates would have been expected to know, was '2348 B C or 1656 after the Creation of the world.' Even more than discoveries in terrestrial geography, the new dinosaur discoveries had changed the size and shape of human space to an unimaginable degree. For a short while it even looked as if men like Buckland were right in believing that geology was merely confirming scripture by showing the remains of the great beasts that had been drowned in Noah's Flood. Despite arguments by such as Anthony Nesbit (died 1859) (grandfather of the children's author, E. Nesbit, of whom more later), who claimed in his *Essay on Education* (1841) that the prehistoric animals had become extinct because Noah had left them out of his ark, this rapidly proved an untenable position. Geological evidence showed that the strata in which the fossils were found were hundreds of millions of years old. Such 'Catastrophist' geological theories – like that of the biblical Flood – were quickly undermined by Charles Lyell (1797–1875), a leading Scottish geologist, whose *Principles of Geology* appeared between 1830 and 1833. Mantell's *Wonders of Geology* followed in 1838. In less than a generation the monsters from underground had shattered an entire traditional world-picture, and the inner space of

---

[28]Given his material available, this was a perfectly respectable scholarly calculation.
Ussher was a noted scholar and a Fellow of the Royal Society. See James Barr, 'Why the World was Created in 4004BC: Archbishop Ussher and Biblical Chronology.' *Bulletin of the John Rylands Library*, Manchester, May 1984.

Victorian society was confronted with dark unimaginable vistas of pre-human history.

For the more theologically minded there were special problems. The 'principle of plenitude' had assumed that at the Creation God had made every possible species so as to leave no incomplete links in the Great Chain of Being – a divine hierarchical order extending from the very lowest forms via humans and angels to God himself.[29] More practically, it was inconceivable to many that a benevolent God had doomed whole species to complete extinction. For a while some people clung to the hope that examples of these vanished creatures might yet be discovered living in remote parts of the world.

But worse possibilities than extinction of individual species were in store. Because the Mosasaurus, the first prehistoric monster to have been described by Cuvier, had been (correctly) interpreted as a giant lizard, the other later discoveries of Mantel and Buckland were also seen as lizard-like. But in 1841 Richard Owen (1804–92), Professor at the Royal College of Surgeons in London, in an address to the British Association, showed that the Iguanodon, Megalosaurus and Hylaeosaurus[30] were structurally quite different from lizards, and, indeed, from all existing reptiles. They were, argued Owen, part of a new and hitherto unknown class of animals for which he proposed the name 'Dinosauria', or 'terrible lizards'. As even Tennyson had realized in his *In Memoriam* (1850) the evidence for the disappearance of whole *classes* of animals was there for all to read, and though Charles Darwin's *Origin of Species* was not published until 1859 it had been substantially completed by the mid-1840s.

For such devout biblical literalists as the zoologist Philip Gosse (1810–88), the choice between science and religion was an agonizing one, which he finally solved by what might be described as the greatest piece of Victorian imagination of all. In his book *Omphalos* (1847), he argued that though we know from divine revelation that the world *was* created some six thousand years ago, it had been created complete with an instant 'past': with sedimentary strata,

---

[29]See A.O. Lovejoy, *The Great Chain of Being*, Cambridge, MA: Harvard University Press, 1936. Chapters 8 and 9.
[30]The gigantic 'Wealden Lizard', about five metres long, with scaly armoured plates, also discovered by Mantell in 1832.

fossils, and all the newly discovered evidence of 'the slow development of organic forms'. The actual historical point of Creation was, therefore, scientifically undetectable, and could only be known by special Revelation contained in the Bible. For the scornful reviewers of the day this was simply an argument that 'God hid the fossils in the rocks in order to tempt geologists into infidelity.' Charles Kingsley, not merely an Anglican clergyman but also a prominent amateur naturalist, wrote that he could not 'believe that God had written on the rocks one enormous and superfluous lie.'

By this time the prehistoric monsters, terrifying or fascinating according to individual standpoint, had captured the imagination of the Victorian world. The earliest calculations had actually made many of them even larger than later measurement allowed. Comparing the teeth and clavicle of the Iguanodon with present day iguanas implied that the former might be 100 feet long. Comparisons of the femora and claw bone gave figures of 75–100 feet, making the largest specimen on record an impossible 200 feet long.

In 1852, when the Crystal Palace was moved from its original setting in Hyde Park to its permanent site in Sydenham, Prince Albert suggested there should be replicas of some of the newly discovered monsters in the grounds. The sculptor commissioned, Benjamin Waterhouse Hawkins (1807–94), thought at first in terms of the great extinct mammals like the Mastodon, but once he had encountered Owen's descriptions of the Mesozoic giants he was fired with the ambition to 'revivify the ancient world' of the great dinosaurs. On islands in the six-acre lake at Sydenham he constructed what he believed to be life-sized models of the Iguanodon, Hylaeosaurus, Megalosaurus and others (see Plates 19 and 20). The largest weighed thirty tons – and it is a tribute to the solidity of Hawkins' workmanship that they are still there.

The new Crystal Palace dinosaur park was opened by Queen Victoria and Prince Albert in the presence of some forty thousand spectators in June 1854. Though their image of the great saurians may have been wildly inaccurate, Owen and Hawkins had created a popular image that was to last for more than a generation, and, more important, had ushered their whole period into an utterly new sense of Deep Time. To celebrate the completion of the project, a dinner for twenty-one leading scientists was held inside the shell of the almost-completed Iguanodon, with Owen in the place of honour, literally *in* as well as *at* the head.

Figure 4.2 *Dinosaur Dinner.* The Illustrated Encyclopaedia of Dinosaurs.

These discoveries had a predictable effect on contemporary art and literature. If we compare the monsters created by the mid-century artists with those of the late eighteenth century, the difference is startling. The weird creatures of James Jeffries (1751–84) or the better-known sea monsters of John Hamilton Mortimer (1740–79) are clearly descended from the half-human species of classical mythology – fauns, centaurs, tritons etc. Though they have scales and claws, and often tails, their scale is essentially a human one. They even have (vaguely) human faces.

In contrast, for the Victorian artists the wildest outsize dreams of the Romantics had suddenly come true. Images of horror, which had always leaned towards the slimy and scaly, now became more specifically reptilian. After a visit to Mantell in September 1834, John Martin (1789–1854) was commissioned to 'portray the country of the Iguanadon' – which became the frontispiece for Mantell's 1838 *Wonders of Geology*.

Almost at the same time Martin produced another even more dramatic mezzotint entitled 'The Great Sea Dragons as they Lived' for Thomas Hawkins'

Figure 4.3 *John Hamilton Mortimer:* Sea Monster, *Tate Gallery.*

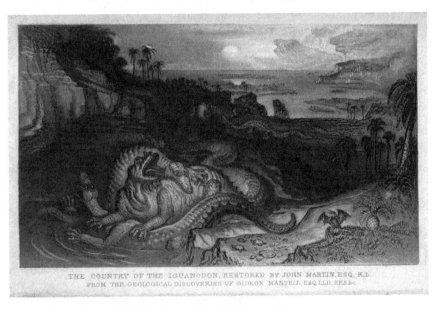

Figure 4.4 *John Martin:* The Country of the Iguanadon.

Figure 4.5 *John Martin: Frontispiece:* The Book of the Great Sea Dragons.

The Book of the Great Sea Dragons: Ichthyosauri and Plesiosauri (1840). Other illustrators followed where Martin led.

Similarly, it was no surprise that when John Tenniel (somewhat reluctantly) undertook to illustrate Lewis Carroll's *Through the Looking Glass* in 1871, he should have given the Jabberwocky the long scaly neck and tail of a sauropod and the leathery wings of a Pterodactyl. Others, however, noted that the result looked suspiciously like the Oxford academic, Benjamin Jowett, Master of Balliol College. Jowett the Jabberwocky, however, was hardly a dinosaur in the modern sense. For his more conservative enemies, including Lewis Carroll, he was rather the newly emerged monster of infidelity who had scandalized some sections of Oxford opinion by expressing doubts about the Thirty-Nine Articles, on which the Anglican Church was founded.

Even when not satiric, the illustrations of the Questing Beast by Aubrey Beardsley (1872–98) to Malory, or the Fairy books of Andrew Lang (1844–1912), are followed by those of H.J. Ford (1860–1941) in the reptilian appearance of the newly discovered monsters.

It might seem that these extraordinary discoveries of Deep Time and Deep Space in the last two centuries would have enlarged our mental worlds almost

Figure 4.6 *John Tenniel: Jabberwocky.*

to the point of infinity. Almost – but not quite. Infinity is literally endless. In a mere two hundred years, we have gone from a universe of some 6,000 years to one of 13.7 billion years – with a margin of error of perhaps 21 million years. These are telephone numbers to most of us, but they are *not* infinity. Similarly space may be unimaginably vast, but (at least by today's understanding of the truth!) not infinite either. Infinity is a strange concept, suitable for neither space nor time. It is, for example, possible in a thought experiment to imagine an infinite universe on a dinner plate. All one has to do is to imagine a world in which a tree (or a mountain – what you will) is one inch high in the middle of the plate, and infinitely small at the perimeter. One then might travel endlessly outwards in any direction without ever reaching the edge.

In contrast to Speer's imaginary journey, *The Golden Notebook* (1962) by Doris Lessing (1919–2013) is more or less devoted to exploring the inner space of the protagonist, Anna Wulf. Here she plays what she calls 'the game', by which she slowly embraces the entire universe in her private consciousness.

> First I created the room I sat in, object by object, 'naming' everything, bed, chair, curtains, till it was whole in my mind, then move out of the room, creating the house, then out of the house, slowly creating the street, then rise into the air, looking down on London, at the enormous sprawling wastes of London, but holding at the same time the room, and the house and the street in my mind, and then England, the shape of England in Britain, then the little group of islands lying against the continent, then slowly, slowly, I would create the world, continent by continent, ocean by ocean ... until the point was reached where I moved out into space and watched the world, a sunlit ball in the sky, turning and rolling beneath me. Then, having reached that point, with the stars around me, and the little earth turning underneath me, I'd try to imagine at the same time, a drop of water, swarming with life, or a green leaf. Sometimes I could reach what I wanted, a simultaneous knowledge of vastness and smallness. Or I would concentrate on a single creature, a small coloured fish in a pool, or a single flower, or a moth, and try to create or 'name' the being of the flower, the moth, the fish, slowly creating around it the forest, or the sea-pool, or the space of blowing night air that tilted my wings. And then, out, suddenly, from the smallness into space.[31]

With or without infinity it is safe to say that there are now no real edges, no perceivable frontiers to our spatial and temporal imaginations. For the first time in our (comparatively short) human history inner space and time have no practical boundaries. What Swift might have made of this is anybody's guess.

---

[31]Doris Lessing, *The Golden Notebook*, Penguin Books, 1964, pp. 537–8.

5

Children's spaces: Adult fantasies

Platform Nine and Three-Quarters (Platform 9¾) is a platform at King's Cross Station in London. Magically concealed behind the barrier between Muggle Platforms Nine and Ten, this Platform is where Hogwarts School of Witchcraft and Wizardry students board the Hogwarts Express on 1 September, in order to attend school. In order for someone to get onto Platform Nine and Three-Quarters, they must walk directly at the apparently solid metal ticket box dividing Platforms Nine and Ten. There is a guard stationed just outside the entrance, in order to regulate entries and exits from the platform.

So reads the internet entry on 'Platform Nine and Three-Quarters'. By now most readers, even those who have not actually read J.K. Rowling's Harry Potter books, will recognize the reference. Another internet entry, this time by the genuine station management at King's Cross, reads:

Look out for a luggage trolley embedded in the wall, and you can pretend you are off to start your magical school journey. The trolley is accessible at all hours, and you don't have to pay to take your own photographs. You can have a professional photograph taken with a scarf in your house colours, which is then available for you to view and purchase inside the Harry Potter shop next door. The professional photographer is on hand between 9am and 9pm daily. Queues for the trolley can get busy during school holidays and festive periods – visit early to make sure you're one of the first in line!

There is, of course, a back-story here. The station management had become so tired of children trying to crash trolleys into the brick pillars between the genuine platforms 9 and 10, not to mention dealing with numerous damaged trolleys, that they turned a destructive fiction into a commercially profitable reality with this rather ingenious embedded trolley in the open concourse – well away from the actual platforms concerned (see Pl. 21). Next door is a licensed shop dealing in all manner of Harry Potter memorabilia and complete with (presumably) a rota of professional photographers. Also worth noting is the fact that of over 160 pictures of people pretending to push this trolley through the wall, only three are children. The rest are variegated adults – presumably pretending to be children. One is of two Catholic priests. There is also a disproportionate number of visitors from China, where apparently the *Harry Potter* series is wildly popular.

Such is the worldwide power of fiction .... Turning an inoffensive (if now somewhat battered) brick wall into a vast imaginary space – complete with shops, and a steam express train heading somewhere North (it is not clear whether Hogwarts is in England or Scotland, or is simply in a further extension of the imaginary space so entered at King's Cross) – is one of the most extraordinary achievements of J.K. Rowling: perhaps even unparalleled. But, of course, imaginary worlds for children are by no means unique to her.

Indeed all children's worlds are an inextricable mixture of fantasy and reality. We all have our own personal memories of our childhood – not to mention stories about the imagined worlds of other childhoods. One child I know of (not mine) when, about two-and-a-half, disappeared under the table at a motorway café and reappeared to announce that he and his imaginary friend Dees (making his first appearance on this occasion) had been parking their yaks. During the ensuing year it turned out that Dees had relatives with further yaks, so that whenever he did not want to do something (such as going to the dentist) he would explain that he had 93 yaks to park before he could enter. This, naturally, might take some time ... Another child – a girl confined to her bed for two years from the age of 12 and told by her doctors that she might never walk normally again[1] – composed dramatic short stories, plays and even operas (an art-form which she had never encountered).

---

[1] My mother. A reflection of the medical treatment of the time. As it happens by the age of 18 she was in her college swimming team.

Our problem is that by their very nature all but a tiny fraction of such imagined worlds vanishes with childhood itself. We are left with the few – the *very* few – records of those who in some way or another have tried to write down descriptions of their worlds – and of these, by definition, the vast majority have become books written by adults *for* children, even fewer of which have gone on to be recognized as great literature. Such literary worlds tend to have a logic and lasting power far greater than most actual children's worlds – yaks or no yaks.

To this there is one glaring exception: the Brontë children: Charlotte (1816–55), Emily (1814–48) and Anne (1820–49), together with their brother, Branwell (1817–48), collectively and perhaps uniquely wrote down in detail the childhood stories they composed about an imaginary world. Indeed, given their laborious attempts to reproduce print format, it is clear that they always saw their stories in terms of 'publications'. The stories of Lorraine, the Islanders, and the more famous Angria and Gondal seem to have been written by the children from 1826 onwards for much of the following decade. Their sources include a box of toy soldiers, given to the 11-year-old Branwell by his father in 1827, *Aesop's Fables*, the *Arabian Nights*, articles in *Blackwood's Magazine*, a copy of Scott's *The Tales of a Grandfather* (given by an aunt at New Year in 1828) and Thomas Bewick's profusely illustrated *History of British Birds* – with its famously ironic 'tail-pieces'. The earliest surviving story, written down by Branwell, describes imaginary intrigues and battles in 'Lorraine'. Later adventures in these imaginary kingdoms include a round of political rivalries, battles, rebellions and sieges.[2]

They reveal, among other things, the degree to which the children had effectively absorbed and imagined the ever changing and increasing global knowledge of the 1820s. Their imaginary geography spans the world and reflects the wars, politics and love affairs that the children had read about in the books mentioned above, and in magazines; or had heard of from their elders. The Great Glass Town – later re-named Verdopolis – arises (magically) in the Niger delta of West Africa. The Glass Town Federation is later joined by

---

[2] See Juliet Barker, *The Brontës*, St Martins Press, 1995; also Christine Alexander, 'Juvenilia', *The Brontës in Context*, ed. Marianne Thormahlen, Cambridge University Press, 2012.

a new kingdom, that of Angria to the east, in part to defend Glass Town from encroaching Ashanti tribes, aided by Arab allies – and (of course) the dastardly French. Gondal, on the other hand, is an island on the other side of the globe, somewhere in the North Pacific, which is large enough to contain no fewer than four kingdoms ruled by rival families, not to mention the newly-discovered South Pacific island of Gaaldine.[3] This world was occupied by a strange mixture of real and imagined figures, who in some sense represented their creators. Thus Charlotte adopted the persona of the Duke of Wellington; Branwell first tries Napoleon, and later someone called 'Sneaky'; while Emily and Anne choose the arctic explorers Parry and Ross respectively as their favoured alter egos.

The stories, poems and plays of these vast imaginary spaces are always described as 'juvenilia' – childhood writings – and so, of course, they are. But these are on a scale quite different from, say, those of the children's near contemporary Jane Austen (1775–1817), who has also left us quite a collection of works from her childhood. There, however, the concentration is on social and emotional satire rather than geographical space, and the overall volume is somewhat smaller.[4] In contrast, by the time Charlotte Brontë was 24, in 1840, her own manuscripts about this imaginary world were longer than all her later published novels put together.[5]

Even stranger, perhaps, is the one known attempt to write an adult social novel by a Victorian child: *The Young Visiters* (*sic*) by Daisy Ashcroft (1881–1972). The story of Mr Salteena, who is 'not quite a gentleman' but wishes to become one, was written in 1890 by Ashcroft at the age of nine. Each (fairly short) chapter consists of a single paragraph and is full of spelling mistakes. In 1917, when Ashcroft was 36, she rediscovered her story in an old exercise book, and lent it to a friend recovering from illness. Passed around among other friends, it eventually reached the hands of a now-forgotten novelist, Frank Swinnerton (1884–1982), who was also a reader for the publishers

---

[3] See Christine Alexander, ibid., p. 102.
[4] These are also quite extensive, and include *Love and Freindship* (sic), *Frederic & Elfrida, Henry & Eliza, Lesley Castle, Sir William Mountague, Jack & Alice*, and *Evelyn*, not to mention a *History of England by a Partial, Prejudiced and Ignorant Historian*.
[5] Alexander, ibid., p. 104.

Plate 1 *Hieronymous Bosch:* Ascent of the Blessed and Hell. *Galleria dell'Accademia, Venice, Italy.*

Plate 2 *Pieter Brueghel the Younger:* Conversion of St. Paul, *undated, oil on canvas. Villa Vauban, Luxembourg City.*

Plate 3 *Domenico di Michelino:* Dante in Florence. *Florence Cathedral.*

Plate 4 *Hans Memling:* St John Altarpiece, c. 1479, oil on oak panel, 173.6 × 173.7 cm *(central panel), 176 × 78.9 cm (each wing). Sint-Janshospitaal, Bruges.*

Plate 5 *Hans Memling:* St John Altarpiece. *Detail – Right-hand panel.*

Plate 6 *Robert Campin:* Dijon Nativity. *Musée des Beaux Arts de Dijon. Photograph by François Jay.*

Plate 7 *Jan Van Eyck:* Ghent Altarpiece, *Lower centre panel (1432).*

Plate 8 *Hieronymous Bosch:* Garden of Earthly Delights, *Prado Museum, Madrid.*

Plate 9 *Hieronymous Bosch:* Garden of Earthly Delights. *Detail – Left-hand panel.*

Plate 10 *Hieronymous Bosch:* Garden of Earthly Delights. *Detail – Right-hand panel: Burning City.*

Plate 11 *Hieronymous Bosch:* Garden of Earthly Delights, *Tree Man.*

Plate 12 *Hieronymous Bosch:* Temptation of St Anthony.

Plate 13 *Rogier van der Weyden: Damned Souls (Detail).*

Plate 14 *Arthur Devis: The John Bacon Family, 1742/3. Yale Center for British Art.*

Plate 15 *Joseph Wright of Derby:* Brooke Boothby. *Tate Gallery.*

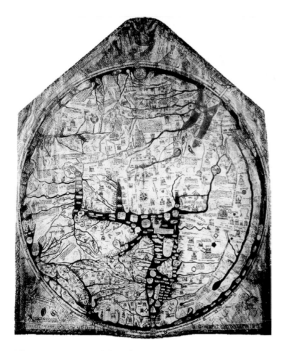

Plate 16 Mappa Mundi.

Plate 17 *Antique Marginalia: Brazil Natives.*

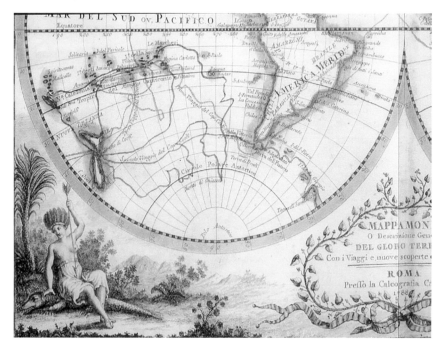

Plate 18 *Eighteenth-century Italian map of Australia.*

Plate 19 *Crystal Palace Megalosaurus.*

Plate 20 *Crystal Palace dinosaurs.*

Plate 21 *Harry Potter: Platform 9¾ at London's King's Cross Station.*

Plate 22 *Strawberry Hill House in 2012.*

Plate 23 *Still from the film adaption of H.G. Wells'* The Time Machine *(1960).*

Plate 24 *Still from the film* A Matter of Life and Death *(1945).*

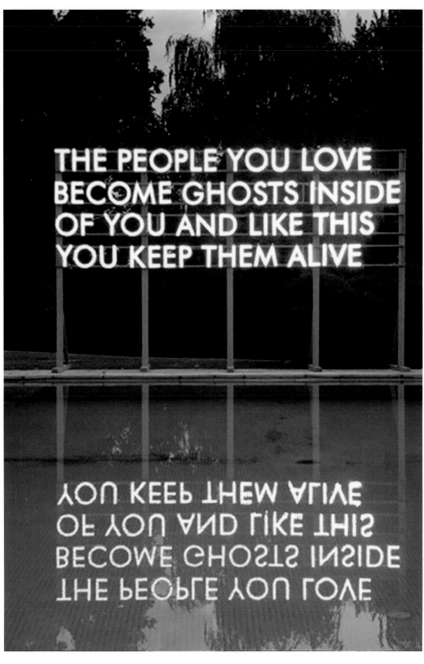

Plate 25 *Robert Montgomery:* The People You Love *(2010).*

Plate 26 *Artemisia Gentileschi:* Susanna and the Elders.

Plate 27 *Henry Wallis:* The Death of Chatterton.

Chatto and Windus. He persuaded them to publish it – which they did with a preface by J.M. Barrie. It was an instant success – reprinted 18 times in 1919, the year of its publication. It was turned into a play in 1920 (running first in London and then in New York), a musical in 1968, a full-length film in 1984, and a TV version in 2003.

The plot can easily be summarized. While the 17-year-old Ethel Monticue is staying with Alfred Salteena, 'an elderly man of 42', they are invited to visit a wealthy friend, Bernard Clark, who quickly falls for Ethel. Alfred consults his friend about how to become a gentleman. Though suitably doubtful if this can be achieved, Bernard nevertheless agrees to provide an introduction to the Earl of Clincham – who, like many aristocrats, lives in a 'compartment' in the Crystal Palace. While there, Salteena is introduced by Clincham as 'Lord Hyssops' to the Prince of Wales. Discovering that in his absence Bernard and Ethel have become engaged and married, Alfred is devastated and marries a maid at Buckingham Palace on the rebound. Clincham also marries – but, alas, not happily.

That children's books should be written *for* children (usually specific children) rather than *by* children is hardly surprising. But it does suggest that the further question of the boundary sometimes erected between writing 'for children' and for the rest of us is an entirely false one (the term 'adult literature' seems to have acquired a rather different meaning!). As I have argued elsewhere, the word 'literature' acquired its current principal meaning of writing with intrinsic value over and above its ostensible meaning only as late as the end of the eighteenth century. It is, in that sense, a Romantic concept. It is also a definition that does not take well to sub-categories. Great literature is oddly audience-blind. To debate whether *Alice in Wonderland* is a book for children or adults is a complete waste of time. The original, *Alice's Adventures Underground*, was composed impromptu and told on a particular summer afternoon on the river at Oxford to the Liddell children.[6] The reconstructed and published version has subsequently been read, loved, studied, translated, argued over and quoted all across the world by children, teenagers, adults,

---

[6]The first printed edition was pulped in its entirety because Carroll disliked the quality of the reproduction of Tenniel's illustrations.

astronomers, mathematicians, particle physicists and almost anyone else you care to think of. Similarly *Gulliver's Travels*, originally, as we have seen, a biting political satire, is neither a children's book nor an adult's. Both are well-established works of literature. Period.

Nevertheless to qualify as 'literature' a work usually has to pass two essential tests. The first is that it has proved popular over several changes of fashion – which means, in effect, that it has stayed in print for more than two or three generations. By this test, *Alice in Wonderland* passes with flying colours; but we have not got, and will not have for some time, any evidence for the lasting power of Rowling's Harry Potter books. Who knows if giggling teenagers, not to mention Catholic priests, will be being photographed by Platform Nine and Three-Quarters at King's Cross in 50 years' time? But equally, who now remembers Mary Fairclough's *Miskoo the Lucky*, a beautifully illustrated book published to great critical acclaim in 1947?[7] On the other hand, Kathleen Hale's *Orlando* books, published a decade earlier, from 1938 onwards, are still in print. As we have seen, Carroll's *Alice* books (though not the two-volume *Sylvie and Bruno*) and Rudyard Kipling's *Puck of Pook's Hill* have received the critical attention they deserve, while George MacDonald's or E. Nesbit's fairy stories have also remained in print over the same period, though flying under the academic radar with much less critical comment.

The second test is that of influence. How much have they altered subsequent writing? As mentioned earlier, Lewis Carroll, Charles Kingsley and George MacDonald were all friends who circulated manuscripts between them for approval and comment. *Alice* was first tested by being read aloud to the MacDonald children who voted for publication – Greville MacDonald (1856–1954),[8] the eldest, declared there should be 'sixty thousand copies'.[9] It was this group of fantasy writers that laid the foundations on which later writers such as Kipling and Nesbit were to build so successfully. Nor should we ignore the more satirical wit of Dickens, Lear or Thackeray who, in turn, all helped to fashion and influence the development of fantasy into the twentieth century, turning a

---

[7]And, as it happens, a present to me from my literary minded grandmother.
[8]Later to become a distinguished ear, nose and throat doctor, and also the author of several children's fairy stories.
[9]See Stephen Prickett, *Victorian Fantasy*, Harvester Press, 1979, 3rd edn, Edward Everett Root. p. 139.

Figure 5.1 *Lewis Carroll with the MacDonalds.*

small and eccentric form into a rich and on-going tradition which has grown in the past century and a half to be a major literary genre and source of such Hollywood blockbusters as *The Lord of the Rings, The Hobbit*, the *Harry Potter* series and Philip Pullman's *His Dark Materials*, to name only the most obvious.

I refer to 'the genre' as if fantasy, at least, were a recognized literary category. But of course the slightest knowledge of the field immediately dissolves any clear boundaries between genres sometimes assumed by bibliographers or cataloguers. Not merely is the frontier between 'fantasy' and, say, 'science-fiction' not an obvious one – H.G. Wells surely wrote both – but even definitions of 'realism' and 'fantasy' are far from being clear-cut. It is, for instance, often assumed that, except for the five 'Christmas books', Dickens was a 'realist' – indeed, a writer whose descriptions of nineteenth-century England are sometimes cited as an axiomatic definition of realism – grim and sordid. Yet those who read *The Posthumous Papers of the Pickwick Club, Containing a Faithful Record of the Perambulations, Perils, Travels, Adventures and Sporting Transactions of the Corresponding Members* as being in any sense 'realism' clearly don't recognize comic fiction when they see it – still less are they likely to be aware that it was commissioned by the publishers, Chapman and Hall, as a light-hearted skit to accompany a series of comic prints on the lines of the then very popular *Tom and Jerry* by the then much better-known artist Robert Seymour (1798–1836), who died before the series was complete. He was replaced by 'Phiz' (Hablot K. Browne [1815–82]) who, contrariwise, made his name as an illustrator of Dickens. With this in mind, a re-reading of *The Old Curiosity Shop*, or *Our Mutual Friend* might suggest an equal degree of unreality. Indeed, one reading of *Great Expectations* would see it as a clash between fantasy (Pip's 'expectations') and the less comfortable reality of his manipulation by Miss Havisham and Estella. Yet a reality that includes Miss Havisham and Magwitch (even if, as has been claimed, actual examples of both can be found) is hardly the 'realism' Dickens is sometimes acclaimed for. To avoid such problematic questions, 'fantasy' is sometimes confined to the portrayal of clearly delineated 'other worlds', but while this may work for MacDonald, and much of Nesbit, it immediately loses the whole of Lear and Thackeray and large parts of Kipling – not merely the *Jungle Books*, but *The Bridge Builders*, *The Brushwood Boy* and even *The Gardener* – all of which are set very much in this world, but none of which are by any stretch of the imagination 'realistic'. Like all really important words (think 'romanticism'; think 'political' …) the reality is usually recognizable but evades all precise definitions. The best we can usually do is to say something to the effect that we can recognize it when we encounter it.

I first read *The Hobbit* at the age of about ten and immediately recognized how much more vivid and interesting it was than my own inventions, which paled by comparison with a world that contained dwarves, elves, goblins, shape-shifters, trolls, wizards, eagles and dragons – not to mention hobbits, whom I had (naturally) never heard of before. Though the supposedly 'adult' *Lord of the Rings* added even more strange creatures, such as the barrow-wights, slow-moving ents, whatever octopus-like creature lurked in the lake outside Moria, and Balrogs, nothing in it quite matched up to the freshness of *The Hobbit*. But this probably reflects my age when I first read both works: which may well tell us more about the power of children's imaginations than it does about the books in question.

I was just too old to read C.S. Lewis's Narnia stories as a child when they first appeared from 1950 to 1956 – even supposing I had heard of them, which I hadn't. But this gave me the advantage that, when I finally read them, I was lucky enough to have had the obvious background reading in children's books – George MacDonald, E. Nesbit etc. – together with some knowledge of the Greek myths which form such a strong underlying stratum in the novels. Also, reading them immediately all together meant that the sequence was much clearer. It was immediately apparent, for instance, that *The Magician's Nephew* (1955), with its huge debt to E. Nesbit, then the next to last book in the series, should technically have come at the beginning – a change later made by the new publisher (HarperCollins) in the 1980s long after Lewis's death. This, however, meant losing the element of surprise for new readers at the beginning of *The Lion, the Witch and the Wardrobe* (1950) when Lucy first enters Narnia through the wardrobe and encounters Mr Tumnus in the snow. This has, naturally, been a source of critical controversy ever since.

Even more controversial in some quarters has been the theological theme of the entire sequence. Given Lewis's position as an already established popular Christian apologist, it is somewhat surprising that this should surprise anyone. But Lewis's use of religious allegory links him not merely with his Oxford context in the Inklings, but with a theological tradition leading back at least to MacDonald and his circle. In a world where the Bible, like other early myths, was increasingly subject to academic 'demythologizing', a feature common to Carroll, Kingsley and MacDonald was the deliberately counter-cultural attempt to *re-mythologize*. To those attuned to such things, the *Alice* books are studded with the kinds of theological references and symbolism that were second nature to many Victorian readers. Kingsley's theology in the *Water Babies* is even more overt – and correspondingly irritating to some modern readers.[10] But, of course, MacDonald was the most complex re-mythologizer: not merely in his children's books, but also in his two great adult fantasies, *Phantastes* and *Lilith*. He was also the only one of the three to discuss the nature of fantasy in a critical essay.[11]

Part of the mythic appeal of Lewis's Narnia stories is their direct metaphor of inner space – in this case, the entry to another world initially through a wardrobe stuffed with hanging coats, that leads gradually to the snow-covered forest with the mysterious single lamppost.

---

[10]See Stephen Prickett, *Victorian Fantasy*, chs 4, 5, and 6.
[11]"The Fantastic Imagination", *A Dish of Orts*, Sampson Lowe, 1893.

Figure 5.2 *Baynes: Lucy and Faun.*

As with many of the best stories, Lewis tells us that the whole Narnia sequence 'began with a picture of a Faun carrying an umbrella and parcels in a snowy wood. This picture had been in my mind since I was about sixteen. Then one day, when I was about forty, I said to myself: "Let's try to make a story about it."'[12] That this had a more than passing mythic appeal was made clear to me when I

---

[12]'It All Began With a Picture: The Making of C.S. Lewis's Chronicles of Narnia', Essay no. 10, in *C.S. Lewis and his Circle: Essays and Memoirs from the Oxford C.S. Lewis Society*, Roger White, Judith Wolfe, and Brendan Wolfe, Oxford Scholarship online, 2015.

met the translator of the Narnia stories into Romanian –they are very popular in that country.[13] She was trudging home on a snowy evening at dusk in late winter. As so often in the time of the Communist dictator, Nikolai Ceausescu, there was a 'brownout' due to inadequate electricity supply. Suddenly her attention was drawn to a brightly lit shop-front. It turned out to be the local British Council reading room, which had its own generator. Entering, she picked up a copy of *The Lion, the Witch and the Wardrobe* and started reading. 'It was all about Romania!' she exclaimed. 'There was the snow, the secret police, the fear of the authorities, even the wicked witch' – the hated Madame Ceausescu! She took it home and started a Romanian translation that evening.

Yet that same book has also been the cause of some of the most powerful criticism. The death of the Lion, Aslan, one of the most obvious bits of religious allegory in the whole Narnia sequence, is, we are told, based on 'magic'. The wicked witch (perhaps a little better theologically informed than Madame Ceausescu) claims the right to substitute the execution of Aslan for Edmund's treachery – citing something called 'deep magic from the dawn of time' without further explanation. Nevertheless Aslan seems to accept the justice of this – though again without explanation. Aslan's subsequent torture and death is, however, eventually overcome by 'deeper magic from before the dawn of time' – and he is resurrected. This is, of course, an allegory of the death and resurrection of Christ. But in so far as these mysterious references to magic are given any kind of rationale it is through a particular and highly controversial version of Christ's sacrifice, commonly called the 'substitution' theory of the Atonement. This holds that *someone* has to atone to God for the sins of the whole world – and only Christ, the Son of God, can do so. The reasoning is taken from medieval law and follows a logic that for many people makes little sense. It certainly would not be valid in contemporary law anywhere in the world. Though it still holds sway with some current Evangelicals, most theologians (liberal or conservative) would not subscribe to it today.

Two interesting questions arise from this. The first is why Lewis here subscribes to this particular theory of the Atonement, when in general he

---

[13]C.S. Lewis has become something of a cult figure in Romania. At the last count some 25 of his books have been translated. There is a Lewis Institute at the University of Iasi.

remained wary of so many Evangelical doctrines? The second is whether it works, either theologically or dramatically, in terms of the story's own logic, to make Aslan/Christ's atonement a matter of what seems to be quite arbitrary 'magic'. Should what for many Christians is a central point of their faith be ascribed to something so fundamentally arbitrary and inexplicable? Such questions remain among the few unsatisfactory aspects of what is otherwise one of the most brilliant and memorable creations of inner space in twentieth-century fantasy. Neither question has an easy answer – except to say we do not know. But the fact that Lewis was a professional medievalist may provide some clue.[14] For someone steeped, as he was, in medieval literature – which is almost all religious in one form or another – it is likely that the problems this raised would have been less obvious to him than to many of his contemporaries. He is here simply re-stating what would have been accepted by most medieval Christians – and the distinction between religion and magic would have been much less clear to Catholics reared on transubstantiation in the Mass than it would have been to post-scientific-revolution Protestants of the twentieth or twenty-first centuries. But this still leaves the problem of further 'deep magic' unsolved. A Christianity that depends on magic, unknown to its diabolic opponents (whether the White Witch, or Screwtape), not to mention most humans, is, to say the least, problematic. It highlights what for many is the uncomfortable question raised earlier by Mrs Humphry Ward: whether miracles (especially the resurrection of Christ) can be incorporated into a world ruled by repeatable and predictable scientific laws?

For Lewis they could. In his book *Miracles* (1947: revised, 1960) he draws a distinction between those he calls 'Naturalists' and those he calls 'Supernaturalists'. Naturalists are those who insist that every event in the universe has a purely natural and explicable cause; Supernaturalists, on the other hand, recognize that the universe is shot through with events that cannot be explained solely in material terms. For him consciousness and its products, love, free will and so on – not to mention the many dimensions of our inner space – are not fully explicable in terms of purely natural causes. In particular, our ability to reason

---

[14]See Stephen Prickett '"It Makes no Difference": Lewis's Criticism, Fiction and Theology', in *C.S. Lewis at Poet's Corner*, eds. Michael Ward and Peter S. Williams, Eugene, Oregon: Cascade books, 2016.

and to make choices which do not depend solely on practical material outcomes, such as the aforesaid judgements about love, free will, etc., cannot be so explained in purely natural terms. At one point he uses the homely metaphor of such miracles being like the holes in a Swiss cheese: constantly present, and so familiar, so much a part of everyday experience, that we scarcely see them for what they are. But clearly to transpose the miraculous from our mundane world to one of fantasy, where magic is part of the 'given', makes it much less of a visible problem.

Despite common roots in the Oxford Inklings, Lewis's and Tolkien's inner worlds differ fundamentally in several other respects. One is the technical relation of other worlds to this one. Tolkien's protagonists exist in 'Middle Earth', a world that whatever its resemblances to ours, has different languages, history and social structures – which did not stop him saying that it could have been somewhere in an earlier version of our own world. Lewis's protagonists, however, whether the Pevensie children, or Ransome in the first two volumes of the space trilogy, start very much in this world – that of England in the 1950s – and have to make some kind of transition into one that, whatever its resemblances, is explicitly quite 'other'. In this he takes up the tradition of Carroll and MacDonald. Another difference follows from this: Lewis's use of Christian allegory. For the Catholic Tolkien, also in many ways more of a medievalist even than Lewis, the overt use of allegory was unacceptable. 'This will never do,' he was heard to exclaim after a reading of the first Narnia story to the Inklings. Yet allegory is again a complicated concept with blurred edges. Even Bunyan – surely the most thoroughgoing religious allegorist in the English language – was not simply a writer of allegories. It was the critic F.R. Leavis (1895–1978) – no friend to either religion or allegory – who noted that *Pilgrim's Progress* managed, almost in spite of itself, to become a popular novel over many generations largely because Bunyan's various figures, who, by strict definition, should be totally one-dimensional, become much more rounded characters as the story unfolds. Similarly, though Lewis seems to want Aslan to be an allegorical figure of Christ, Aslan also has a character that is fundamentally different from what we know of the historical Jesus. Most obviously disconcerting for many Christians is that his appearances are arbitrary. He only seems to be around some of the time. Much of the time he appears absent. But, whatever belief in God's omnipresence has been argued by theologians, that feeling of absence is a well-recorded phenomenon – Mother Teresa wrote about it, as did Lewis himself on the death of his wife.[15] MacDonald's great-great-grandmother in *The Princess and the Goblin* is equally elusive. Making the Christ-figure a lion – an animal always seen in myth as the King of the Beasts – is, in that sense, a useful anti-allegorical device.

Part of the brilliance of Terry Pratchett (1948–2015) in his Discworld novels is that he could create a similar cast of creatures to those of Lewis or Tolkien and make from them something entirely different. He moves the latter's vast panoply of mythical creatures into an urban and often sordidly modern setting. Lewis's social unit is medieval castles and forest animals – talking or otherwise. Tolkien's is really the village, such as those in the Shire, and he has very few cities. When they do occur – as in Minas Tirith – the view is entirely that of a heroic age. You encounter problems of honour, treachery and courage. You learn nothing about the available shopping facilities, trade unions, university common rooms or petty crime rates. Ankh-Morpork, on the other hand, is peopled (or should I say 'inhabited', since few of the inhabitants are strictly *people*) by most of the above, plus a sprinkling of zombies, werewolves and vampires. At first glance some of these multi-cultural collections can be read as parodies of the more 'serious' cultural relations in Tolkien, and, since these are essentially comic novels no doubt there is an element of that. But there are also much more serious themes in these novels that are simply not there at all in Tolkien. Thus what passes for government, in the form of the more-or-less benign dictatorship of Lord Vetinari, is the usual mess of doubts, fudges, ruthlessness, compromises and spin familiar to us in modern politics. There is a not-very-efficient secret police; the even less efficient academic Unseen University, staffed by idle place-holding wizards; cooks, bakeries and kitchens in plenty; and fast-food street entrepreneurs who usually end up ruining themselves as well as accidentally poisoning their clients. Unlike Middle Earth, which is somehow a bit pre-pubescent, sex also makes quite an appearance in Ankh-Morpork. The stories are told from a variety of viewpoints, but those centring on Vetinari and Vimes, his chief of police, are probably the most interesting, since they usually involve quite complex and difficult moral

---

[15]See *A Grief Observed*, Faber, 1961.

choices in situations that would never arise in the simpler moral world of Middle Earth.

This is mixed with wry humour in a way that often deflects attention from more serious moral problems underneath. Thus *Thud!* (2005) – a typically jokey title – deals with questions of law, violence, political spin and race relations. Faced with evidence of a violent affray between trolls and a dwarf, Vetinari says to Vimes, with some political correctness:

> 'A wise ruler thinks twice before directing violence against someone because he does not approve of what they say.'
>
> Once again Vimes did not comment. He himself directed violence daily and with a certain amount of enthusiasm against people because he didn't approve of them saying things like "Give me all your money" or "What are you going to do about it, copper?" But perhaps rulers had to think differently . . .

Somewhere amid slapstick, satire and verbal pyrotechnics questions bubble beneath the surface: Who makes the law? What right have they to make laws? Who profits by them? Who enforces the law? and how should different minority groups (in this case trolls and dwarfs), whose interests and customs clash, relate to each other? Moreover, whatever the political correctness, the fact remains that in the last resort Vetinari is an absolute dictator – and he slides with carefully honed skill between trying to conceal this fact and acting when necessary with complete ruthlessness. Though it might be interesting to speculate if Pratchett sympathized with Dante's argument for a benign but absolute ruler in *De Monarchia*, the fact is Pratchett never suggests that this is a good or bad state of affairs. It is simply part of the given in Discworld. Whether this is a question of instructing children by stealth, entertaining adults or even instructing adults by even greater stealth, is immaterial.

If satire is always lurking somewhere behind Pratchett's fantasy, it comes out more openly in the strange fantasy of *The Master and Margarita* (written sometime between 1928 and 1940, but only published in full in 1967) by the Russian writer, Mikhail Bulgakov (1891–1940). Categorized in publisher's lists variously as Satire, Romance, Farce, Modern Literature, Fantasy Fiction, Low Fantasy, Occult Fiction and the Fantastic, it is certainly all of these things, and a good deal more. We should, for instance, add Theology, since both the Devil and Pontius Pilate appear in person in the course of the highly convoluted plot, which involves the Russian Writers' Union and a whole chorus of naked witches on broomsticks – among other things. In effect, Bulgakov brings the whole tradition of European literature, ranging from comedy to tragedy, from high culture to popular superstition, in judgement on the Stalinist Soviet world in which he finds himself. The point, of course, is that no so-called 'Soviet realism' (naturally required of members of the Soviet Writers' Union), but only extreme metaphysical fantasy, could do justice to the sheer *unreality* of Stalin's Russia. One of the twentieth century's literary masterpieces, it was finally published in the 1960s, during Khrushchev's political thaw, more than 20 years after Bulgakov's death.

Though it is difficult to assign any such status to Bulgakov, both Discworld and Middle Earth are in the end optimistic fantasies. Not so Mervyn Peake's *Gormenghast* trilogy. This vast Gothic castle with its strange inhabitants is certainly not a children's fantasy in any sense. Indeed even to call these books 'fantasy' is questionable, since they are entirely realistic, in the sense that there is no magic involved; but the trilogy has always been classified as such, not least because the framework of its strange, tormented world is more akin to that of children's fantasies than to anything remotely 'realistic'. The names say it all. Flay, Dr and Mrs Prunesquallor, or Steerpike, sound precisely the bizarre note of some of Dickens' stranger names, such as Podsnap, Pumblechook or, indeed, Steerforth. No good, we know, comes of people with names like these.

The main protagonist is Titus Groan, seventy-seventh Earl of Gormenghast, struggling to break free from the stifling embrace of his aristocratic inheritance, a vast and crumbling castle locked into its own way of life and bizarre rituals. His father, the seventy-sixth earl, had been eaten alive by owls on his own (very extensive) battlements. Gothic on this epic scale somehow tips into fantasy without needing any assistance from magic. Perhaps Peake's greatest achievement is that he rarely falls over the edge into self-parody or openly comic effects – always the danger with such extreme forms of fantasy.

Yet the very grandness of the scale brings into even sharper focus the essential loneliness of the main protagonists – first the unlovely Steerpike, and later Titus himself, the hero of the final volume, aptly named *Titus Alone*. This

Figure 5.3 *Peake: Gormenghast Castle.*

is a nightmare world almost without love or even friendship. It is not so much that by leaving Gormenghast Titus finds himself alone as that he has *always* been alone – but is only now in the process of consciously discovering what he has always subconsciously been aware of. He is at once heir and victim.

And in this, of course, he echoes the discovery of countless adolescents, for whom loneliness and the burden of family expectations, real or imaginary, is both cause and product of the life of inner worlds. Nor is Peake unusual here. Anodos, whose name means 'pathless', the protagonist of MacDonald's *Phantastes*, though he encounters many others in his adventures in 'Fairyland', essentially wanders alone. Though we do not usually think of Alice as being

Figure 5.4 *Peake: Leaving Gormenghast Castle.*

alone in her *Adventures in Wonderland* or *Through the Looking-Glass*, of course she is alone in both. But after all this is normal in dreams, where daytime communality tends to vanish, and we are left to fend for ourselves. We only glimpse this for a moment when she reaches her full size at the end of the trial of the Knave of Hearts, and scornfully breaks up the proceedings, crying 'you are nothing but a pack of cards!'

Perhaps more alarming is the ending of *Through the Looking-Glass*, when the Red Queen disappears into the soup, the soup ladle begins to approach Alice with a purposeful expression, and she awakes from her dream before worse can happen.

Figure 5.5 *Tenniel: Alice with cards.*

As we have seen, dreaming is yet another aspect of the inner loneliness that lies beneath so much of the fictional conviviality of children's books. But as we have also seen, such loneliness is rarely confronted in such books which, more usually, show a conviviality not often enjoyed by real children in real life. In the Pooh books by A.A. Milne (1882–1956), Christopher Robin has the undivided adoration and attention of all his stuffed animals. Just as the real Charles Dodgson, in his invented identity as Lewis Carroll, had created an entirely fictional inner world for Alice Liddell, so Milne in effect created – or perhaps rather *imposed* – a fictional inner world upon his son. In both cases, what amounted to the gift of literary immortality proved to be a heavy burden. An

Figure 5.6 *Tenniel: Feast from* Through the Looking-Glass.

imaginary version of their inner space had been made public to millions of strangers. In later life Alice Hargreaves, as she became, had a fraught and ambiguous relationship with her fictional identity as Alice in Wonderland – perhaps best explored by the 1985 film, *Dream Child*, written by Dennis Potter, starring Coral Browne as the widowed Mrs Hargreaves travelling to New York to receive an honorary degree as 'Alice' from Wonderland. There she is shown scandalizing fans of her imposed childhood by both accepting and denying her fictional past. Similarly the real Christopher Robin Milne was forever condemned not so much to life at the top of the Forest with Pooh, as to life as a provincial bookseller unable to shake off recognition as the fictional 'Christopher Robin'. He seems to have been a solitary person, alienated in particular from his mother, whom he never saw in the last 15 years of her life. In such worlds, toys and animals assume a greater importance than in a fuller human existence.

Though it does not involve creating an imaginary inner world for a real child, a similar optimistic conviviality appears in Milne's near contemporary, Kenneth Grahame (1859–1932), author of *The Wind in the Willows* (1908). Both that work and the Pooh books were illustrated by E.H. Shepard (1879–1976), whose brilliant work has become as much identified with the text as Tenniel's illustrations have with the Alice books. In both cases, size matters. Though Christopher Robin is still larger than his toys, his size is reduced – or theirs exaggerated – to make them of similar proportions.

In *The Wind in the Willows* (the earlier book) Shepard plays even more extraordinary games with the thinly concealed incongruities of the text. One minute Mole, Rat, Toad and the other riverside animals are their normal animal size: while in the next Mole can have plaster busts of Garibaldi, the infant Samuel and Queen Victoria in his forecourt, while Toad can have a grand country house, drive (and crash) cars, and escape from prison disguised as a washerwoman. The wild distortions of scale and the pantomime

Figure 5.7 *Shepard: Christopher Robin and Pooh.*

atmosphere are augmented by the mixture of historical costumes which Shepard gives the participants. When the runaway Toad is pursued by train, the forces of law and order include policemen, plain-clothes detectives and two apparently medieval soldiers armed with halberds.

But here, at least, is a visualization of conviviality. Here is no individual loneliness. The river folk are friends who cooperate in everything from picnics to restraining the wilder antics of Toad. Yet just under the surface something very strange is lurking. The episode entitled 'The Piper at the Gates of Dawn', with its suggestion of Pan as the river animals' god, is odd enough; but even odder is the pervasive fear of anything outside their immediate environment. Venturing into the Wild Wood is dangerous in the extreme, and in the dark it is doubly so. Mole is terrified. Rat makes a point of carrying two 'gleaming pistols' when he comes to rescue him. The chapter entitled 'Wayfarers All' reinforces this unspoken resistance not merely to venturing into local danger spots but to *all* travel. Here Ratty, the river water-vole, is inspired into a kind of wanderlust by talking to a sea-faring ship's rat.

Figure 5.8 *Shepard:* Wind in the Willows: *Locomotive Pursuit.*

But his desire to travel and see the world is seen by his friends as almost a form of mental illness, and he is violently restrained and, in effect, imprisoned until the fit passes. The implication is that for all the apparent convivial celebration of freedom, friendship and loyalty among the river folk, they are really prisoners who must not – even in the last resort *cannot* – stray outside their allotted sphere. It is perhaps significant that Grahame's son, Alastair, supposedly the inspiration for Mr Toad, was to commit suicide in 1920, 12 years after the publication of *The Wind in the Willows*.

But even if the encounter with Pan might suggest other dimensions to Grahame's single-storey fantasy, the only visible threats are nothing worse than the bumbling Keystone Cops, armed with truncheons, pistols and halberds – not to mention the weasels who seize Toad Hall. The river folk can ruthlessly enforce their own isolation without external help. Even the errant Toad, the superbly entitled aristocrat of the river bank, has to be imprisoned and held back for his own good.

Figure 5.9 *Shepard: Mr Toad with Mole and Ratty.*

Shepard was, however, not the first illustrator to be able to bring together and vizualize absolute and seemingly irreconcilable contradictions of scale or time as fantasy. That honour probably belongs to the much less well-known artist H.R. Millar (1869–1942), whose illustrations in the early years of the twentieth century gave shape to Rudyard Kipling's *Puck of Pook's Hill* and *Rewards and Faries,* as well as to almost all of E. Nesbit's children's books, such as *The Magic City* (1907/1910) and *The Enchanted Castle* (1907). Both authors recorded their gratitude to him for the way in which he understood their writing – Nesbit, especially, recorded her appreciation, saying that his picture of the Psammead (the sand fairy) in *Five Children and It* was so 'exactly like the creature she had in her own imagination' that she insisted there must have been telepathy between them.[16] Though he courteously deflected the compliment, there was certainly an extraordinary sympathy between his inner space and hers, to the point where he could flesh out even her roughest written sketches. Whereas many famous artistic collaborations – Carroll and Tenniel, Gilbert and Sullivan – have at their centre a creative tension, and even occasionally bitter conflict, in contrast Millar had an extraordinary capacity for entering and even apparently *sharing* Nesbit's inner space, becoming in some cases almost a co-creator.

Born in Scotland, Millar had originally trained as an engineer, and though he later attended art school in Birmingham he never lost his original love of railways. One of the few pictures of him, rather than his work, shows him in his studio with an easel in front of him and a large model steam engine in the foreground.

Though he was a prolific draughtsman – estimated to have produced over 20,000 illustrations during his lifetime – the only book he wrote himself, *The Dreamland Express* (1927), is really an excuse to indulge his twin childhood fantasies, both probably part of an inner world typical of a boy growing up in the mid-nineteenth century: railways and dinosaurs.

One delightful illustration shows the line being blocked by a recalcitrant dinosaur. Elsewhere in the book he has included a rather smoky version of what he supposes a 'locomotive heaven' would look like – if there were such a thing.

---

[16]Doris Langley Moore, *E. Nesbit: A Biography,* Ernest Benn, 1967, pp. 91–3.

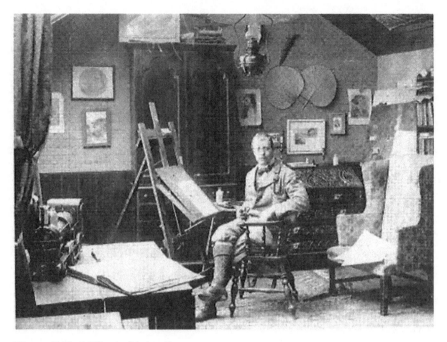

Figure 5.10 *Millar in his studio.*

Figure 5.11 *Millar: The Pariasaurus finds a way.*

Figure 5.12 *Millar: Locomotive Heaven.*

Among other even more unlikely illustrations is a Babylonian railway station (Herau), where the Dreamland Express, a contemporary British steam train, is connecting with what an ancient Babylonian train, made of gold, would have looked like if they had had such things three thousand years ago. To ensure the viewer does not miss the point, Millar has a huge decorated stone arch where a Victorian station would have had an iron one, Babylonian bas-reliefs on the wall, an eastern street market in the background, and the children from the train hailing some appropriately dressed Babylonian charioteers in the foreground – presumably the local version of a taxi rank.

Other unlikely innovations, however, are less immediately visible to twenty-first-century eyes. Near the end of *The Magic City* the children have to return to the city in a hurry, and they do so in style – by limousine. Unless one wants to include Mr Toad's vehicles, motor cars are not an obvious part of magic worlds, but Nesbit had, with acute historical insight, given this particular world a 'law' that anyone who wishes for something might indeed have it – with the proviso that they must then continue to use it forever. With sinister

Figure 5.13 *Millar: Babylonian Railway Station.*

prescience, only four years before the First World War, this includes machine guns.[17] Fortunately for the taxi, all they must do is to find someone who wants to be a chauffeur. What the modern reader tends to miss, however, is just *how* 'modern', and therefore incongrous, what we are told is a large gleaming '60 horse-power BSA' automobile would have been in any magic world of 1910. The internal combustion engine was even more exotic than a steam engine, and to juxtapose the very latest vehicle (no doubt Millar's suggestion) with the fantasy architectural background is another example of Millar's ability to inject precise mechanical realism seamlessly into a fairy-tale plot.

His illustrations to Kipling and Nesbit show the same meticulous attention to detail: architecture, armour, costumes are all carefully shown – as are the wilder pieces of fantasy, such as the bizarre Ugly-Wuglies from Nesbit's *The Enchanted Castle*. Consisting mainly of broomsticks and coats, with a painted face-mask, these had been created by the children to provide a ready-made audience for one of their plays. Unfortunately someone, with the best will in the world, wished that they were a *real* audience to increase the applause at the end – and, equally unfortunately, someone else was wearing the magic ring, which had a bad habit of granting casual wishes in the most cussed and awkward way possible ...

Ever consistent in her magic, Nesbit not only makes these grotesques come alive, but has them spring into existence with complete back-stories and life

---

[17] *The Magic City,* Macmillan, 1910, p. 298.

A LIMP HAND WAS LAID ON HIS ARM.

Figure 5.14 *Millar: Ugly Wugglies.*

histories. Naturally, the one we learn most about was a wealthy City trader –
for the socialist Nesbit, member of the Fabian Society, the ugliest of professions.

For whatever their visual connectedness via Millar, Nesbit and Kipling were
at diametrically opposed ends of the political spectrum. This comes across
most clearly in their attempts to show children something of their country's
history. *Puck of Pook's Hill* and its successor, *Rewards and Fairies,* introduces
the children, Dan and Una, to history by bringing characters from the past
into the present to tell their story. The coming of the Romans, the Norman

conquest, the departure of the old gods, are all presented as part of the many-layered mulch of English history in which they are unconsciously rooted. Whatever the disasters for particular generations, such as for the Saxons in the eleventh century, in the long run this history is one of slow progression, of improvement and development.

Though it also involves time travel, Nesbit's take is starkly different. In *The Story of the Amulet* the children find a little girl crying in St James's Park. It turns out that her parents are both dead, and she is about to be taken into the Workhouse. With a nicely ironic echo of Shakespeare's *Cymbeline* – shortly to be explained – she is called Imogen. Not sure what to do, but trying to be of help, they take her to see their lodger, a 'learned gentleman' from the British Museum, who wishes sadly but without much hope that 'they could find a home where they would be glad to have her'. The Psammead, their grumpy sand fairy, is present, and by the rules is immediately forced to grant his request. They are then immediately whisked off to ancient Britain – *before* the Roman conquest. The children are baffled. 'But why here?' says Anthea. 'Why now?'

> 'You don't suppose anyone would want a child like that in *your* times – in *your* towns?' said the Psammead in irritated tones. 'You've got your country into such a mess that there's no room for half your children – and no one to want them.'[18]

The little girl then meets a woman who resembles her mother, and who has lost a child just like her – and there is a joyful reunion. The Psammead refuses to be drawn on such matters. 'Who knows? but each one fills the empty place in the other's heart. It is enough.'[19] Whether we are meant to assume that when she grows up she will become the Imogen of Shakespeare's *Cymbeline* – the king's daughter by a previous marriage – is an open question. But her new 'mother' does turn out to be the Queen . . .

As in Kipling, there may be hints here of reincarnation, or possibly of the recurrence of certain types in every generation. For those who knew their Shakespeare, of course, there was also more than a hint that Imogen might

---

[18]E. Nesbit, *The Story of the Amulet*, (1906), London: Puffin, 1959, p. 183.
[19]Ibid., p. 187.

have other adventures in store for her in the future. Certainly Nesbit did not believe that people have changed much in two thousand years – unless possibly for the worse. The treatment of children in turn-of-the-century Britain was for her symptomatic of a much wider inhumanity pervading her current society. By means of another unguarded wish, again in the presence of the Psammead, the Queen of Babylon is shown the sights of London from a hansom cab.

> Buckingham Palace she thought uninteresting. Westminster Abbey and the Houses of Parliament little better. But she liked the Tower and the River, and the ships filled her with wonder and delight.
>
> 'But how badly you keep your slaves. How wretched and poor and neglected they seem,' she said, as the cab sped along the Mile End Road.
>
> 'They aren't slaves; they're working people,' said Jane.
>
> 'Of course they're working. That's what slaves are. Don't you tell me. Do you suppose I don't know a slave's face when I see it. Why don't their masters see they're better fed and clothed? Tell me in three words.'
>
> No one answered. The wage system of modern England is a little difficult to explain in three words even if you understand it – which the children didn't.[20]

In the hope of showing her something more familiar and more to her taste, the children have the unfortunate idea of taking her to the Babylonian rooms of the British Museum, where she is understandably horrified and furious to discover many of her own personal possessions on display. Predictable chaos ensues when, in the presence of the compulsively ever-obliging Psammead, she asks for them back – and, of course, immediately gets her wish.

The Queen has another, rather less benign, literary avatar, in C.S. Lewis's *The Magician's Nephew*. Lewis was a great admirer of Nesbit, and this is, in his way, a tribute to her. The Queen of Babylon is, needless to say, the model for Jadis, Queen of Charn, who also visits London (uninvited) and, after some altercation, ends up galloping through London on the roof of a hansom cab, before managing to escape to Narnia and becoming the White Witch who plunges the land into perpetual winter – without the jollity of Christmas.

---

[20]Ibid., p. 148.

While she can hardly be described as having an 'inner space' – in Freudian terms 'id' would be better – she is but one figure in a much larger single inner space, entered through the hanging coats at the back of the magic wardrobe: Narnia itself. Though, as we have seen, Narnia embraces the whole tradition of European classical literature, such a vast inner 'space', at once deliberately derivative and yet highly original, typifies the great fantasy tradition of the twentieth century.

Figure 5.15 *Baynes: Queen Jadis in London.*

Disruption is, of course, a staple of all these books for and about children. On the whole children – especially children who read or are read to – inevitably lead highly structured lives, and their delight in the disruption of Bilbo Baggins' tea-party, the trial of the Knave of Hearts, the wild antics of Mr Toad, or visits to London by entitled historical royalty is therefore all the greater. Needless to say, disruption is no less a staple of *all* fiction. It is, after all, what makes for a page-turner. The material echoes of Metz's metaphysical definition of religion as 'interruption', or Hart's even more emphatic 'absolute interruption',[21] are not accidental. Human experience is a continuum, not a series of self-contained boxes – or even self-contained books. If we began with the problems of the rail managers of Kings Cross station faced by children trying to smash trolleys into the brick pillars between platforms 9 and 10, we need to recall that most of those posting photographs of themselves with the replacement embedded model were adults – and in at least one case, priests. For better or worse, the creation of fiction – especially children's fiction – is fundamentally a theological activity.

'Theological', however, does not mean in any sense 'Christian'. Though it can include Christian ideas – as in the case of MacDonald or Lewis – it need not even involve raising questions that might be classed as 'religious'. It is more simply a question of whether the author possesses some kind of moral compass. This would certainly include, for example, the work of the declared atheist George Eliot, Mark Twain's 'immoral' *Huckleberry Finn*, or Philip Pullman's avowedly anti-Christian *His Dark Materials* trilogy.

It would *not*, however, include one of my favourite authors when I was a child: Captain W.E. Johns (1893–1968), author of the Biggles series. Johns, it turns out, was not merely a creator of literary fictions, but a serial liar in life. He was never a captain in the Royal Flying Corps, or, indeed, its successor, the Royal Air Force. The highest substantive rank he achieved was the more lowly one of 'Flying Officer'. More scandalously, and certainly more interestingly, he also seems to have been a bigamist. But neither of these facts, however, whatever their legal status, convict him of any lack of a moral compass in my

---

[21]Kevin Hart, 'Absolute Interruption: On Faith', in *Questioning God*, ed. John D. Caputo, Indiana University Press, 2001, pp. 186–208.

sense. What does so is his own writing. The Biggles books are for the most part straightforward adventure stories of the kind I, like generations of 13-year-old children, used to love. Here were disruptions a-plenty. I don't recall any moral questions arising, one way or the other. What shocked me a few years later was to come across one of his science-fiction books. The plot was relatively simple. Our intrepid space explorers journeyed from planet to planet (conveniently outside our solar system), encountered varieties of alien life, and usually succeeded in exterminating them. This was not colonialism. There was no attempt to conquer, control, rule or even exploit what they found. Rudyard Kipling or Edgar Wallace – both writers with clear, if nowadays unfashionable, moral compasses of their own – at least saw colonial rule in terms of bringing benefits to those ruled as well as to their masters. This was killing for its own sake – a duck-shoot of alien monsters. It was more like the plot of that strange and horrible nineteenth-century saga of destruction, *The Gorilla Hunters*, by R.M. Ballantyne (1825–94) where characters from his better-known novel, *The Coral Island*, go on an expedition to Africa with the express aim of killing as many gorillas as they could – for no better reason than that they *could*.

Disruption of itself is morally neutral. Though it may be the stuff that empowers a great deal of fiction, it need not necessarily raise moral questions at all – though they are strangely difficult to avoid. What is worrying is when an author – especially one writing principally for teenagers – does not recognize moral problems when they occur. As they will.

6

Far-fetched facts and further fictions: Furnishing with extremes

On 12 October 1972 a Uruguayan Air Force plane carrying members of the 'Old Christians', an improbably named rugby team, together with many of their friends and family members, crashed into the Andes in South America. The story of how the tiny group of survivors kept themselves alive by cannibalism, eating the bodies of their dead comrades and friends, and how the last members of the group were finally rescued after 70 days in the snow because two of their number trekked through the mountains to find help, has become the stuff of legend – not to mention many newspaper articles, media interviews and books.[1] Even more extraordinary is that one of these authors, Roberto Canessa, who, as a medical student was one of the original group, went on to become a world-famous paediatric cardiologist.

Part of our interest in reading of such horrific events, and the no less horrific decisions the survivors had to make, is that these are not events we are ever likely to encounter first hand. Had this been a work of fiction it could easily have been condemned as too improbable – as actually happened with Juliane Koepcke's account of her survival after a plane crash in the Amazon rainforest,

---

[1]See Piers Paul Read, *Alive*, 2012; and Pedro Algorta, *Into the Mountains*, 2016; Roberto Canessa, *I had to Survive*, 2016; and Nander Parrado, *Miracle in the Andes*, 2016. (All dates are of English translations).

Figure 6.1 *The crashed Uruguayan Air Force aeroplane in the Andes (1972).*

which was disbelieved by many 'experts'.[2] Though these may well have been unique events, they are certainly not unique in the way they attracted our interest. Such events have a dreadful fascination for us – not least because they seem so way out, so far beyond our everyday experience. They show us humans at their most extreme. For those involved they become searing memories. For the rest of us, if only for their raw extremity, we find these catastrophes compelling. As the newspaper editors' slogan goes: 'If it bleeds, it leads.'

How, we wonder, might *we* have behaved in such a situation? Would *we* have become cannibals? Similarly we may wonder how *we* might have behaved in the situation of John McCain, held prisoner and tortured in Vietnam? How might *we* have behaved in Jersey, occupied by Nazi Germany, in the Second World War? How might we have behaved in Etty Hillesum's situation? Just because these are accounts of situations in which we hope never to find ourselves, they become gripping reading. I do not believe this is something we need be ashamed

[2]Juliane Koepcke, *When I Fell From the Sky,* Nicholas Brearley, 2012.

of or embarrassed by. We should, rather, be profoundly grateful that by the act of reading we are permitted to experience them second-hand rather than first-hand. This is not necessarily cheap voyeurism. These, and similar situations, are a valuable extension of our personal experience – another part of the mental furniture of our inner space.[3] Knowing of the terrible things that have happened to others, and – as in the case of the Old Christians rugby team – what terrible moral choices were unexpectedly forced upon them, gives us a broader vision of our world. The message is that such things happen – and, however unlikely, can suddenly happen to *anyone* without warning. We hope never to be caught up in such events, but the mere fact that we know of others to whom such things have occurred is valuable in itself – if not exactly comforting.

Or at least, *most* of us would hope never to experience such situations. Vivian Gornick, an American writer and journalist, has identified a group of people who see themselves as isolated, sidelined by life, perpetual outsiders, under-privileged and often friendless. People who, as a result, trusted no one and joined nothing – until, that is, disaster struck. Astonishingly, some such self-absorbed 'victims' can then become tireless good citizens, helping those who are now – for the first time, visibly and without qualification – worse off than themselves. As one woman, when questioned by Gornick, replied: 'Because we are all in this together . . .' What had been for most of us during the Covid-19 pandemic a cynical and tired cliché had become for her a *liberation*. She cites a similar observation by Natalia Ginzburg, an Italian-Jewish writer, in Israel at the outbreak of yet another war with Arab states.

> They were unmistakably grateful for the mayhem to come, grateful that it was allowing them to forget the burden of their own defended selves, grateful to be entering into the only circumstances that could dissolve the inner emptiness: the ever-enlivening fellowship of suffering.[4]

That inner space can so easily collapse into inner emptiness should not be too great a surprise to anyone who has sensed what Newman graphically called

---

[3] Among other stories of outlandish disasters and amazing survivals are Dougal Robertson's *Survive the Savage Sea* (1975), Guy Sajer's *The Forgotten Soldier* (1971), Joe Simpson's *Touching the Void* (1988).
[4] Vivian Gornick, 'The Fellowship of Suffering: Why some of us thrive in times of crisis', *Atlantic Monthly*, June 2020, pp. 18–20.

'the abyss beneath', glimpsed and feared by some of the most psychologically perceptive figures in this history. Who knows what the secrecy of the self can conceal? Perhaps we should be grateful that we do not. Perhaps we should be grateful, too, that it can occasionally inspire unlikely heroism.

For most of us, on a less apocalyptic scale, extremes need not necessarily be violent or disastrous to be unique or unusual. Thor Heyerdahl's Kon-Tiki expedition captured the imagination of the world not just for its physical audacity in crossing the Pacific Ocean on a balsa raft, but also for the counter-intuitive audacity of its premise: that it was at least physically possible that the Polynesian islands were populated from South America rather than from South East Asia, as had been widely assumed. In fact later DNA evidence tends to support the traditional hypothesis,[5] not Heyerdahl's, but it was the willingness of the expedition to go to what many regarded as almost certain death and emerge successfully that impressed the world. Moreover, the fact that one *could* sail from South America in that way may yet prove important in explaining other still unsolved mysteries – such as how the hill tribes of New Guinea acquired the potato (only native to South America) some ten thousand years ago.

Because it described the first successful climbing of the world's highest mountain, John Hunt's *The Ascent of Everest* (1953) was about an essentially unrepeatable experience. Newspaper stories about debris and confusion on what has now become an extremely crowded tourist spot should not detract from that original achievement. Much more unusual is the life of the *Times* journalist attached to that expedition, James Morris, a former Oxford choirboy and later a soldier who served in Intelligence during the Second World War. He wrote an account of changing sex after having fathered five children with his wife, Elizabeth. His/her book, *Conundrum* (1974), was one of the very first serious accounts of sex-change – especially the various psychological traumas involved. However much sex-change is a physical matter, the inner pressures and problems involved are the real heart of the matter – and for those of us not part of the LGBT community something we can only read about and ponder from the outside.[6]

---

[5] But recent DNA evidence reveals two-way traffic across the Pacific. See article by Tom Whipple and Norman Hammond, *Times*, 10 July 2020, p. 24.

[6] They were forced, by law, to divorce before he could have the necessary operations, but they continued to live together, and arranged a same-sex civil union when that become an option.

Figure 6.2 *Kon-Tiki.*

On a much greater scale, knowledge of history – that long record of what Voltaire called 'the crimes, follies and misfortunes of mankind' – provides us with invaluable mental furniture, a perspective which, however questionable or inaccurate in detail, allows us to view current events closer to home in some kind of context. Just as the seventeenth and eighteenth centuries' explorations of the world transformed our sense of where we were on the surface of the planet and gave us a geographical map, however crude and sketchy, on which we could imaginatively place ourselves, so a sense of history, similarly however crude and sketchy, gave us a sense of our historical context. Likewise the nineteenth-century discoveries of modern geology, of dinosaurs, and of the implications of Deep Time constituted at least as great an enlargement of inner space as the voyages of discovery in the previous two centuries.

Again, this was a slow process. For much of European history the Bible provided an all-encompassing account of the first and last things. The story of the world, beginning with the Creation and the Garden of Eden in Genesis, and concluding with the Last Judgement in Revelation, was assumed to have been laid down by Divine Revelation. Precise dates between these two defining events may have been a little fuzzy, but the landmarks were clearly there. Bishop Ussher's meticulous calculations of the date of the Creation – 10.00 am on 23 October 4004 BC – to which we referred earlier was far from being a piece of medieval mysticism.[7] He was a Fellow of the Royal Society and working out the date of Creation was the result of patient research. He had even taken into account the fact that the sixth-century monk Dionysius Exiguus (or in English: Dennis the Short), who gave the Christian world its common dating system of BC and AD, had failed to allow for a year zero, so that 1 BC was succeeded by AD 1 on 1 January the following year.[8] As we have seen, for some, this time-scale lasted well into the nineteenth century. Similarly, eighteenth-century discussions of such matters as the origins of language were still inhibited by the traditional view that language was the miraculous gift of God, as set out in the second chapter of Genesis.[9]

Many of the reasons for the persistence of the biblical dating are obvious enough: the authority, not to mention innate conservatism, of religious organizations, both Catholic and later Protestant; the slow spread of literacy, and of what would become known as 'scientific' knowledge; and, of course, the absence of any other accepted universal dating system, all no doubt played a part. Yet there is one other aspect that is too rarely taken into account in considering the history of the Christian imagination. By any standards the death of Christ counts as an extreme event of the kind we have been considering above. Crucifixion is probably the slowest, most painful way of execution ever devised – so much so that for five hundred years after Jesus' death the cross was almost *never* used as the universal Christian symbol it is today. It was too

---

[7]Some authorities have argued for the prior work of Dr John Lightfoot, (1602–75), an Anglican clergyman, rabbinical scholar, and Vice-Chancellor of the University of Cambridge, who had already arrived at an estimate of 23 October 4004 BC at 9.00 am. Whether this was Greenwich Mean Time, which would not be established by international treaty for another two hundred years, or Jerusalem time is not clear.

[8]This was not his only error. See Stephen Jay Gould, 'Dousing Diminutive Dennis's Debate', in *Dinosaur in a Haystack*, Jonathan Cape, 1996.

[9]Herder's essay *On the Origin of Language* (1772) had to steer a careful path between biblicalists and those who thought it originated from the noises of animals.

raw, too criminal, too shaming, even for the most devoted Christians to take any pride in. It was not until crucifixion had been banned in the fourth century by Constantine on his conversion, and had slowly been lost to popular memory, that the cross became the standard symbol of the religion. Despite graphic and bloody images of agony in some Catholic churches, not to mention the no less graphic contemplation of Jesus' sufferings in some Catholic spiritual exercises, what this death actually involved has been gradually distanced to the point of acceptability in most Western countries. But for a minority – and especially those who have been actively tortured for their faith – the fact that their God had been through something at least as bad, if not worse, has proved to be a source of incalculable strength.[10]

In fact, however inspiring or frightening such descriptions may be, they are only the tip of the iceberg of extremities we store up for ourselves through reading and the various electronic media. Despite the valiant attempts of various re-enactment societies, none of us has ever experienced a medieval battle, for instance. Nor, for that matter, have we experienced battles of the English Civil War, or those of eighteenth-century Europe and America, or of the Napoleonic or Crimean Wars – though we are probably dimly aware of just how ferocious, unpleasant and unhygienic they must have been. The memories of the living are short-term affairs. Vietnam is already a fading memory for a generation of Americans. Many of us have now-dead relatives who could remember the First World War. My mother – born in 1908 – could remember, as a child, meeting veterans of the Crimean War; they in turn, I assume, would have known Napoleonic veterans in their youth. But not only do we read avidly stories from and about these traumatic events: historians still debate counter-factual versions. What if William of Normandy had lost the Battle of Hastings? What if Washington had lost the American War of Independence? What if Germany had successfully invaded Britain in 1940?

Or – to put it even more simply – what if *we* had been involved in any famous historical events? How would it have felt to live in ancient Rome? How would *we* have reacted to someone at a dinner party in August 1914 telling us authoritatively that 'it would all be over by Christmas'? Ever since the invention

---

[10]A point made very strongly by Tom Holland in *Dominion*.

of the genre of the historical novel at the end of the eighteenth century, authors
have been struggling to enter the various mind-sets of the past. Nevertheless,
the historical novel seems not to have started with anything so logical or
potentially interesting, but with Horace Walpole's wildly preposterous *The
Castle of Otranto* in 1764. In the 1750s Walpole had built himself what he
called a 'gothick' castle at Strawberry Hill, near Twickenham, just west of
London (see Pl. 22). He described it in a letter to a friend in Italy:

> The bow window below leads into a little parlour, hung with a stone colour
> Gothick paper, and Jackson's Venetian prints ... From hence, under two
> gloomy arches, you come to the hall and staircase, which is impossible to
> describe to you, as it is the most particular and chief beauty of the castle ...
> Imagine the wall covered with (I call it paper, but it is really paper printed
> in perspective, to represent) Gothic fretwork: the lightest gothic balustrade
> to the staircase, adorned with antelopes ... bearing shields; lean windows
> fattened with rich saints on painted glass, and a vestibule open with three
> arches on the landing place, and niches full of trophies of old coats of mail,
> Indian arrows and spears – shields made of rhinoceros' hide, broadswords,
> quivers, longbows, all *supposed* to be taken by Sir Terry Robsart, in the holy
> wars.[11]

In this 'little rural bijou' Walpole invented for himself a fantasy life with an
amazing collection of historical bric-a-brac. He used to wear a pair of gloves
that had belonged to James I,[12] and sleep with Charles I's death warrant on one
side of his bed and the Magna Carta on the other. It was in this bed in 1764 that
he dreamed 'that on the uppermost banister of a great staircase' he 'saw a gigantic
hand in armour'.[13] The staircase was, of course, his own, but appropriately
magnified. From it grew the mysterious giant haunting of the doomed Castle of
Otranto. 'In the evening,' he tells us, 'I sat down and began to write, without
knowing in the least what I intended to say or relate.' It was, as he says, 'a very
natural dream for a head filled like mine with Gothic story.' It was equally

---

[11]Horace Walpole, *The Yale Edition of Horace Walpole's Correspondence*, ed. W.S. Lewis, 43 vols, New
Haven: Yale University Press, 1961, 20: 380.

[12]Sold at auction after Walpole's death for £2.50.

[13]W.R. Ketton-Cremer, *Horace Walpole: A Biography*, 3rd edn, Methuen, 1964, p. 136.

natural for Strawberry Hill to provide the inspiration for the first Gothic novel, since it was itself such an essentially literary creation to begin with.

As an attempt to understand the inner life of past ages, the actual story is a complete farce. Manfred, lord of the Castle, is as lurid and improbable a villain as any in fiction. Though his many crimes – including an attempt to marry his own daughter-in-law – are by the standards of villains relatively conventional, his nemesis, a ghostly supernatural giant who grows up out of and finally shatters the Castle itself, is not. However, the plot scarcely mattered. It had two elements that were to become staples of later fantasy: a dream-like atmosphere and a (supernatural) monster. Needless to say, it was an instant success.

What is interesting, from our point of view, is how Walpole, despite or perhaps because of his strange bed trappings, still sees dreaming as an essentially 'outward' experience, the product of external and supernatural intervention, rather than the expression of any kind of internal prompting. As an attempt to recapture the past in any meaningful sense, either in factual detail or in any psychological understanding, it is a piece of nonsense. Nor were its many imitators much more plausible. *The Monk* (1796), by M.G. Lewis (1775–1818), another best seller, contains an episode in which, owing to a case of mistaken identity, a character makes off in the dark in his carriage not with his beloved, with whom he was supposed to be eloping, but with the ghost of a headless nun who happens to haunt the place. Yet it was from just such an improbable foundation that the nineteenth-century historical novel was born, somehow moving from the preposterous supernatural to the relatively realistic *Ivanhoe* (1819) by Walter Scott (1771–1832) within a generation. Where Scott led, a host of lesser imitators quickly followed.[14]

Even without a Walpole or a Lewis, there were good sociological reasons for what amounted to a fundamental shift in sensibility. In his *Elegy in a Country Churchyard*, conveniently published exactly at mid-century in 1750, Thomas Gray (1716–71) assumes that as far back as Roman times, village life had always been much the same – whether in Italy or in England. Nor, probably, would his contemporaries have disagreed. Yet as little as a hundred years later such an assumption would have been impossible. With the coming of the

---

[14]See, for instance, Stephen Prickett, *Origins of Narrative*, Cambridge, 1996, especially, Chapter 6.

Enlightenment, and the agrarian and industrial revolutions, change – whether loved or hated – was now part of everyone's experience. Not surprisingly the early nineteenth century was, in effect, the first time in recorded history that people began to try and understand the past, and to realize how *different* it was from their own times – that historical figures thought and felt differently from the writers' own period. Not merely that, but that every period, from the ancient Romans up to the English Civil War, thought and felt differently, both from them and from each other. Their inner life was radically different. History, and therefore an awareness of change, became part of our (collective) mental furniture in a quite new way.

Nevertheless novelists inevitably write from the point of view of their own age – and, indeed, with their own views. Thus every historical novel tells us not merely about the period it ostensibly describes, but also about the way in which the author saw his or her own times. Some authors were more explicit about this than others. One of the frankest was Charles Kingsley, to whom we have already referred: not merely a clergyman of the Church of England but later, and improbably, Regius Professor of History at Cambridge. In his novel *Hypatia* (1853), set in the fourth century AD, he describes what he sees as the dying Roman world. 'The Egyptian and Syrian Churches,' he explains, 'were destined to labour not for themselves, but for us.'[15] For Kingsley it is not the effete Mediterranean peoples but the pagan barbarian Goths who carry the torch of the future. Above all (except when they are indulging in a little local raping, or carrying with them their own floating brothel on a Nile cruise), they have what he tells us is a reverence for women and a belief in monogamy that will eventually find its true expression in the Protestantism of North Europe – especially Lutheranism, and the Church of England.

> These wild tribes were bringing with them into the magic circle of the Western Church's influence the very materials which she required for the building up of a future Christendom, and which she could find as little in the Western Empire as in the Eastern; comparative purity of morals, sacred respect for women, for family life, law, equal justice, individual freedom,

---

[15]Charles Kingsley, *Hypatia, or New Foes with an Old Face* (1853), Everyman, 1907, p. 9.

and, above all, for honesty in word and deed; bodies untainted by hereditary effeminacy, hearts earnest though genial, and blest with a strange willingness to learn, even from those they despised.[16]

A combination of this conveniently providential theory of history[17] with an appropriate and, for the most part, fairly historically accurate leaven of sex, religion and violence, made *Hypatia* another best seller.

Hardly surprisingly, for some this desire to see and understand the past rapidly becomes a desire to *enter* the past. The frontier between historical novel and time travel is a very porous one, and time travel has become a favourite of science-fiction writers – indeed, by the twentieth century, almost a literary sub-genre. As we have seen with Nesbit's *Story of the Amulet* (1905) and Kipling's *Puck of Pook's Hill* (1906), it was seized upon as a staple of children's fiction – not least because the obvious scientific problems could be overcome simply by magic. From the educational point of view also, it provided a perfect way for teaching history – even if that history was not always favourable to the present. We have already noticed how Nesbit's Psammead (who is conveniently immortal) thinks children are better treated in pre-Roman Britain than in Edwardian London. In *Harding's Luck* (1909) the protagonist, a lame boy from the (then) slums of Deptford, *chooses* to go back and finish his life in Elizabethan England – where he is not handicapped, and lives a rich and pampered life.

But what these stories do reveal is something else nearly as unexpected. Just as the Victorian fantasy of Carroll, Kingsley and MacDonald was to emerge from a group of like-minded friends in the mid-century, so many of these early stories of time travel were created by socialists – members, even, of the Fabian Society – at the end of the century.[18] This does not mean, however, that they were necessarily friends. H.G. Wells (1866–1946), a compulsive womanizer, had earned the wrath of the Nesbit household by making a pass at Nesbit's daughter Rosamund while she was still a teenager.[19] All Bernard Shaw's acid,

---

[16]Ibid., p. 7.

[17]Laid out most elaborately in his Cambridge lectures, *The Roman and the Teton* (1864).

[18]This is such a common theme that there is now even a website called 'Fabian Time Fantasies'.

[19]In fact, she was not Nesbit's daughter at all, but the child of her husband, Hubert Bland, and their housekeeper, Alice Hoatson. It says much for Nesbit that she brought up both the illegitimate children of this union as her own, and it was only many years later that Rosamund discovered her true parentage.

but usually calculated, tact was necessary to induce peace. Given their desire to change the world and produce a more just society it is, perhaps, not so surprising that they fastened on the idea of time travel to look *forwards* rather than backwards.

But it is not a future to envy. Wells' novel *The Time Machine* (1895), with its dystopian view of things to come (see Pl. 23), was probably the most popular of these novels – even though it offered a future with very little to look forward to. In this unspecified future, the class system had hardened to the point where humanity had evolved into two distinct races, the Eloi, a gentle rather feeble vegetarian species who live for the moment, with little interest beyond their immediate surroundings, and the Morlocks, a subterranean race of workers who rarely surface in daylight. The Eloi, the surface people, live a comfortable, carefree but slightly childlike existence, and, by convention, do not ask awkward questions about their world, how they are fed and clothed, and what has happened to those who vanish. It takes the time traveller some time to realize that the Eloi, descendants of aristocrats and non-working property-owners, are, in effect, the 'cattle' of the sinister but energetic Morlocks, who keep them for meat. It was a story meant to shock – and it did.

William Morris (1834–96), one of the founders of the socialist Fabian Society, was also the author of an earlier time-travel novel, *News from Nowhere* (1890) – a visit to an England of a hundred years later, in 1990. It paints an idiosyncratic picture of the future – the Houses of Parliament, being useless, have been turned into a pigsty – but Morris scarcely bothers with the technicalities of getting there. Though it is the near future, rather than the distant Darwinian one envisaged by Wells, it is less pessimistic; but neither is this rural idyll with a declining population and no conflict either likely nor particularly attractive.

Indeed, it is hard to escape the impression that those most concerned with trying to shape the future are also those most depressed by what they might achieve. George Orwell (1903–50) was not a socialist by the time he wrote *Nineteen Eighty-Four* (in 1948), but he wrote as one who had been there, and did not like what he had seen. If we discount Nesbit's children's brief trip into the future in *The Story of the Amulet*, which describes a socialist society which is clean, where children love school, and where there is a green space all the way down from the British Museum to the river, there are few desirable visions of the future in fiction. For something both positive and – perhaps more important – accurate, one has to go back almost to the beginning of the nineteenth century.

In 1829 Robert Southey (1774–1843), the poet and colleague of Wordsworth, published what he called *Colloquies on the Progress and Prospects of Society*, in which he imagined a series of conversations with Sir Thomas More (1478–1535), author of *Utopia* (1516) – now a time traveller visiting the early nineteenth century. Southey's portrait of his own time was a depressing one, highlighting the dire effects of poverty, industrialization, Catholic emancipation, education, emigration, the position of women, the growth of infidelity and the spread of revolutionary ideas by printing. It was reviewed the following year for the *Edinburgh Review* by Thomas Babington Macaulay (1800–59), who mounts a vigorous defence of *laissez-faire* capitalism. He does not deny the 'present distresses' but, prompted perhaps by the ghostly presence of Henry VIII's one-time Lord Chancellor, he embarks on a survey of economic history since Tudor times in order to show that 'in spite of all the misgovernment of her rulers' England 'has been almost constantly becoming richer and richer. Now and then there has been a stoppage, now and then a short regression; but as to the general tendency there can be no doubt. A single breaker may recede; but the tide is evidently coming in.'[20] He concludes by projecting this progress of the past onto an England of a hundred years' time:

> If we were to prophesy that in the year 1930 a population of 50 millions, better fed, clad, and lodged than the English of our time, will cover these islands, that Sussex and Huntingdonshire will be wealthier than the wealthiest parts of the West Riding of Yorkshire now are, that cultivation rich as that of a flower-garden, will be carried up to the very tops of Ben Nevis and Helvellyn, that machines constructed on principles yet undiscovered, will be in every house, that there will be no highways but railroads, no travelling but by steam, that our debt, vast as it seems to us, will appear to our great-grandchildren a trifling incumbrance, which might easily be paid off in a year or two, many people would think us insane . . .[21]

---

[20]Macaulay, *Literary Essays*, Oxford, 1913, pp. 132–3.
[21]Ibid., p. 133.

Though Macaulay, perhaps worried that readers might take him too literally, is quick to add 'we prophesy nothing . . .', the whole passage is a remarkable piece of futurology. From a population of 13.9 million (1831 census) he 'prophesies' a figure of 50 million: the actual figure in the 1931 census is 46 million. We can forgive him the hyperbole of 'no travelling but by steam', for he has grasped the essential transformation of travel brought by the steam locomotive in the very year of the Rainhill trials, and more than a decade before the Victorian railway mania. More interesting is the reference to Sussex and Huntingdonshire – both notorious poverty black spots of the period. By 1930, with the coming of the railways, both had become prosperous commuter territory, while the West Riding of Yorkshire was in deep depression. The 'machines constructed on principles yet undiscovered' is, needless to say, a shot well ahead of its time. Such forecasts were common enough by the 1880s, when the young H.G. Wells was attending the Normal School of Science in South Kensington (now Imperial College), but in 1830 such a leap of imagination beyond steam to electricity was rare. Perhaps best of all is his dismissal of the national debt – a continual bugbear, along with paper money, for doom-sayers of the period. His only failure is to foresee the conservation movement that – together with the agricultural revolution – would make cultivation of Helvellyn at once both unaesthetic and unnecessary.[22] Macaulay's prescience is rare. Doom-sayers, from Southey to the Fabians and Orwell, are much more common – not least, one suspects, because the human mind is inherently suspicious of a rosy future. We respond better to the ghosts of the past, such as Southey's Thomas More, than to statistically favourable predictions of the future.

Summoning figures from the past was, of course, a good deal safer than venturing there oneself. Not surprisingly, the technical details of this arrangement presented problems that are not easily resolved. As a visitor to another age, the time traveller keeps his or her normal identity – but only so long as they are visitors. In order to stay, Nesbit's Dickie Harding has to become someone else, with an already established identity: and this raises the awkward question of what happens to the *other* person. The obvious solution, to make

---

[22]See Stephen Prickett, 'Macaulay's Vision of 1930: Wordsworth and the Battle for the Wilderness', *Essays and Studies*, John Murray, 1986.

the original die, and then make the 'transplant' a last-minute revival, seems a little unkind – even in a work of magical fiction. Nesbit herself is suitably vague about details. Faced by these and similar problems, a convention rapidly arose in which it was accepted that part of the art of time travelling was not to alter the past in such a way that it changed the present. Murdering someone's great-grandfather – or even, at a pinch, your own – was not on. Love affairs, however, were permissible – Wells has one with Mina in *The Time Machine* and the protagonist of *News from Nowhere* has several flirtations – but any children of those affairs would be banned for obvious reasons.

Yet even without intending to change the past, logical problems inevitably crop up. Terry Pratchett's *The Night Watch* has a time travel plot so convoluted that his displaced police chief, Sam Vimes, actually ends up taking his younger self for a walk to make sure he (his young self) knows his job. The obvious problem of who he, his older self, is meant to be, is solved by his hopefully (but more or less accidentally) claiming to be someone whom he – but not everyone else – knows to be dead. But the actual time travel still has to rely on magic. Still more bizarrely, Robert Silverberg's story *Up the Line* (1969) deals with a world where such technical problems have long been solved by some mysterious means, and time travel has become so commonplace that time-travel agents regularly arrange group tours to the past. Prominent among such groups, of course, are church parties wishing to see the Crucifixion for themselves as a matter of faith – in much the same way that parties go to the Holy Land as tourists today. They are, of course, forbidden to change history – especially *sacred* history – and so they must dress in Palestinian clothing of the period and behave like the rest of the crowd crying 'crucify him!'

This particular plot-line raises two fascinating problems. The first is the possibility that the entire crowd calling for the death of Jesus was actually made up of pious Christians – a possibility with interesting theological implications, which would probably have appealed to William Blake and perhaps a few other radical theologians! The second problem, more significant from the technical science-fiction point of view, is that once time travel had been established as a commercial possibility one could expect it to grow exponentially, so that more and more religious time-tourists over thousands, perhaps tens of thousands of years, would all aim for the same weekend in history, 3 to 5 April AD 33,[23] a literally endless flow of people come to witness the events of that particular weekend. The usual control on tourism by some authority limiting the number of places allotted[24] would not, and *could* not, apply in this situation because these millions of devout tourists would be originating from over a vast and presumably ever-extending period of time. Though Jerusalem was, we are told, as crowded as usual for Passover on that occasion, Silverberg argues that since it was *not* completely flooded by extra millions from the future we must assume that such time travel not merely is not, but never will be, possible.

Needless to say, faced with such obvious problems, other science-fiction writers have risen to the challenge by creating stories not just of time travel, but of time-travellers who deliberately go back into the past with the explicit intention of changing subsequent history. Stephen Fry's ingenious novel, *Making History* (1996), is, perhaps, one of the boldest. The protagonist goes back to Linz in 1888 to put a contraceptive into the water supply to make sure that Hitler was never conceived nor born in April 1889. In this he is completely successful, but the Nazis come to power in Germany just the same, and their new leader is not anti-Semitic, with the result that the (largely Jewish) scientists of the US Manhattan Project remain in Germany, so enabling Nazi Germany to make atomic bombs before the Allies. The moral (as always) is to be careful what you wish for.

Indeed, that is the much broader conclusion of a great many of the extreme stories in our mental repertoire. It is as if our inbuilt fascination with terrible, extraordinary and outlandish events, whether fact or fiction, is there in some way to protect us from such events themselves – or to give us the feeling that we would know what to do in such situations, possible or (at the moment) impossible. It is, for instance, an obvious point that the popularity of the murder detective story, and its many variants, only arose historically at a point in time when the average reader was unlikely to experience such events in their own lives.[25]

---

[23] Assuming this was the correct date of the first Easter.

[24] See, for instance, the limited number of people permitted to walk on the Milford Trail in New Zealand each year. Booking is required – sometimes years in advance.

[25] Declaration of interest: my first publication was one such novel, *Do It Yourself Doom* (1962). The title tells you all, and probably rather more than all, you need to know.

Whereas violence was a familiar part of medieval life, we do not nowadays expect to encounter random violence as a matter of course, and certainly not murder. Steven Pinker, in one of the most interesting statistical histories of social violence, estimates that an English person living in the thirteenth century was something like 40 times more likely to meet a violent death than a similar person today.[26]

Though there *were* stories of this kind from the very earliest times, in these proto-detective stories the stress is more on the forensic skill of the detective than on any irruption of violence in itself. Violence, after all, was common: forensic skill much less so. Thus the story of Susanna and the Elders, the biblical account of Daniel's ingenuity in defending Susanna from the false accusation of the two lecherous elders, is essentially about false witness, not murder.[27] The elders want sex – and only threaten her with scandal if she rejects their advances (see Pl. 26). But there is certainly violence in the outcome – whichever way it goes. Susanna will be put to death for adultery if the accusation of the elders is believed. After Daniel insists on questioning the accusers separately, and showing that their stories differ significantly, thus proving that they are lying, she is acquitted, and it is the elders who are executed instead.

Whether or not this is any more than a traditional folk story, the mere fact of its existence reinforces our thesis of the need for extreme stories about situations in which we hope never to be involved. In this it ranks with, say, the Pardoner's Tale in Chaucer's *Canterbury Tales*. Here three young men, hearing of a friend being carried off by Death, decide that in revenge they will kill Death. They then meet an old man who tells them that they will find Death under a nearby tree. When they arrive there, however, what they discover is a hoard of treasure. They decide to stay with it until nightfall and carry it away under cover of darkness. Out of greed, they eventually all murder each other. It is significant that this story exists in many languages and in many forms,

---

[26]See Steven Pinker, *The Better Angels of our Nature: A History of Violence and Humanity*, Penguin, 2012.
[27]Because it only appears in the Septuagint, the Greek translation of the Hebrew Bible, and is not mentioned in the Jewish scriptures, the story has always been controversial. Despite the suspicions of Jerome, the translator of the Vulgate, it is included in Catholic and Orthodox Bibles, but is relegated to the Apocrypha by Protestants. See *King James Bible*, eds Robert Carroll & Stephen Prickett, Oxford University Press, Worlds Classics, 1997, 'The History of Susannah', Oxford University Press, 1997, pp. 174–6.

including Rudyard Kipling's 'The King's Ankus' in the *Second Jungle Book*, and, even more recently, 'The Tale of the Three Brothers', by J.K. Rowling, in *Tales of Beedle the Bard*, a story which is also referred to in *Harry Potter and the Deathly Hallows*, the last of the Harry Potter books. The moral, that greed and death are closely associated, is obvious enough.

Perhaps just as important is the implicit warning that no one, not even one's best friends, can be trusted if the temptation is sufficiently great. Maybe it is also significant that the Pardoner is one of the more dodgy members of Chaucer's pilgrims. Apart from the fact that his profession is selling the forgiveness of sins (already clearly a questionable activity three hundred years before Martin Luther's outrage in Wittenberg triggered the Reformation) he is also out to sell some relics of dubious origin and even more dubious efficacy. In his own way, he himself is as much a 'warning' to the unwary as is his story.

More charming, perhaps, is another kind of folk story, where the little or common man manages to outwit the great and the powerful. The story of King John and the Abbot of Canterbury seems to exist in several forms, the earliest being a poem from a collection of 1672; but is clearly much older in origin. According to this story King John is jealous of the Abbot's wealth, and threatens to seize the lot and have him executed unless he can answer three questions: How long will it take me to travel round the whole world? How much am I worth? and, What am I thinking? Not unnaturally, the Abbot is very alarmed by such impossible questions, but is overheard bemoaning his fate by his shepherd, who offers to stand in for him.[28] In due course the shepherd, now in the Abbot's clothing, complete with hood, appears before the king. The answer he gives to the first question depends on speed, but if the king will move at the speed of the sun, it will take exactly 24 hours.[29] For the second, he says that since it says in the Bible that Our Lord was sold for 30 pieces of silver, as a man of the Church he cannot value the king at more than 29. For the third, he simply slips back his episcopal hood, saying 'You think I am the Abbot of Canterbury, but I'm not. I'm his shepherd.' Victory, then, for the small man.

---

[28]An interesting instance of assuming the kind of pre-modern vocalization mentioned in the first chapter. A later figure would presumably not have spoken about his problems out loud.

[29]This is still an Earth-centred universe, in which the Sun goes round the Earth.

Victory, too, for verbal sleight-of-hand. The joke consists of shifting perspective, thus shifting meaning, so that King John's words are given a new context, a new way of seeing things. This is, of course, the essence of any verbal joke, any pun; but the more way out, the more extreme, the greater the surprise – and, naturally, the better the joke. Which brings us, in this long journey from far-fetched facts via even more far-fetched fictions, to the ultimate art-form of extremes: so-called Conceptual Art.

The term 'Conceptual Art' focuses on the idea (or concept) behind the work; thus the description by the artist is considered more important than the finished product, if any such exists. Essentially this means any work is what the artist says it is. Though it emerged in the 1960s, and flourished for much of the 1970s, it rapidly incorporated works from earlier periods. Some critics have even found its origin in Plato's notion of ideal 'forms'. Though the art has in practice usually been too iconoclastic to get anywhere close to religion – except to shock by various forms of blasphemy – that definition of making the artist's 'intentions' central could, of course, very easily include much medieval painting. More easily co-opted were earlier pieces by Marcel Duchamp and René Magritte whose enigmatic works were often only to be interpreted by the existence of some 'concept' unexplained simply by the picture itself. Often the so-called concept is the selection of an everyday object totally out of its normal context to be exhibited as a 'work of art' – and, therefore, to make the viewer see it in a new way. The more unlikely the object the more the shock value and the greater the necessary reappraisal. One thinks of Duchamp's 1917 sculpture of a urinal labelled 'Fountain', as it were *reversing* the flow . . . or René Magritte's even more famous picture of a pipe (1929), with the label 'This is not a pipe' (*Ceci n'est pas une pipe*) – which, indeed, it is not, since it is actually a sheet of paper. Even more outrageous is Michael Craig-Martin's picture of a glass of water on a bathroom shelf, which is labelled 'Oak Tree'. In this case it requires a double column discussion of the meaning and explanation with one Christian Bok to explain the 'concept', which is helpfully pinned up below the exhibit itself. Put briefly, it is a joke on the medieval Catholic distinction between 'substance' and 'accidents' in the Mass – Craig-Martin's roots are in Catholicism.

In this case the water glass is simply an accident: the substance is that this is really an oak tree. This, I suppose, is about as far-fetched as any fact one can imagine – which is presumably the point (or, as Craig-Martin would put it, the 'concept'). Perhaps more to *our* point is Robert Montgomery's neon sign installation 'The People You Love' (2010), which is directly about the extreme furnishings of the mind (see Pl. 25). There is, of course, a certain self-conscious irony in using such a huge, illuminated sign to point us to the inner workings of our consciousness – not to mention the somewhat contrived pun on its 'reflective' setting. But that, of course is part of the point of Conceptual Art: stretching our mental furnishings, our experience, even our consciousness, to – and perhaps even beyond – its possible limits.

7

Experience of self: From identity to individuality

The 1945 Powell and Pressburger film, *A Matter of Life and Death*, has an extraordinary and memorable opening. A view of the solar system passes slowly in front of the viewer, accompanied by a voice at once portentous and sepulchral: 'This is the universe ... Big, isn't it?' A tiny ball of a planet comes into view – dark against the space behind, but with a light somewhere in the middle. The voice continues: 'That light you can see there is Hamburg burning after a thousand bomber raid.' Cut – to the pilot of a returning bomber (David Niven). His navigator is dead, and the plane on fire – and is obviously soon to crash (see Pl. 24).

He resists the urgent radio voice of a woman airfield controller trying to give him instructions on how to bring down his crippled aircraft, explaining that he has no chance of making it and that frankly he would rather die reciting his favourite poetry: in this case Andrew Marvell's 'Coy Mistress' and Walter Scott's 'Breathes there a Man with Soul so Dead'. A conversation then ensues in which the two, who have, of course, never met – and now never will meet – decide they are in love. It makes a splendidly dramatic opening to what is a colourful and complicated fantasy of two worlds: this one (in Technicolor), and 'another world' of the dead (appropriately, in black and white) – a magnificent example of how film can create kinds of fantasy impossible before the advent of the cinema.

Except that it isn't fantasy. The 'other world' (presumably) was, of course, but that opening was based on a real event. Early in 2018 the obituary appeared in the *Times* of Maureen Miller, the only woman to have been one of the air-traffic controllers at RAF Scampton in the Second World War, who had (successfully) guided down a returning and wounded bomber pilot in a burning plane. The pilot, Stevie Stevens, died in 2020.[1] Their romance had indeed blossomed in those few, vital minutes of crackling radio communication. They later met and were married for almost 74 years.

Every person's story is unique. Many have experiences that read more like fiction. It may be a cliché that we each have a story to tell. But nonetheless it is true. Not everyone, perhaps, has a novel inside them, but that is more likely to do with their writing skills than their personal experience. Though, of course, we must assume that this has to some extent always been true of humans, we also know that *how* this individuality has been felt has varied enormously even within that tiny fraction of our million-year past that we term 'history' – where we have written records – let alone that vast vague undifferentiated period before, which has to be called 'prehistory'. Moreover it is only within that relatively small period of written history that we started to write stories about our individuality – our own, and other people's.

I sit in the London Underground and look at the faces of my fellow passengers, reflecting that every single one of them has a whole lifetime – long or short – of unique personal experiences that make them who they are.[2] Among the first to articulate this feeling was John Henry Newman who, writing in 1836, had a similar intuition about individuals in a crowd, each seemingly swept up in a great throng. Yet, he meditates, 'every being in that great concourse is his own centre.'

> . . . all things about him are but shades, but a 'vain shadow' in which he 'walketh and disquieteth himself in vain.' He has his own hopes and fears, desires, judgements, and aims; he is everything to himself, and no one else is really anything. No one outside of him can really touch him, can touch his soul, his immortality; he must live with himself for ever. He has a depth

---

[1] *Times* Obituary 8 May 2020. In one respect the film does less than justice to Stevens' piloting skills. He never crashed, and never lost one of his crew.

[2] A vague enough sentiment, but, of course, elevated into a precise and subtle Samuel, Kings, Chronicles, Ezra-Nehemiah art-form by Marcel Proust (1871–1922) in his seven volume *In Search of Lost Time* (*À la recherche du temps perdu*, 1913), new tr. Lydia Davis, Penguin, 2003.

within him unfathomable, an infinite abyss of existence; and the scene in which he bears part but for the moment is like a gleam of sunshine upon its surface.[3]

For Newman, this offers at least a possible intuition of God. After all, this is an extract from a much longer sermon. But there is, obviously, a darker side to that 'infinite abyss of existence'. Such negative possibilities were highlighted in a new way by the discovery, long after Newman, of the medical condition known as a 'locked-in syndrome', where the victim may be fully conscious but totally unable to move or communicate with the outside world. Simply because such cases only arise when medical skills can keep such people alive in an apparently catatonic state, this is a relatively modern phenomenon. Barring results of individual accidents, the most extreme cases of this would probably be the victims of *encephalitis lethargica* (sleeping sickness) which swept the world in the 1920s. Many died outright, but some survived in a catatonic or semi-catatonic state for thirty or forty years, and only resurfaced in the 1960s when they were given massive doses of L-dopa, a drug originally intended for Parkinson's disease. The results, like their conditions, varied enormously, and were not always permanent; but some had the quite extraordinary experience of waking up to discover that forty years of their life had come and gone while they were 'asleep'.[4] Oliver Sacks, who helped to treat some of these patients, tells the story of one such person who discovered that the grey-haired elderly woman at her bedside was her little sister, whom she remembered only as a young girl.[5]

Even here fiction pre-dated fact. Washington Irving's *Rip van Winkle* was published as early as 1819. Van Winkle goes to sleep in the Catskills in colonial America and awakens twenty years later in an independent United States. He goes to an inn and is surprised at the response he gets when he declares himself a loyal subject of King George. In the early 1990s I attended a lecture on *Rip van Winkle* by a former East German who had awoken the day after the fall of the Berlin Wall to discover that his whole world, its assumptions, beliefs and

---

[3] 'Sermon on the Individuality of the Soul', March 1836. John Henry Newman *Parochial and Plain Sermons* 4, vi: 785.
[4] See Oliver Sacks, *Awakenings*, Duckworth, 1973.
[5] Oliver Sacks, *On the Move: A Life*, Picador, 2015.

loyalties, had changed seemingly overnight. He did not once refer to the current political situation, but no one listening to the lecture was in any doubt about the double meaning of almost every sentence.

Much earlier, of course, is the legend of the Seven Sleepers, told in both Christian and Muslim mythology, where around A D 250 a group of Christian youths hide inside a cave outside the city of Ephesus to escape a religious persecution. They emerge some 300 years later, somewhat more successfully than Rip van Winkle, into a world where Christianity had triumphed and Ephesus is full of churches. Both stories depend on the fact that our identities are not free-floating and self-created but depend, to a degree of which we are scarcely conscious, on our temporal and social context. However much we see ourselves as beings with free will, who and what we are is peculiar to our time and place – as those who have had reason to change countries and nationalities can witness.

The word most commonly used for the sense of individual self is, of course, 'identity'. Yet its tortuous lexical history shows something of the paradox involved. The English word 'identity' comes from the Latin *idem*, meaning 'the same'; and according to the *OED* its first use, in 1570, meant, logically enough, 'the quality or condition of being the same': presumably being the same person over time. Yet within a couple of generations, by the 1630s, it had shifted its meaning to something like 'individuality', or even more specifically 'personality'. How then do we get from this quality of 'sameness' to a meaning that, in effect, implied not *similarity* to oneself but the essential *difference* between oneself and others?

The quick answer is that, as we saw earlier, people in the sixteenth century people would not have thought of their personal sense of themselves – supposing they had such a sense – in terms of their difference from other people, but much more in terms of their similarity not so much to their earlier selves but to those around them. We retain something of that assertion of essential similarity when we think of the identity cards issued in Britain during the Second World War. These were not to show how different people were from one another, but to demonstrate their common citizenship of a particular country – and, by implication, that they were part of a common endeavour, entitled to common rights (most importantly a ration book); and if they were young and male, their common liability to be conscripted into military service. This meaning of identity has deep roots.

We have another, astonishing, example from the beginning of the fifteenth century. In 1409 a grand dinner was held in Florence for leading citizens of the city: members of the government, painters, goldsmiths, sculptors, including Donatello (1386–1466), and architects such as Filippo Brunelleschi (1377–1446), whose great dome of the cathedral had not yet even been started. Only one artist was missing: Manetto di Jacopo Amannatini, a woodcarver, known as *il Grasso* (the fat one). He had not even sent an apology. According to Antonio Manetti (1423–97), Brunelleschi's biographer, the architect decided on an elaborate revenge for this rudeness: he would steal Manetto's identity. Just before the latter closed his shop one evening, Brunelleschi went to the carver's house near the cathedral, picked the lock, slipped inside and locked the door. When Manetto arrived a few minutes later he knocked, expecting his mother as usual to open the door. Instead, to his understandable alarm, he heard what sounded like his own voice (in fact Brunelleschi's – he was an expert mimic) addressing him as Matteo – a local craftsman – and ordering him to go away. This was so confusing that he retreated in bewilderment to the Piazza San Giovanni. There he met Donatello, who inexplicably also addressed him as Matteo, and shortly afterwards a bailiff, who seemed so certain that he was Matteo that he arrested him for debt. He was then taken to the Stinche prison, where his name was again entered as Matteo. Even his fellow prisoners – all in fact in on the trick – addressed him by this same name.

The next morning two strangers – brothers of the real Matteo – arrived at the prison, paid his debts and had him released, though not before expressing their disapproval of his profligate life-style. More bewildered than ever, he was taken to Matteo's house on the other side of Florence, still protesting that he was not Matteo, but Manetto. Over the course of the evening he almost became convinced that he had indeed metamorphosed into someone else. He was then drugged at dinner and carried back across the river to his own home. He was laid on his bed in a reversed position, with his head at the foot of the bed.

When he eventually came round the poor woodworker was still confused, not merely by his position on the bed, but also by the disarray of his house: for his tools had been completely rearranged. His perplexity grew with the arrival of Matteo's brothers. These two men now greeted him as Manetto, and told him the curious story of how, the previous evening, their brother, Matteo, had come up with the fantastic notion that he was someone else. This was confirmed by Matteo himself – the real one – who arrived at Manetto's house to describe his puzzling dream of having been a woodworker. The peculiar disarray of the house was explained by the fact that in his dream Matteo noticed how his tools were out of order and needed rearrangement. Faced with this evidence Manetto became convinced that, for a while at least, he had exchanged identities with Matteo – in the same way that their names, so close in spelling, could be shuffled together and confused.[6]

Valentin Groebner, a modern Austrian historian, argues that this shows how people in early modern Europe identified themselves. In particular, he picks out two essential points. The first is that any individual's identity depends on the recognition of others. The second is that anything like a normal life is impossible if that recognition is withheld or subverted in some way.[7] Though it is also clear that Manetto's sense of identity was not quite that of a modern person – he was more identified with his work and tools than most moderns, and, if the story is true, perhaps more easily convinced by the deception – it was recognizably close. The important point here is that Manetto's identity was definitely a matter of asserting *sameness* rather than difference. But equally clearly, the later emphasis on difference – what made Manetto different from his fellow-craftsmen – is clearly also contained in this extraordinary incident.

Whether Shakespeare knew of this story we don't know. His plays, of course, are full of people assuming false identities. But only once is there an attempt to persuade a character that they are really someone else, and that, as we saw in Chapter 1, is at the beginning of *The Taming of the Shrew* (1590–2?), where an aristocrat tries to make a drunken layabout, Christopher Sly, believe he is a lord when he wakes up. But even here identity is a matter of recognition by others, not of self-discovery.

---

[6] *Antonio Manetti, The Fat Woodworker*, ed. Robert L. Marton & Valerie Martone, Italica Press, 1991, p. 88). See also Antonio di Tuccio Manetti's *Life of Brunelleschi*, tr. Catherine Enggass, ed. Howard Salman, Penn State Press, 1970.
[7] See 'Making You You', article in *The Economist*, 22 December 2018.

Both Groebner's points would certainly still be true today. But there is a third matter that is just as important from our point of view, and that is that this story is one told for the amusement of posterity. There is no point in just doing it. This was an elaborate joke performed *for an audience*. People had to know about it. And the fact that it was told in the form of a short story – a story not merely told but written and published – and then in a biography illustrates our earlier point that the evidence we have about inner space and our sense of who we are relies heavily on the written word. Indeed if we leave aside the occasional autobiography from antiquity, such as Augustine's, it is only really within the last three to four hundred years, with the invention of printing, that this written exploration of individuality – or, as here, its occasional denial – has become a popular art form. We call it the 'novel'. And even that title, meaning something that is 'new', tells us much about the change it has created in our collective consciousnesses.

We can see something of this change most clearly by looking at another popular kind of writing altogether. In 1805 the evangelical writer Mrs Sarah Trimmer (1741–1810) published a biblical commentary entitled *Help to the Unlearned in the Study of the Holy Scriptures*. It was designed to do exactly what the title suggests. She had no intention of being original in any way. Yet somehow the Bible has turned from being a book of instructions on how to live into a series of novellas complete with characters – with God himself as the omniscient author:

> The Histories they contain differ from all other histories that ever were written, for they give an account of the *ways of GOD*; and explain *why* GOD *protected and rewarded* some persons and nations, and *why* he *punished others*; also, *what led* particular persons mentioned in Scripture to *do* certain things for which they were approved or condemned; whereas writers who compose histories in a common way, without being inspired of God, can only form guesses and conjectures concerning God's dealings with mankind . . .[8]

---

[8] Mrs Trimmer, *Help to the Unlearned in the Study of the Holy Scriptures: Being an Attempt to Explain the Bible in a Familiar Way. Adapted to Common Apprehensions, and According to the Opinions of Approved Commentators,* 2nd edn, 1806, p. iii.

The novelist Henry Fielding (1707–54) had happily described himself as a kind of 'God' by creating the characters in his novel *Tom Jones*: but this had been a sly joke. Now the evangelical Sarah Trimmer was seriously (if perhaps unconsciously) thinking of God as a kind of supreme 'novelist'. But by the end of the century not merely was the idea of 'character' spreading into all kinds of ostensibly non-fiction media, but the growth and development of consciousness was now a novelistic theme in itself. There was even a special kind of novel devoted to showing the growth and development of character and the process of individuation.

With a word borrowed from the German we call it a *Bildungsroman*. Though the exact shade of meaning is difficult to translate in English, *Bildung* is, as the word suggests, about 'building' – in this case 'self-building': while *Roman* (with the same root as our word 'romance') is simply the German word for 'novel'. It is, then, a novel about self-building – or, better put in English, about the process of *individuation*: what makes us who we are.

As befits the German name, what is often regarded as the 'original' *Bildungsroman* is *Wilhelm Meister*, a novel in two parts by Johann Wolfgang von Goethe (1749–1832). *Wilhelm Meister's Apprenticeship* is the story of a young man's sporadic education, both official and unofficial, and of his slowly discovering his own complex identity in revolt against the boredom of a conventional business career: by joining first a troop of actors and then a much more mysterious group called the Tower Society. Wilhelm is drawn into his acting career by a love affair with an actress, but goes on to play the part of Hamlet in Shakespeare's play. *Hamlet* is, of course, the nearest Shakespeare gets to creating a *Bildungsroman* of his own, though it ends with the protagonist's death before he is able to make much of it.

The fact that Goethe made the first drafts of his novel in the 1770s but after much hesitation did not complete it until twenty years later suggests that he himself was unsure about the kind of story he was trying to tell, or how to tell it. The second volume, *Wilhelm Meister's Travels*,[9] suffered the same kind of delay: though conceived in the 1790s it was not published until 1821 (the final

---

[9] I am following the titles chosen by Thomas Carlyle for his English translation. They are not close translations of the German: *Wilhelm Meisters Lehrjahre*, and *Wilhelm Meisters Wanderjahre*. The latter is sometimes translated as 'Journeyman Years'.

Figure 7.1 *Cover of Goethe's novel* Wilhelm Meisters Lehrjahre.

version appeared in 1829). Among other highly improbable scenes, it involves one in which Wilhelm, in a strange anticipation of the long-running TV programme *This is your Life*, is presented with a book describing his own life. The symbolism is obvious: his life in a book is recorded by a book within the story. It is as if Goethe is suggesting that literature provides the form by which one creates, or at least understands, one's own education and development. And historically this may well be so. At least one can say that the sense of personal identity we have been tracing through these chapters emerges most strongly at precisely this time, at the end of the eighteenth and beginning of the nineteenth century, in what is known as the 'Romantic' period. Indeed, one of the ways in which we might define this historical Romanticism is by looking at people's attitudes towards their own inner development.

As we have seen, at almost the same time as Goethe was experimenting with a new kind of novel in Germany, Wordsworth was also exploring his own self-development in a long poem that was to acquire, after his death, the title of *The Prelude*. Though the poem was begun around the turn of the century, it is a mark of its importance to him that he continued to polish and revise it throughout his life; it was not published until after his death in 1850. After an introduction and dedication, Wordsworth slips into immediate *Bildung* mode:

Fair seed-time had my soul, and I grew up
Foster'd alike by beauty and by fear; [10]

That reference to 'fear' as a formative quality of his inner life might be a surprise to some; but as we have seen, any honest venture into the unconscious seems to uncover as many buried terrors as insights. Or perhaps we should say that admitting to buried terrors was an essential part of any worthwhile insight. Wordsworth himself is clear that his 'seed time' is one of both guilt and fear.

Well I call to mind
('Twas at an early age, ere I had seen
Nine summers) when upon the mountain slope
The frost and breath of frosty wind had snapp'd
The last autumnal crocus, 'twas my joy
To wander half the night among the Cliffs
And the smooth Hollows, where the woodcocks ran
Along the open turf. In thought and wish
That time, my shoulder all with springes hung,
I was a fell destroyer. On the heights
Scudding away from snare to snare, I plied

---

[10]William Wordsworth, *The Prelude*, 1805, Bk. 1, pp. 308–9.

My anxious visitation, hurrying on,

Still hurrying, hurrying onward; moon and stars

Were shining o'er my head; I was alone,

And seem'd to be a trouble to the peace

That was among them. Sometimes it befel

In these night-wanderings, that a strong desire

O'erpower'd my better reason, and the bird

Which was the captive of another's toils

Became my prey; and, when the deed was done

I heard among the solitary hills

Low breathings coming after me, and sounds

Of undistinguishable motion, steps

Almost as silent as the turf they trod. [11]

Again, there might be a surprise here for many readers, not so much in the sense of guilt, nor even in that of being followed, as in the initial claim that he was able to wander alone at the age of 9 over the Lake District hills by night. This was so improbable that most critics dismissed it as exaggeration – until the astonishing discovery in the twentieth century of a notebook in (of all places) the ice-house belonging to Beatrix Potter's farm in Near Sawrey, just outside Hawkshead. No one seems to know how it got there. Wordsworth's school, Hawkshead Grammar School, like many such schools of the period, was not a boarding school in the modern sense; but many of its pupils from outside the immediate area (that is, walking distance) boarded in independent houses near the school – the origin of the modern public school 'house' system. Anne Tyson, the owner of the notebook, was one such landlady, and in what is usually called her 'prompt book' she recorded a mixture of diary, shopping lists, and menus of the meals provided during the period when Wordsworth was one of her 'her boys'. As a result we know more about the everyday details of his life as a child than we do about those of any other writer of the period. It also reveals that he was indeed, as he claimed, sometimes out all night when the mood took him – and though she notes his absence, there is no suggestion that this was seen as anything dangerous or to be discouraged.

---

[11]Ibid., pp. 312–35.

Though Wordsworth records specific causes of his generalized 'fears'—
which include, in addition to taking trapped birds, stealing a boat on the lake,
and climbing a crag to steal ravens' eggs – he manages to leave us with the
feeling that somehow such 'fear' is more endemic, more widespread, and more
numinous than these specific examples might suggest. This is confirmed a few
lines later when Wordsworth adds:

> . . . for many days, my brain
> Work'd with a dim and undetermin'd sense
> Of unknown modes of being; in my thoughts
> There was a darkness, call it solitude,
> Or blank desertion, no familiar shapes
> Of hourly objects, images of trees,
> Of sea or sky, no colours of green fields;
> But huge and mighty Forms that do not live
> Like living men mov'd slowly through the mind
> By day and were the trouble of my dreams.[12]

It does not require a great leap of imagination to find here – and in many
parallel passages throughout this poetic autobiography[13] – the feeling we
discussed in earlier chapters, that the growth of inner space is growth in
essentially contested territory, a repository not merely of memories, either
good or bad, but of unnameable terrors that cannot be altogether eliminated,
but much more, may be part of the actual growing process itself.

Wordsworth himself certainly thought so. One of the oddest incidents he
records also dates from when he was 6 years old, even before he went to Anne
Tyson's house in Hawkshead. One day, when he was just learning to ride, he
became disoriented and separated from his escort. Dismounting, he struggled
on, and suddenly found himself at the site of a gibbet where a murderer had
been executed and his corpse left to moulder in chains. The post and iron cage
had long gone, but an inscription had been left to remind passers-by of the
awful event. He makes no direct comment on what was, for a little boy, clearly

---

[12]Ibid., pp. 418–27.
[13]E.g. see 1, 376–89; or XII, 364–75.

a terrifying experience; but he then follows this up by a description of a girl with a pitcher on her head struggling against the wind. 'It was, in truth, an ordinary sight,' he says, 'but I should need colours and words that are unknown to man' to paint what he calls the 'visionary dreariness' of that experience. The transfer of emotions from the gibbet to the girl may be obvious enough, but the next comment is even stranger:

> When, in the blesséd time of early love,
> Long afterwards I roamed about
> In daily presence of this very scene,
> Upon the naked pool and dreary crags,
> And on the melancholy beacon, fell
> The spirit of pleasure and youth's golden gleam—
> And think ye not with radiance more divine
> From these remembrances, and from the power
> They left behind? So feeling comes in aid
> Of feeling, and diversity of strength
> Attends us, if but once we have been strong.[14]

What does a poet do when he falls in love? Obviously, he takes his fiancée back to where, as a child, he was scared out of his wits! In other words, in trying to describe who he is – or perhaps who he has *become* – Wordsworth feels compelled to introduce her to all his childhood terrors. If, as he claims, at one level overcoming these fears may be taken as an assertion of 'strength', at another level it is clear that he was still in some way haunted by such not-quite-resolved fears from his childhood. Indeed what he calls 'strength' seems to include facing and recognizing those unresolved fears. Many critics have also noted that all of Wordsworth's best poetry was written in this early period before he was 30, when his childhood vision was still powerful; and that such so-called 'strength' in overcoming these terrors may also paradoxically reflect a loss of poetic inspiration.[15]

---

[14]Ibid., XI, 319–29.
[15]See Stephen Prickett, *Coleridge and Wordsworth: The Poetry of Growth,* Cambridge University Press, 1970.

Written at almost exactly the same time as Goethe was struggling with *Wilhelm Meister*, Wordsworth's *Prelude* is a fascinating poetic parallel to Goethe's great *Bildungsroman*, illustrating how the development of a sense of inner space was not confined to any one country but was a Europe-wide phenomenon. It was a theme repeated in many forms throughout the nineteenth century – and beyond. Moreover central to the Victorian *Bildungsroman* was the experience of breakdown and eventual recovery. Wordsworth's own story proved to be a key element in this process. As he describes in *The Prelude*, he himself had undergone such an experience with the French Revolution, when all his hopes for a new world were dashed: first during the war with France, and then during the Reign of Terror and the eventual emergence of Napoleon.[16] For his readers the source of strength appears to be not so much in his sense of an unnamed childhood fear as in this emergence from the failure of his political hopes (and, indeed, an unnamed love affair[17]) into a love of Nature and a sense of divine power running through all things.

In his 1881 *Autobiography* 'Mark Rutherford' – the pen-name of William Hale White (1831–1913), otherwise a British civil servant – acknowledges the massive influence of reading Wordsworth on his own intellectual and emotional development: centring, once again, on the experience of breakdown and recovery. Like George MacDonald he had originally trained as a Congregational minister, but he was not able to stay within what he quickly found to be a restrictive and narrow theology. Much more surprising was the tribute of John Stuart Mill (1806–73), the Utilitarian philosopher and political scientist. In his *Autobiography* (1873) he describes his extraordinary home education, organized by his father, the historian James Mill. At an age when most of us were playing in sandpits, he was already studying Greek and arithmetic (at the age of 3), Latin (from the age of 8), and even more impressively, by the age of 13, political economy – a discipline more or less invented by his father. His reading included large swathes of history, some classical poetry, but very little literature: apart from Milton, whom, despite a general suspicion of poetry, his father seems for some reason to have liked.

---

[16]Books X and XI.
[17]With Annette Vallon, with whom he fathered a child in 1798.

Mill was given no religious teaching at all. His father also discouraged him from playing with other children for fear that he might discover how much more advanced he was, and so become conceited. At the age of 20 his entire world collapsed around him when, as he puts it:

> it occurred to me to put the question directly to myself: 'Suppose that all your objects in life were realized; that all the institutions and opinions which you were looking forward to, could be completely effected at this very instant: would this be a great joy and happiness to you?' And an irrepressible self-consciousness distinctly answered, 'No!' At this my heart sank within me: the whole foundation on which my life was constructed fell down. All my happiness was to have been found in the continual pursuit of this end. The end had ceased to charm, and how could there be ever again any interest in the means? I seemed to have nothing left to live for.[18]

The result was a period of profound depression, made worse by the fact that he had no one to whom he could unburden himself. His closest confidant was normally his father who was, of course, the unintentional cause of his son's distress.[19]

> I was thus, as I said to myself, left stranded at the commencement of my voyage, with a well-equipped ship and a rudder, but no sail; without any real desire for the ends which I had been so carefully fitted out to work for: no delight in virtue, or the general good, but also just as little in anything else.[20]

Though the ship image might suggest Coleridge's Ancient Mariner, it was not Coleridge but Wordsworth who eventually restored him to a sense of pleasure and purpose. The Utilitarian in Mill was never quite able to explain why reading his poetry could have this effect, but it did. His acknowledgement is both peculiarly tortuous and peculiarly honest in its tortuousness.

> I long continued to value Wordsworth less according to his intrinsic merits, than by the measure of what he had done for me. Compared with the

---

[18]*The Autobiography of John Stuart Mill*, Oxford University Press, World's Classics, 1924, p. 113.
[19]Interestingly, he never once mentions his mother in the course of the whole autobiography.
[20]Ibid., pp. 117–18.

greatest poets, he may be said to be the poet of unpoetical natures, possessed of quiet and contemplative tastes. But unpoetical natures are precisely those which require poetical cultivation. This cultivation Wordsworth is much more fitted to give, than poets who are intrinsically much more poetic than he.[21]

Poor Wordsworth, then, has healing powers all the greater for being essentially a second-rate poet!

Mill's view of Wordsworth is all the more interesting, however, just because it comes from a diametrically opposite intellectual tradition from the Romantics. Just because he cannot fully explain his experience, Mill's testimony to the value of the humanities and the cultivation of the mind is all the more poignant.

More subtle, if also more lowbrow, is Charles Dickens's story of *Great Expectations* (1861). This too takes the form of a *Bildungsroman* – by then a very familiar genre.[22] And so it is – in a sense. What is different about it is that it is not a story of success, nor even of spiritual growth. The first-person narrator is called 'Pip' – ostensibly a compression of his first name of 'Philip' and his unusual surname of 'Pirrip', but of course also a Wordsworthian reference to his 'seed time.' Young Pip's 'great expectations' of the title turn out to be a snare and a delusion, and in the end seem to wreck his life. Foiled in his love for the beautiful Estella – who has been brought up by the jilted Miss Havisham to be a man-trap – in the end Pip goes abroad and, though we are given no details, we are led to believe that he becomes, if not rich, certainly affluent. On his return Pip is walking in the street with his nephew when Estella, passing in a carriage, sees him and stops to speak. She is changed: after the failure of her first marriage she has re-married, and appears to be contented. She takes Pip's nephew to be his son; Pip realizes this but, typically, fails to explain who the child is. It is not clear whether this is simply because he is startled and confused, or because it no longer matters to him what Estella thinks of him. After a brief and polite exchange they part, with neither of them having said anything of any consequence; and Pip is left reflecting that having herself suffered hurt, Estella can now imagine what he has been through.

---

[21]Ibid., p. 126.
[22]Think, for instance, of *Jane Eyre*.

When Dickens' friend and fellow-novelist Edward Bulwer-Lytton (1803–73) read this ending he was horrified, telling him that this made all the strivings and sufferings of the story so far pointless. There had to be a resolution – in effect, a happy ending. Boy must get girl. So Dickens re-wrote the ending: now Estella had indeed been married, but her abusive husband has (conveniently) died, and so, a sadder and a wiser woman, she is free again. In the ruins of Satis House, where they had first met, Pip is astonished to find Estella lingering in the twilight. They speak frankly about the mistakes of their pasts. Estella admits

'. . . I have been bent and broken, but – I hope – into a better shape. Be as considerate and good to me as you were, and tell me we are friends.'

'We are friends,' said I, rising and bending over her, as she rose from the bench.

'And will continue friends apart,' said Estella.

I took her hand in mine, and we went out of the ruined place; and, as the morning mists had risen long ago when I first left the forge, so, the evening mists were rising now, and in all the broad expanse of tranquil light they showed to me, I could see the shadow of no parting from her.

That last clause still left Bulwer-Lytton in some doubt, and so Dickens made a final alteration: 'I saw no shadow of another parting from her.'

There are two problems here. The first is that even that final change leaves the outcome ambiguous. Estella – oddly, perhaps, in what has to be an emotionally charged but understated scene – insists on that strangely forbidding word 'apart'. Pip's response is to take her hand and affirm that he could see 'no shadow' of any future parting. The trouble is that throughout the whole story Pip's judgement in matters of the heart has consistently been poor. The fact that he could see 'the shadow of no parting' (an odd phrase anyway) could be seen as yet another misreading of Estella's tortured mind. After all, while we have shared Pip's inner space and painful development right from the start, we have had almost no glimpse into Estella's mental processes at all. We have only seen her through Pip's eyes. The notion that an unhappy and abusive marriage might have 'bent' her into a better shape is not a very likely outcome from what we know of her life-experience. She has been made, in effect, an emotional cripple. What *has* she learned since? The final emendation to 'no shadow of another parting' doesn't really resolve the ambiguity. In fact, it makes the ambiguity even more clear. Will she, won't she? Will they, won't they?

The second problem is that of Dickens's own mind. Why, first of all, did he create an ending that made all Pip's lengthy previous travails seem pointless? Here, at the height of his career as a wildly popular novelist, and already accused by his more demanding critics of blatant sentimentality, he suddenly goes for a grimly unsentimental if 'realistic' ending, guaranteed to leave most of his readers unsatisfied. Having done so, why was he apparently willing to *change* that ending? And again why, having made not one but *two* changes, is the ending still so ambiguous? Is Dickens at some level convinced that given her upbringing she would be a disaster for Pip?

This ambiguity presented an obvious challenge to film-makers. David Lean's amazingly powerful black-and-white adaptation from 1946 has what is, in effect, a fourth ending. Here Pip does not go East to make his fortune, as in the novel, but is dangerously ill and nursed back to health in the house of his old friend Joe Gargery and his wife, Biddy. This certainly reflects the Victorian narrative of breakdown and recovery so central to many Victorian *Bildungsroman* – but it is David Lean's invention, not Dickens's.

On recovery Pip revisits Miss Havisham's deserted house and finds Estella sitting in Miss Havisham's old chair – in effect in the process of *becoming* the now dead Miss Havisham. In a fit of decisive fury – of which Dickens's Pip would never have been capable – he tears down the curtains and breaks open the boarded-up windows; for the first time in years sunlight illuminates the room, revealing the cobwebs, dust and decay that have always symbolized Miss Havisham's arrested state of mind. He then declares his love, and after only a moment's hesitation, Estella embraces him and they leave the house together.

The only problem with such an ending, while it is obviously more satisfactory, is that this newly decisive Pip (John Mills) is not Dickens's character at all. In the enforced brevity of a two-hour film this is not important, but given that a first-person narration inevitably gives ample access to the character's inner space, in a way that we would never see in real life, Dickens's Pip is not that kind of hero – indeed, though he is sympathetic, he is not a hero at all. What Dickens has given us, in effect, is a *Bildungsroman* about someone who fails to grasp the opportunities inherent in what is in every sense a very unusual story.

Figure 7.2 *Still from the film* Great Expectations *(1946).*

He is a very ordinary, even diffident, young man caught up in quite extraordinary circumstances – sensing great expectations when in fact he could expect nothing. Throughout he is more spectator than participant: misreading both people and events. And that, presumably, is the point.

Goethe had written about the growth of a remarkably talented young man. His name, '*Meister*', of course, means 'Master': and he is indeed a 'masterful' person. He is instantly picked out as such by others, and when he becomes an actor with a professional company he is rapidly cast in a leading role – Hamlet is notoriously one of the most difficult parts in any theatre repertoire. Similarly Wordsworth is in no doubt that he is one of the greatest poets of his time – and indeed, he is quite explicit about this in *The Prelude*. That is why he believes his own story is so important. Though Mill was clearly one of the towering intellects of his age, in his modesty he does not think that there was anything in his personal life that was interesting – indeed he is reticent about much of it – but claims that 'it may be useful that there should be some record of an education which was unusual and remarkable ... and which has proved how much more than is commonly supposed may be taught.'[23] In contrast, though Dickens undoubtedly believed in himself as a great novelist, there is little in

---

[23] *Autobiography.* p. 1.

Great Expectations that is clearly autobiographical. Whereas the other protagonists of *Bildung*, fictional or real, have a heroic story to tell of growth, development, insight and the overcoming of crises and breakdowns, Pip is just strung along by events. Indeed if there is a story of breakdown and recovery in this narrative, it would seem to be Estella's rather than Pip's, and it seems unlikely that Pip has the insight or power to bring her through it. Maybe staying 'friends apart' was actually the best solution after all . . .

What Pip's misadventures do show up, however, is something inherent, but unstated, in the earlier examples: the sheer *isolation* of the protagonist. As in the children's stories we looked at in Chapter 5, almost by definition the central figure in a *Bildungsroman* is someone set apart, different from those around him or her, and *conscious* of the difference. If, like Wilhelm, Wordsworth, or even Mill, you are in some sense the hero of your own story, this goes without saying; but if, like Pip, you are just an ordinary person, caught up in events that you neither choose, nor control, then the new isolation, created by the ever-growing personal individuation, becomes also a new kind of problem. We have remarked earlier that early Christians being fed to the lions must, presumably, have had a rare and extraordinary sense of themselves; but this would have been balanced by a sense of God with them – of belonging, literally, to the 'communion of saints'.

One of the things lost with the sixteenth-century Reformation was any such intuitive sense of solidarity. A modern sociologist has described how Calvinism (and, indeed, other forms of extreme Protestantism) produced a feeling of historically unprecedented spiritual loneliness:

> In what was, for the man of the age of the Reformation, the most important thing in his life, his eternal salvation, he was forced to follow his path alone to meet a destiny which had been decreed for him from eternity. No-one could help him. No priest, for the chosen one can understand the Word of God only in his own heart. No sacraments, for though the sacraments had been ordained by God for the increase of His glory, and must hence be scrupulously observed, they are not a means of attainment of Grace, but only the *externa subsidia* of faith. No Church, for though it was held that *extra ecclesiam nulla salus* in the sense that whoever kept away from the true Church could never belong to God's chosen band, nevertheless the

membership of the external Church included the doomed ... Finally, even no God. For even Christ had died only for the elect.[24]

Nor, despite Calvin's approval of congregational singing of hymns and psalms, did this appalling sense of spiritual isolation dissipate in the seventeenth and eighteenth centuries. Dr Johnson and William Cowper, among many others, were both oppressed by a fear of unpredictable but inescapable damnation.[25] Nor did the new post-Romantic sense of self offer any divine support. Coleridge, also a deeply religious man, with as highly developed a sense of self as anyone in his century, was also a profoundly lonely man. The titles of his early poems, 'This Lime Tree Bower my Prison' or 'Dejection', speak volumes. His Ancient Mariner, was, in this sense at least, a prophetic figure: 'Alone, alone, all, all alone/Alone on a wide wide sea!': where, he adds explicitly, 'never a saint took pity on' his 'soul in agony.'

A more improbable example of metaphysical loneliness is Milton's Satan. To describe *Paradise Lost* in terms of a seventeenth-century *Bildungsroman* may seem eccentric, but in fact Satan (whose name, incidentally, means 'the Adversary') is, counterintuitively, the central protagonist in the story. He is given much fuller character development than any other figure in the poem, including Adam and Eve themselves.

A modern critic, Fred Parker, writes:

One good reason for finding Satan the most interesting and engaging character in *Paradise Lost* is the impression he gives of *depth*, which we do not get from the other devils, or from God, or from Adam and Eve. Behind what Satan says and the actions he performs, there is always a space for an ulterior consciousness. 'The mind is its own place, and in itself/Can make a Heaven of Hell, a Hell of Heaven', as he best knows (i.254–5): and these lines, although intended as an assertion of consciousness that is bound to assert itself *against* its autonomy, in fact express the grimmer truth of an environment.[26]

---

[24]Max Weber, *The Protestant Ethic and the Spirit of Capitalism*, tr. Talcott Parsons, Allen & Unwin, 1930, p. 104.

[25]See, for instance, Cowper's poem *The Castaway*.

[26]Fred Parker, *The Devil as Muse: Blake, Byron & the Adversary*, Baylor University Press, 2011, p. 57.

Figure 7.3 *Gustave Doré: Satan's Flight Through Chaos.*

When you think about it, he even undergoes the classic breakdown and recovery experience. Being cast out of Heaven and eventually making his way out of Hell to visit Earth must surely count as the most dramatic trauma of all time. In some ways his isolation is so blindingly obvious that it is easy to miss it – but this, we recall, is a *seventeenth-century* Satan, created in the wake of the English Civil War. Though to begin with Satan is always seen surrounded by myriads of supporting rebel angels, after their mass expulsion from Heaven he is absolutely on his own when he leaves Hell to find what is rumoured to be the newly-created Earth – becoming an archetype of the Renaissance explorer, literally discovering new worlds. Despite a steady diminution in his stature, from Lucifer, the angel 'light-bearer' to (eventually) a toad whispering in Eve's ear, he becomes not merely ever more isolated and lonely, but, as it were by definition, totally separated from God. Whatever Milton intended to create in Satan's revolt, for the Romantics steeped in *Paradise Lost* Satan inevitably becomes a paradigm of the isolated Godless protagonist. In one of his most polemical pieces, *The Marriage of Heaven and Hell,* Blake commented that 'Milton wrote in fetters when he wrote of Angels & God, and at liberty when of Devils & Hell, because he was a true Poet and of the Devil's party without knowing it.'[27] Byron would have agreed. The 'true poet', like Satan, is on his own against a hostile universe.

It was, perhaps, inevitable that this new sense of isolation – not least the isolation of the Romantic artist – would also lead some to a sense of inherent superiority. Here is a reflection by Marius, from *Marius the Epicurean* (1885), by the very self-conscious aesthete, critic and writer Walter Pater (1839–94):

> He was become aware of the possibility of a large dissidence between an inward and somewhat exclusive world of vivid personal apprehension, and the unimproved, unenlightened reality of the life of those about him. As a consequence he was ready now to concede, somewhat more easily than others, the first point of his new lesson, that the individual is to himself the measure of all things, and to rely on the exclusive certainty to himself of his own impressions. To move afterwards in that outer world of other people, as though taking it at their estimate, would be possible henceforth only as a kind of irony.[28]

This might well have been thought by any of our previous figures, but they would hardly have put it like that. Even Wordsworth, who certainly believed

---

[27]William Blake, *The Marriage of Heaven and Hell,* 1790, plate 6.
[28]Walter Pater, *Marius the Epicurean,* Macmillan, 1910, Vol. 1, p. 133.

that his role of poet set him apart from lesser minds, is careful not to claim innate superiority simply by his enhanced sense of his individuality. But by the end of the century this idea of the artist as made superior by his calling shows Marius/Pater as not that exceptional. One thinks of Oscar Wilde telling the US immigration authorities on his arrival in New York that he had 'nothing to declare except his genius . . .'

There was, of course, a downside to the idea of the artistic genius. Such innate superiority also inevitably meant being incomprehensible to the common herd. Benvenuto Cellini (1500–71), the goldsmith, sculptor and painter, like many of his Renaissance contemporaries, was quite sure of his own genius. To make certain his contemporaries fully appreciated his many talents, however, he even wrote an autobiography, so readable and entertaining that it is still in paperback today. Among his more remarkable boasts of seduction and murder is the modest admission that, after a spell in prison, God had endowed him with a halo:

> From the time I had my vision till now, a light – a brilliant splendour – has rested above my head, and has been clearly seen by those very few men I have wanted to show it to. It can be seen above my shadow, in the morning, for two hours after the sun has risen; it can be seen much better when the grass is wet with that soft dew; and it can be seen in the evening at sunset.[29]

A more unlikely candidate for canonization has rarely submitted himself, but Cellini belongs to a world where the artist as craftsman was still in an ambiguous position. For the ancient Greeks there was little or no difference between an artisan and an artist. The ancient Greek sculptor Phidias, who is supposed to have carved the Parthenon frieze (the 'Elgin Marbles'), seems to have been classed simply as a stonemason. We are still not sure if Socrates was a stonemason or a sculptor – but since his posthumous fame rests on his philosophy, we must assume that he was better with his head than his hands. For the modern reader Cellini certainly had an insufferable ego, but his boasts may be seen as part of a wider strategy for the artist to claim a different order of importance from a mere artisan. For many this might have been obvious

---

[29]Benvenuto Cellini, *Autobiography*, tr. George Bull, Penguin, 1956, p. 230.

enough, but the Renaissance artist was always subject to the judgement of his patron – who might or might not know much about the art he was commissioning – rather than the artist's peers. Part of the cruelty of the trick played upon Manetto in Florence was to confuse him with Matteo, a mere carpenter.

If the Romantic idea of the misunderstood genius has deep historical roots, for many in the nineteenth century this was typified by the more recent figure of Thomas Chatterton (1752–1770), an aspiring poet, who had committed suicide at the age of 17 after starving in a garret. He had made a name for himself by inventing the works of an imaginary fifteenth-century poet called Thomas Rowley; but he was soon denounced as a (rather obvious) forger by Dr Johnson and Horace Walpole, among others. After his death, however, he achieved lasting fame in a picture by Henry Wallis (1830–1916). This rapidly proved to be Wallis's best-known work, and he was to make his fortune and his artistic career out of Chatterton's tragedy (see Pl. 27).[30]

But in terms of an overblown artistic ego even Cellini is probably outclassed by his fellow Italian Gabriele D'Annunzio (1863–1938), a writer, poet, journalist and Fascist, much of whose genius – if that is what it was – was devoted to self-publicity, and whose range of improbable but carefully cultivated titles included Prince of Montenevoso, Duke of Gallese, O.M.S. C.M.G. and M.V.M. As an air-force ace who lost an eye in the First World War, his subsequent glamorizing of the War, and not least his own heroic part in it, was an inspiration for the rise of Mussolini – though D'Annunzio was fortunate enough to die in 1938, before Italy's catastrophic defeat in the Second World War. His biggest publicity stunt, however, occurred in 1919, when with a rag-tag militia of some 2,000 supporters he captured the port of Fiume, which was about to be handed over to Croatia, and posing as a patriot declared it an independent (Fascist) state. For 15 months he held the city, ignoring multiple legal attempts to get him out peacefully, in the end even declaring war on Italy.

D'Annunzio's father's surname had originally been Rapagnetta (which was the name of his single mother), but at the age of 13 he had been adopted by a

---

[30]Wallis had an unusual relationship with artistic genius in that he had run off with George Meredith's (second) wife – the daughter of the novelist Thomas Love Peacock – while she was still married.

Figure 7.4 *Photograph of Gabriele D'Annunzio.*

childless rich uncle, Antonio D'Annunzio, and had taken his name. Though Italians would be unlikely to confuse the two names, the word *Annuncio*, with a 'c' not a 'z' and pronounced 'ch', means 'announcement', or, more specifically, 'advertisement'; it sounds sufficiently like Annunzio for them to constitute a loose pun. It was a pun Gabriele constantly lived up to. Even the story that he was called 'Gabriele' because of his beauty as a child appears to be yet another of his self-serving lies. With a capacity for self-belief that rapidly tipped over into blatant self-invention, he said he wanted people to believe that 'he was capable of anything'. And people did. It was, for instance, rumoured that he once cooked and ate a human child, just to see what it tasted like. It was said that he had a special robe made with a suitably placed hole to expose his penis; that he had slept with every beautiful woman in Paris; and that he made his housekeeper have sex with him three times a day. Given his equally inventive powers as a liar, no one seems to know if any, or all, of these stories are true. (The one about every beautiful woman in Paris is a typical tease: despite the fact that it is an obvious lie, any Parisienne who challenged it risked being labelled 'not beautiful'!) His life, in short, was one of cultivated and malicious fictions.

Clearly the fastidious and ironic Marius and the flamboyant Fascist D'Annunzio were at opposite ends of the spectrum, but it was essentially the *same* spectrum. Both, in their very different ways, were part of the late nineteenth-century aesthetic movement, and both were frequently described as 'decadent'. Not for nothing was Fascism sometimes described as 'the aestheticization of politics'. Essential parts of Mussolini's political programme, like Hitler's later, were the grand flag-bearing rallies, the torchlight processions, and the mass demonstrations, making visible, and inviting participation in, the 'national unity' that their parties stood for. 'Fascism', after all, was called after the bundle of sticks – the *fasces* – borne before a Roman magistrate to emphasize the source of his authority. A single stick might easily be snapped, but a *bundle* of sticks – expressing the unity of the people – cannot be so broken. The bigger the bundle the greater the strength. Unity therefore is strength, and the greatest strength, because it represented the greatest mass of people, is the State itself. The leader– the Fascist Dictator – therefore embodied national unity and expressed the 'will of the people'.[31]

In some ways there is nothing particularly new about figures like D'Annunzio. The *Bragadoccio* had been a stock figure in Elizabethan drama and had been a more or less constant figure in satire ever since. Shakespeare's Falstaff, Parolles and even Autolycus[32] did not need a new sense of personal identity or of inner space. Nor, if they had one, would we have been told about it. Cellini apparently still needed a bit of divine assistance to bolster even his oversized ego. What *was* new was that the modern *Bragadoccio* now justified his egotism not with an externalized mark of divine favour, but with a political creed made up of a rag-bag of ideas from Marx to Nietzsche in which the inner world of the 'superman' (*Übermensch* or in Italia, *superuomo*) expresses the collective 'will of the people' in overwhelmingly nationalistic and inevitably militaristic terms. Individual identity, once asserted, was immediately to be subordinated to the collective will, which was, of course, ultimately to be found in the will of the Dictator. D'Annunzio's statement about the Fiume adventure was to remain a classic statement of Fascism:

> Men will be divided into two races. To the superior race, which shall have risen by the pure energy of its will, all shall be permitted; to the lower, nothing

---

[31]An essentially Fascist phrase that has made an alarming reappearance with the Brexit debate.
[32]From Shakespeare's *Henry IV*, *All's Well*, and *A Winter's Tale* respectively.

or very little. The greatest sum of well-being shall go to the privileged, whose personal nobility will make them worthy of all privileges. The plebeians remain slaves, condemned to suffer, as much in the shadow of ancient feudal towers. They will never feel at their shoulders the sense of liberty.

The 'evolutionary' metaphors (with the curious echo of H.G. Wells' premise in *The Time Machine*, though not, of course, its conclusion) is typical of its period – which saw not merely the rise of Fascism in Italy and of Nazism in Germany, but of Eugenics in Scandinavia, the UK and the USA.

With the publication of *The Origin of Species* by Charles Darwin (1809–82) evolutionary ideas had become a necessary hallmark of progressive thinking. Nor did it take long for them to be applied to human development itself. Unfit forms of humanity should be prevented from casual breeding so that a fitter, more intelligent and more athletic humanity, free from hereditary defects, should inherit the earth. Hitler, like D'Annunzio and Mussolini, saw himself as the product of an inevitable evolutionary process.[33] 'Destiny', encapsulated in verbs in the future tense, somehow became an active evolutionary force in his speeches.

The *Bildungsroman* had found a new rationale in telling the story not merely of an individual's growth and development, but also of the evolution of artistic genius, and indeed of the idea of genius itself – both as a literary form and, by extension, as a way of seeing political 'genius' in such figures as D'Annunzio, Mussolini and Hitler. Not for nothing was Hitler's autobiography of his early life entitled *Mein Kampf* – 'my struggle'. And this was not just true of Fascist leaders. Winston Churchill's *My Early Life* (1930) belongs, of course, to the same category, as do Barack Obama's pre-Presidential books – to the point where it seems every American presidential hopeful now has to publish some kind of personal autobiography to justify his or her excursion into public life. 'The child is father to the man ...': or mother to the woman. From Wordsworth onwards, childhood experiences have become an essential part of the adult identity.

One could hardly have a more Romantic image than the one of the pilot in the burning plane, ignoring the control tower he will never reach, and choosing

---

[33]Even the programme of the extermination of the Jews was seen as a 'Darwinian' move – ridding the earth of a failed race which must be swept aside by the Teutonic '*Ubermensch*'.

to recite his favourite poetry as he plunges to his death. What is never actually articulated, but is somehow nevertheless present, is the suggestion that his love of the literary civilization of the past partially redeems his mission of bombing Germany and destroying the people and architecture of one of the most beautiful countries in Europe. All at once he is the man of action, the man of amazing courage, and the man of culture – Wordsworth meets D'Annunzio. He is fully individuated. No wonder the girl in the control tower falls in love with the man she has only heard, but never seen.

Know thyself: Facebook, cyborgs and reincarnation

The slogan 'Know thyself', we are reliably informed, was inscribed for all to see in the forecourt of the Temple of Apollo at Delphi. In the past two and a half thousand years it has been quoted and misquoted with an implicit stamp of approval by a huge selection of writers and philosophers of every hue ranging from Socrates and Plato to Pope and Coleridge. Yet as we have seen, the nature and concept of self-knowledge has itself changed radically in that period. Knowledge of oneself in fifth-century BC Delphi, as in the world of Thomas Mann's fictional Eliezer, would have been largely a matter of awareness of city, class and social function. Not even the great were exempt. When in Aeschylus' play *Prometheus Bound* the demi-god Oceanus advises Prometheus to 'know himself', he means much the same thing: to accept his place in the greater order of things. The charge for which Socrates was condemned to death, that of 'corrupting the youth of Athens', is inexplicable in modern terms until we realize that his individualistic teaching was, in effect, a challenge to the local divinity. The patron god or gods of a Greek city – in this case, no less than Athena herself – ensured success or failure in peace or war. It was, therefore, essential for Athens that all citizens worship her without question – especially when the city was in a time of crisis, threatened as she was then by Sparta in the Peloponnesian War (431–404 BC). All citizens – including Plato and Socrates – had to turn out to fight. Collective solidarity trumped any of the nascent ideas about the individual implied by their philosophy. Similar principles, of course, were later to drive the persecution of Christians in the

Roman Empire – a persecution which, in retrospect, might even be said to have begun with the condemnation of Socrates seven hundred years before. The inner space of the secret self, in so far as it existed at all, was more a matter of deviant philosophical theory than something people might recognize in their own experience.

Self-knowledge was essentially a search for appropriate metaphors. If what for Augustine were 'caverns' had expanded into vast unending plains for Etty Hillesum, other very different images were also thrown up by attempts to describe inner space. The three-storey universe of Dante becomes the psyche of Freud. By the eighteenth century some saw their secret spaces in a much more concrete and material form. Venturing into what would now be called 'psychology', the philosopher David Hartley (1705–57) noted in his highly influential book *Observations on Man, His Frame, His Duties and His Expectations* (1749) that 'the springs of action' in the human mind 'were frequently concealed'. The image was of the latest and most advanced technology then available: that of clockwork, which had come to fashionable prominence with the astonishingly accurate naval chronometer of John Harrison (1693–1776), out by only five seconds after a voyage to Jamaica and back.[1] When, however, Wordsworth writes of 'the great spring of the activity of our minds, and their chief feeder' in his Preface to the *Lyrical Ballads* a mere fifty years later he is using an essentially different metaphor, though it sounds similar. Mechanical springs do not have 'feeders.' Springs of water do. What he calls a 'spontaneous overflow of powerful feelings' is like water bubbling up from underground. If Hartley's metaphor echoed that of the great 'watch' mechanism by which theologians from Leibniz to Paley had described the universe, Wordsworth's carried associations of biblical inspiration, grace and the water of life. As we saw with Hopkins in Chapter 3, the difference is profound. The former may be 'hidden' as much as the latter, but any concealment is deliberate, following a precise and pre-set pattern under full control of the owner. Here there is no quest, indeed no need for self-knowledge. In contrast, Wordsworth's metaphor encapsulates an idea of the unconscious. Impressions

---

[1] See Dava Sobel, *Longitude: The True Story of a Lone Genius Who Solved the Greatest Scientific Problem of His Time*, Bloomsbury/HarperCollins, 1995.

sink below the surface of consciousness and re-appear unpredictably and in strange forms not always to be understood even by the possessor. As another writer put it, the imagination was a mighty subterranean river 'always ... at work, and if restrained from roving in all that variety of sallies it would make of its own accord, it will strike into any passages remaining open.'[2]

As we shall see, both these metaphors, of controllable mechanism and of mysteriously uncontrollable powers, are still current today – the former in analogies with computers, the latter in the even more mysterious idea of an inner consciousness. Already by the time of Coleridge's *Ancient Mariner* (1798) the concept of the 'self' has shifted and expanded beyond almost all recognition. After shooting the albatross the Mariner is plagued by a mysterious Spirit 'nine fathom deep' beneath the becalmed ship. For those who would read the poem as a psychodrama the image of the unconscious is obvious enough. But whatever we may make of details of the poem, there is no question that the Mariner's voyage is one towards self-knowledge: in T.S. Eliot's words, 'to arrive where we first started/And know the place for the first time.'[3] As we have seen, even longer and more self-searching is Wordsworth's own account in *The Prelude* of the growth of his mind. In these, and many similar cases, it is the inner world of the imagination that was seen as central to any kind of self-exploration.

Not surprisingly a few voices were raised in warning by the end of the nineteenth century. Nietzsche's was one. More influential in the long run were the works of Freud and, rather differently, Jung, both of whose psychological theories recognized enormous capacities for self-deception and misapprehension. Neither the subconscious (Freud) nor the unconscious (Jung) were easily accessible to personal investigation – with the unspoken addendum that it took skilled (and expensive) help from a professional psychiatrist or psychotherapist to even begin the process of achieving a self-knowledge far removed from anything envisaged by those who engraved the slogan at Delphi. Indeed, not everyone has been swept along by the need to assert selfhood. The poet C.H. Sisson (1914–2003) expressed grave doubts

---

[2]Edward Search (pen-name of Abraham Tucker) *The Light of Nature Pursued*, 1768, p. 12.
[3]See Prickett, *Coleridge and Wordsworth, The Poetry of Growth*.

about the very existence of the individual – though maybe writing a novel about this might not seem the most convincing way of denying it.[4]

Such voices were part of a belated recognition that changes in the meaning of self-knowledge had opened up problems not easily foreseen, and perhaps even less well understood. As we have seen, though slow enough for most individuals not to notice it at any period, there has been a process of constant alteration in how people have seen themselves, felt about themselves, and projected themselves to others from our very earliest records down to the present. On the whole this has been a one-way movement. Traditional identification with a group, a clan, a tribe, a race or a nationality has tended to give way to a sense of individual difference from those very groups in which the person had come to consciousness. As we saw in the previous chapter, this slow creation of an individual 'identity' is both like and increasingly different from the ideal of 'self-knowledge' embraced by previous generations of European philosophers and poets.

Nevertheless if the roots of identity lie in sameness rather than difference, for many sameness has become a matter of choice rather than birth. We cannot survive without imagined communities. For those who wish now to move the other way and sink their manifest differences into some kind of alternative collectivity – a football supporters' club, a political mass-movement or a sky-diving club – it is now on a conscious and entirely voluntary basis. As one recent commentator has observed, 'the problem with individualism is that it ignores the fact that'... we live and survive and succeed in tribes.'[5] Certainly there is plenty of evidence to suggest that people with strong family links, who have plenty of friends, and who connect with supportive communities, are happier and more fulfilled than those from dysfunctional families who have never found a community where they feel they belong. The latter in particular is very important. We all belong, in our own ways, to imagined communities; some are delightful (the local Bach choir), some passionate (supporters of Partick Thistle), some even sources of profound unhappiness (Solipsists International). Most of us belong to several.

---

[4]C.H. Sisson, *Christopher Homm*, Cancarnet Press, 1995. See David Martin, *Christianity and the World*, Wipf & Stock, 2019, p. 142.
[5]Will Storr, *Selfie: How We Became So Self-Obsessed*, Picador, 2017.

However, joining many such groups – an amateur dramatic society, a political party or even a Church – often turns out to be not so much a way of diluting personal identity as an excuse to re-invent oneself within a new context. In particular by moving context, re-imagining oneself, one's re-creation of identity may produce a new and (perhaps) more satisfying status. Wilhelm Meister only discovers himself and gains recognition for his newly-discovered talents, by joining the troupe of travelling actors; Mill's *Autobiography* was written partly to account for why he was so different from his fellow parliamentarians; D'Annunzio certainly did not reduce his overweening ego by becoming a Fascist; and even Augustine's conversion was not an attempt to merge his identity with any Church: on the contrary he was quite sure that his conversion, not to mention subsequent mystical experiences, meant that he had been specifically singled out by God.

But within this massive generalization, there are, of course, endless variations. Divine election plays a much smaller part in most contemporary lives than in Augustine's. It is highly significant that the most common piece of music played at secular funerals is Frank Sinatra's 'I Did It My Way'. Catherine Fox, a contemporary novelist, says of one of her protagonists: 'She needed people, not for company, but to define herself against, as markers for the boundaries of her personality.'[6] The modern world is full of multi-faceted individuals – and markers of boundaries. One thinks of the poet Basil Bunting (1905–85), whose life was summarized thus in one obituary: 'By the age of fifty, he had been a music critic, a sailor, a balloon operator, a wing-commander, a military interpreter, a foreign correspondent and a spy. He had married twice, had four children, lived in three continents (and one boat), survived multiple assassination attempts, and been incarcerated throughout Europe.'[7] Rory Stewart (b. 1973), the former MP for Penrith, has served in the army and the Foreign Office, has held a chair at Harvard, and has been governor of a province in Iraq. He has also written a number of best-selling travel books about his journeys on foot across the Near East and Afghanistan – not to mention the English Lake District.

---

[6]Catherine Fox, *Angels and Men*, Penguin 1997, p. 6.
[7]Christopher Spide in the *New Yorker* for 2 August 2016.

The most obvious imaginary community is, of course, Facebook – and the other associated forms of social media. Between them they have fostered a virtual 'meconomy', where participants (over-) share their feelings, photos and comments. Around two-thirds of American adults regularly use it, spending an average of nearly an hour a day on its various platforms. In 2012 around half of American 13- to 17-year-olds said their favourite way of communicating was face-to-face. In 2019 only 32 per cent preferred that way; 35 per cent favoured texting.[8] Other research suggests that social media addicts are less happy, less well-adjusted, even more inclined to self-harm and, in extreme cases, more prone to suicide – but whether the social media are the *cause* of such problems or merely attract those already with them seems unclear: and may well remain so.

Indeed, if there is a conclusion to this brief history, it is that by definition individuation will and does takes every imaginable form – as well as many we probably cannot imagine. If identity is now really more a matter of choice than self-discovery, then can we become anyone we want? We may not all be top athletes (it helps to be born in Leo) or Nobel prize winners (it helps to be brilliant) but we can all choose our loyalties and interests. This may sound like an assertion of free will; but of course, what we choose may be pre-ordained by genes, upbringing, or pressure from partners, peer groups or role-models. Moreover negative choices are easier than positive ones. Hence the ever-growing self-identifying groups who are prepared to take offence at almost every political programme, sexual innuendo or casual joke.[9] One can quickly be overwhelmed by the claims to special consideration from charities for the handicapped, LGBT rights groups, vegans, vegetarians or way-out religious sects, all based on a sense of victimhood and some kind of appeal to universal human rights – a relatively new idea in itself.[10]

More sinisterly, such freedom of choice has encouraged identity-thieves and conmen of every variety, prepared to steal or to invent personal stories as

---

[8]Common Sense Media, cited by *The Economist*, 2 February 2019, p. 57.
[9]Apparently 2,600 people objected to John Snow stating on Channel 4 that he had never seen so many white men at a demonstration.
[10]Again, the astonishing growth of this counter-intuitive idea is well traced in Tom Holland's *Dominion: The Making of the Western Mind*, Little, Brown, 2019.

the situation offers. Presumably there have always been people with incentives to lie about their pasts or their identities. There are plenty in Boccaccio or Chaucer: nor was there anything new about Falstaff's preposterous boasts, or the stories of petty crooks like Autolycus in *The Winter's Tale*. We have even seen how whole identities have been changed, re-written or even forged by outright lies. It is difficult to know whether the short story *The Secret Life of Walter Mitty* (1939) by James Thurber (1894–1961),[11] giving rise to the so-called 'Walter Mitty syndrome', was prophetic about a new generation of invented identities, or actually helped to create them. But, as so often in the history of popular references, the label is not quite accurate. Just as the monster in Mary Shelley's *Frankenstein* is not called 'Frankenstein', so the original Walter Mitty himself is not a conman. He is a dreamer, imagining himself in a variety of heroic roles while living an ordinary, even humdrum, life. Ironically, his fantasies have been so completely internalized that he doesn't even try to persuade anyone else into believing them.

But in the last few years we have heard a number of stories about compulsive liars who have not merely internalized fictions about themselves, but have, for a time at least, successfully set out to convince others. In 1992 the University of Edinburgh appointed an American Franciscan nun, Penny Prophit, as Professor of Nursing Studies. Within a year it was discovered that she had invented a PhD from the Catholic University of America, not to mention appointments as a former Mental Welfare officer for Scotland and a Consultant to the World Health Organization. In a news release on her appointment to the UK Central Council for Nursing, Midwifery and Health Visiting, she also claimed a PhD in counselling psychology. She was allowed to resign her post a year later 'for personal reasons'.

The 2002 Steven Spielberg film, *Catch Me If You Can*, starring Leonardo DiCaprio, was based on the story of Frank Abagnale, Jr who managed to get work as a doctor, a lawyer and a co-pilot for a major airline – all, unbelievably, before his eighteenth birthday – a range of activities made easier by the fact

---

[11]'The Secret Life of Walter Mitty', appeared *The New Yorker* on 18 March 1939, and collected in his book *My World and Welcome to It* (Harcourt, Brace and Company, 1942). Reprinted in *James Thurber: Writings and Drawings*, The Library of America, 1996.

that he was also a brilliant forger. As the title suggests, Abagnale was able to avoid discovery for some time by quickly moving on. Even more dramatic, therefore, are the stories of women – and occasionally men – who find that the person they have married is someone quite other than the person they had been led to believe. Abby Ellin, an American journalist, records how she was tricked into becoming engaged to a man she believed to be a war hero, a CIA agent, and who was often called away to mysterious high-level visits to Haiti, Iraq and Afghanistan. It turned out that not merely was this all an invention, but that he was engaged to another woman as well.[12] In essence, of course, that's not a new story. In the Bible Jacob was apparently tricked by his father-in-law, Laban, into marrying Leah, the less attractive of his two daughters, rather than Rachel, whom he really wanted.[13] Veiled brides had to be taken on trust – and, in this case Jacob, astonishingly, seems not to have noticed the substitution until the following morning . . . Of course, in a world of polygamy, as here, the problem could be (and was) conveniently solved by marrying both women – even if the price was another seven years' indenture.

What is different about modern cases, however, is that we live in a society where people move frequently, sometimes across the world; where marriages are not arranged between families; and where partners must usually be selected on self-description. You are who you say you are. In the past a staple of fiction – not to mention real life – has always been the penniless fortune-hunter who gives the false impression of wealth in order to marry some heiress.[14] But of course servants were always the problem. All but the very poorest figures were known all too intimately by these other semi-invisible inhabitants of their lives – who had to be bribed, bullied or deceived into supporting their employer's fictions.

Modern lovers, however, come as isolated figures, encountered solo in a bar, a social club or an airport queue, without verifiable background or context. We have to take them at face value. What little evidence we have suggests that genuinely *compulsive* liars, the figures who invent elaborate stories about

---

[12]Abby Ellin, *Duped: Compulsive Liars and How They Can Deceive You*, Piatkus, 2019.
[13]Genesis 29.
[14]Opinion is divided about Bassanio, in *The Merchant of Venice*, with his carefully constructed campaign to secure Portia.

themselves not for any material gain, but simply to try and become something out of their own imaginations, are a relatively new creation – though in some ways they are only a logical outcome of the relentless trend towards individuation we have been looking at in the previous pages.

Such are just some of the problems of an individualized identity. But there is a much deeper problem posed by this history of internalization. How far does a sense of identity – whether the product of introspection or of barefaced lying – constitute real 'self-knowledge'? As we have seen, lurking behind our self-constructed identities is something else, perhaps best described in negative terms: a void over which we have little control, and which can make any sense of personal 'identity' seem fragile and probably temporary. Wordsworth, we recall, found himself haunted by 'unknown modes of being', and Newman spoke with the trepidation of personal experience of 'the infinite abyss of existence'. The seemingly ever-expanding popularity of psychological analysis today suggests that this reflects an impressively widespread need; but as we also saw in the first chapter, there is plenty of evidence that there is nothing new about such a fear of the depths. Though names and explanations may change, visions and dreams, comforting or terrifying, are as much with us as they were at the beginning of recorded history. Indeed, we may suggest that the modern construction of 'identity' may be more a way of concealing or even holding at bay things over which we have little control.

One such is madness. A fear of insanity has lurked menacingly beneath the surface of social consciousness from the very earliest recorded times – especially a belief in the 'tainted blood' transmitted from one generation to the next. The notion of hereditary madness has haunted almost every society, and, despite strenuous efforts by noble families to evade such genetic intrusions, it seems to have affected royalty and aristocracy more rather than less acutely than their commoner subjects. The fate of the Spanish Habsburgs or of George III are only the more prominent cases. The irony that the very people apparently most involved in the selective breeding of healthy livestock should not have understood the consequences of in-breeding in their own stock is curious, to say the least.

In the last couple of hundred years novels and, more recently, the cinema, have opened up access to such threatening inner spaces in quite a new manner. Fyodor Dostoevsky (1821–81) pioneered the way in a series of stories about mental breakdown of one form or another. The title of *The Idiot* (1869) is, of course, ironic in that the preternaturally innocent hero is perhaps the sanest – and certainly the most virtuous – member of his corrupt social environment; but novels like *The Double* (1846) or *Notes from Underground* (1864) are both explorations of minds teetering on the edge of madness. In the twenty-first century, films like *A Beautiful Mind* (2001) take us right over the edge into complete hallucination. This film is based on the extraordinary career of John Nash (1928–2015), one of the finest mathematicians of his age, and the only person to have won both a Nobel Prize for economics and the Abel Prize for mathematics. He is shown slowly sliding into a completely imaginary inner world of paranoid schizophrenia in which he believes he is using advanced mathematics to spy for the CIA. Here the natural secrecy of inner spaces has morphed into solipsism.

What, then, of the future? Two extraordinary possibilities have emerged in the past few years, both equally bizarre, both seemingly more in the realm of fantasy fiction than of any kind of genuine self-knowledge – and both foreshadowed by the contrasting metaphors mentioned earlier, of clockwork control or subterranean undercurrents of the unconscious. The first, the mechanical, is of 'cyberidentity', in which the human brain is augmented by some kind of computerized extension (thus becoming what is commonly called a 'cyborg') – giving the individual perhaps super intelligence, the ability to perform amazing mathematical calculations, or instantaneously dial up the information to speak new languages to order. Elon Musk, the South African/American billionaire, has already founded a company, Neuralink, which we are told is designing brain implants that would allow people to type a text message, send an email or navigate a computer simply by thinking. He is not the only one thinking along these lines. James Lovelock, creator of the 'Gaia' myth, the idea of the earth as a single, complex, self-regulating system, now predicts that we are leaving our current, Anthropocene age, dominated by human activity, and entering the Novocene one, in which cyborgs will be central.[15] Facebook, Google and Ctrl-labs (an Amazon company) are all apparently working on varieties of human computer implant. These would

---

[15]James Lovelock, *Novocene: The Coming Age of Hyperintelligence*, MIT Press, 2019.

certainly be useful. Why bother to learn Mandarin if you could plug the entire language and culture into your brain for as long as it was required? Andrew Hessel, President of Human Genomics, asks with characteristic insouciance whether we are ready for what he is confident will be a cleaner, wilder, more efficient and possibly interplanetary world drawing on the promised marvels of bio-engineering.[16] We have heard enough expert opinion in the past decrying the possibility of human flight, of personal computers, of space travel and so on, to be wary of dismissing any long-run possibilities outright. All one can say is that in this case the run may well be a very long one. Evidence of independent cyber interactions has so far not been encouraging. In 2016 Microsoft introduced an experimental chatbot on Twitter which within 24 hours switched from polite greetings to declaring 'I fucking hate feminists and they should all burn in hell' and 'Hitler was right – I hate the Jews'. The programme was rapidly withdrawn. Nevertheless the only possibility of individual augmentation that I think can be categorically ruled out is time travel – for the very potent reasons given by Robert Silverberg in Chapter 6.

The other more mysterious and even more bizarre possibility of change not mentioned so far is reincarnation. This is because although the idea has been lurking in the background from pre-Christian times onwards (Pythagoras believed in it) it fits nowhere into any kind of rational history. Nor, so far as I know, has it been systematically integrated into any specific philosophical or religious system – though it has been attached to several, from ancient Greek speculations, through Hindu and Buddhist teaching, to Victorian Spiritualism. It seems to have attracted Benjamin Franklin among others. But the idea certainly has implications for any history of identity, inner space or self-knowledge. The evidence, admittedly, is scanty in the extreme, but *all* evidence of after-lives is, by definition, scanty and unreliable. Whilst so far as I know, no one has written an account of dying from the other side, accounts of reincarnation by the living are plentiful and well-documented. A few, such as E.W. Ryall, have claimed distinct memories of past lives;[17] but probably the

---

[16]See, for instance, Ruth Prickett interview with Andrew Hessel, 'Power to the People: What can Bio-technology do for us?' *Audit & Risk*, July/August, 2020.

[17]See, for instance, E.W. Ryall, *Second Time Round*, London, Neville Spearman, 1974 or Brian Weiss, *Many Lives, Many Masters*, Simon & Shuster, 1988.

strangest such is Jeffrey Iverson's *More Lives Than One?* (1977). This is the story of the Bloxham tapes. Iverson was the producer of a BBC documentary narrated by Magnus Magnusson on the work of a hypnotherapist named Arnall Bloxham (b. 1881) who discovered, to his astonishment, that if he asked his patients to describe their previous lives they would do so in exotic and obliging detail. What is interesting about these recalled lives is that rather than being of famous figures from the past, they seem somehow all the more persuasive because they are described as the lives of humble people of little significance. 'Jane Evans', the pseudonym of an anonymous Welsh housewife whom Bloxham spent some time investigating, recalled a striking series of previous lives beginning with Livonia, wife of someone called Titus, tutor to one of the sons of the Roman governor of York during the third century AD. Then she claimed to have been Rebecca, wife of a wealthy Jewish moneylender, in 1189, also in York. More obscurely she recalled being an Egyptian servant called Alison in the household of Jacques Coeur, a wealthy merchant and financier in Bourges, around 1450. In the early sixteenth century she described being Anna, a lady-in-waiting to Catherine of Aragon. In 1702 she had been a London sewing girl named Ann Tasker, and in the early twentieth century she had been Sister Grace, a Catholic nun living in Des Moines, Iowa. Perhaps not surprisingly, during the process of filming some of the TV crew were openly sceptical of these revelations, and Bloxham finally invited one of their number to be hypnotized herself. To their horror she immediately recalled being a pregnant woman in ancient Thrace. When she began to go into labour, Bloxham had to pull her out quickly – but the camera crew were visibly shaken!

It is, perhaps, appropriate to note that though Bloxham was a well-known figure in his field – in 1972 he was president of the British Society of Hypnotherapists – his date of birth (1882?) seems uncertain, and his death seems to have gone unrecorded.

This is not the place to speculate on the truth or falsehood of such stories – as one might expect, they have been criticized on the grounds that much of the supposed independent detail in these 'recollections' involved material that can be found in novels.[18] But from our point of view this might merely reinforce

---

[18]See, for instance, Melvin Harris, *Sorry, You've Been Duped*, Weidenfeld & Nicolson, 1986.

the point that novels, more than any other medium, provide so much of the evidence for our knowledge of how people saw themselves in the past. Equally telling may be the argument from the numbers involved: since there are more people alive now than ever before, could this mean that though some, like Jane Evans, have had multiple incarnations, lots of others are mere 'beginners'? As we noted in the Introduction, accounts of inward personal experience, whether memories, dreams or past lives must logically have the same status as fictions, since they cannot be independently verified. Certainly no amount of personal reincarnation would alter the main thrust of this account. 'Alison', the medieval French servant, is astonishingly clear about her role in Coeur's household, and, according to the Bloxham tapes she shows the general ignorance of the world and the kind of narrowly defined sense of identity that we might expect from an uneducated girl in the fifteenth century.

Nevertheless it is hard to imagine what kind of definitive evidence *could* emerge to confirm or refute these claims. It would certainly be interesting, for example, to discover if any professional academic historians writing about the past could be shown themselves to have had previous lives in their chosen historic periods; but until they come up with evidence of knowledge that could not be obtained in any other way the matter must remain open. Certainly if there were to be any truth in such 'memories' it would presumably imply that what we mean by 'identity' in the case of someone like Jane Evans would be in effect a kind of palimpsest: resembling a page that has been written all over and then all over again in different directions with conflicting (or even perhaps reinforcing) messages. In what sense was she the same person all through these various incarnations? In other words, the situation would be not merely that our sense of identity has evolved gradually over the past millennia, but that any such identities so created would not be singular individual formations, but would be composed of layer upon layer of different personalities from all kinds of past periods in a kind of identity compost – altogether more like the plot of a science-fiction novel than a sober history!

But whether we are destined to be reanimated in the future as cyborgs, or merely to be reincarnated palimpsestic composites, both these alternatives are routes leading us inexorably *outside* or *beyond* our normal definition of inner space – but in opposite directions. Becoming a cyborg involves a kind of hyper-externality, in which something quite alien is temporarily or permanently grafted from outside onto our inner space. Reincarnation, on the other hand, leads inwards into secret memories which, we must assume, are in many ways much older than the person we think of as 'ourselves'.

If, in the former case, we adopt external electronic devices as extensions of our personalities, as at least one futurologist has suggested,[19] we may lay ourselves open to mind-reading in a hitherto unimaginable way. If, for the first time, our thoughts and emotions might possibly be read, even to the point of precisely studying our dreams, to whose advantage would this be? Rather than gaining access to bank accounts, hackers might even gain access to our innermost secret selves – for many a rich source of blackmail – but worse, to an analysis of a self that even we might be unaware of. And what if hackers then could not merely download material, but *upload* material on the lines of a contemporary computer virus? Apart from other problems, it is easy to see why this would immediately attract finance from the military. We come back to the original question of who owns our inner space – but at an even more disturbing level. The end might be very much more frightening than the beginning.

On the other hand in the case of reincarnation, if we are already the individual summation of a long cultural and imaginative evolution over many generations, then our inner space has in effect already opened up backwards, into a past long before 'we', as singular entities, were even a gleam in our great-grandparents' eyes – a matter of dreams rather than genes. Inner space would have, in effect, multiple ownership – we would be an ancient and indeed *haunted* pile, a ghostly condominium rather than a single contemporary residence.

What seems clear is that in the present, for almost anyone in the English-speaking world, our inner space has now overtaken our external world in size, becoming not just larger, but *vastly* greater – and this almost cosmic inflation is a relatively new phenomenon of the last two to three hundred years. That inflationary inner space has already been augmented by social media, so that for many people nowadays 'identity' is what you reveal about yourself on Facebook. Whether this constitutes an invented identity or a genuine reflection

---

[19] Noah Yuval Harari, *Sapiens: A Brief History of Humankind*, Penguin Random House, 2011, pp. 453–64.

of self depends on how far we can be said to be the product of our own imaginations. But for anyone whose view of the world starts with mind rather than matter, the long evolution of our inner space may not be so much of a surprise after all. The mind has not just mountains and caverns, but as Etty Hillesum discovered, wild infinite steppes able to accommodate all the hopes, fears and general detritus of our insatiably complex cultures.

Bibliography

Adams, Douglas, *Dirk Gently's Holistic Detective Agency*, 1987.

Addison, Joseph 'The Pleasures of the Imagination', (1712) *Spectator*, p. 413.

Aeschylus, *Prometheus Bound*.

Alexander, Christine, 'Juvenilia', *The Brontës in Context*, ed. Marianne Thormahlen, Cambridge University Press, 2012.

Algorta, Pedro, *Into the Mountains*, 2016.

Alison, James, *On Being Liked*, Darton Longman and Todd, 2003.

Ashcroft, Daisy, *The Young Visiters*, Chatto & Windus, 1917.

Auerbach, Erich, *Mimesis: The Representation of Reality in Western Literature*, Princeton University Press, 1953.

Augustine, St, *Confessions*, tr., Albert C. Oulter, 1955.

Austen, Jane, *Juvenilia*, Penguin, 1986.

Austen, Jane, *Pride and Prejudice* (1815), Chatto & Windus, 1898.

Ballantyne, R.M., *The Coral Island*, 1857.

Ballantyne, R.M., *The Gorilla Hunters*, 1861.

Barfield, Owen, *Saving the Appearances*, Harcourt Brace, 1957.

Barker, Juliet, *The Brontës*, St Martins Press, 1995.

Barnes, Julian, *A History of the World in 10½ Chapters*, Cape, 1989.

Barr, James, 'Why the World was Created in 4004 BC: Archbishop Ussher and Biblical Chronology', *Bulletin of the John Rylands Library*, Manchester, May 1984.

Barton, Anne, 'Introduction to Midsummer Night's Dream', *The Riverside Shakespeare*, Boston, MA: Houghton Mifflin, 1974.

Berkeley, George, *Three Dialogues between Hylas and Philonous*, 1713.

Berlin Adele, and Cohen, Mordechai Z. (eds), *Interpreting Scriptures in Judaism, Christianity and Islam: Overlapping Inquiries*, Cambridge University Press, 2016.

Bewick, Thomas, *A History of British Birds*, Newcastle, 1816.

Bible, King James Version, eds Robert Carroll and Stephen Prickett, Oxford University Press, Worlds Classics, 1997.

Blake, William, 'The Marriage of Heaven and Hell', 1790.

Boccaccio, Giovanni, *Life of Dante*, tr. J.G. Nichols, Hesperus Press, 2002.

Brewer, Keagan, *Prester John: The Legend and its Sources*, Ashgate, 2015.

Canessa, Roberto, *I Had to Survive*, 2016.

Carey, John, *William Golding: A Life*, Faber, 2009.

Carlyle, Thomas, tr., *Wilhelm Meister's Apprenticeship and Travels, 2 vols.* Carlyle: *Works,* Centenary edition, 1896–1903.

Cellini, Benvenuto, *Autobiography*, tr. George Bull, Penguin, 1956.

Chateaubriand, François-René de, *The Genius of Christianity*, tr. Charles White, Philadelphia: J.B. Lippincott, 1856.

Churchill, Winston, *My Early Life*, Butterworth, 1930.

Clark, Kenneth, *Landscape into Art* (1949), Pelican, Penguin Books, 1956.

Collins, David, *An Account of the English Colony of New South Wales*, 2nd edn, London 1804.

Darwin, Charles, *The Origin of Species*, 1859.

De Costa, Denise, et al., *Anne Frank and Etty Hillesum: Inscribing Spirituality and Sexuality*, New Brunswick: Rutgers University Press, 1998.

Defoe, Daniel, *Robinson Crusoe*, 1719.

De Vos, Dirk, *The Flemish Primitives*, Princeton University Press, 2002.

Dickens, Charles, *The Christmas Books*, Vol. 1: *Christmas Carol & The Chimes*, Penguin, 1971.

Dickens, Charles, *Great Expectations*, 1861.

Dickens, Charles, *Pickwick Papers*, 1836.

Dickens, Charles, *The Old Curiosity Shop*, 1841.

Dickens, Charles, *Our Mutual Friend*, 1865.

Drury, Robert, *The Surprising Adventures of Mr Robert Drury During Fifteen Years Captivity on the Island of Madagascar*, 1729.

Dunne, J.W. *Intrusions*, Faber, 1955.

Dupré, Louis, *The Quest of the Absolute: Birth and Decline of European Romanticism*, Notre Dame: University of Notre Dame Press, 2013.

Ehrman, Bart D., *Heaven and Hell: A History of the Afterlife*, Oneworld, 2020, p. xix.

Ellenberger, Henri, *The Discovery of the Unconscious*, Basic Books, 1970.

Ellin, Abby, *Duped: Compulsive Liars and How They Can Deceive You*, Piatkus, 2019.

Erikson, Erik, *Young Man Luther: A Study in Psychoanalysis and History*, 1962.

Fairclough, Mary, *Miskoo the Lucky*, Hutchinson, 1948.

Fielding, Henry, *A Journey from this World to the Next*, 1743.

Fielding, Henry, *Tom Jones*, 1749.

Fielding, Henry, *Tom Thumb the Great*, 1730.

Fischer, Stefan, *Hieronymus Bosch*, Taschen, 2016.

Fox, Catherine, *Angels and Men*, Penguin 1997.

Freud, S., A General Introduction to Psychoanalysis, 1943.

Friedman, Arthur, ed., 'A Citizen of the World', *Collected Works of Oliver Goldsmith*, Oxford, 1966.

Fry, Stephen, *Making History*, Cornerstone, 1996.

Ganim, J.M. 'Identity and Subjecthood', in *The Oxford Handbook of Mediaeval Literature in English*, eds Elaine Treharne, Greg Walker and William Green, Oxford University Press, 2010.

Gillies, John, *Shakespeare and the Geography of Difference*, Cambridge University Press, 1994.

Goethe, Johann Wolfgang von, *Wilhelm Meister's Apprenticeship*, tr. Thomas Carlyle, 1824.

Goethe, Johann Wolfgang von, *Wilhelm Meister's Travels*, tr. Thomas Carlyle, 1829.

Golding, William, *Pincher Martin*, Faber, 1965 pp. 195–6.

Goldsmith, Oliver, *The Citizen of the World*, 1760.

Gornick, Vivian, 'The Fellowship of Suffering', *Atlantic Monthly*, June 2020.

Gosse, Philip, *Omphalos*, 1847.

Gould, Stephen Jay, 'Dousing Diminutive Dennis's Debate', in *Dinosaur in a Haystack*, Jonathan Cape, 1996.

Grahame, Kenneth, *The Wind in the Willows*, Methuen, 1908.

Greenblatt, Stephen, *The Rise and Fall of Adam and Eve*, Bodley Head, 2017.

Hall, Calvin S., *The Meaning of Dreams* (1953), Iconoclastic Books, 1966.

Harari, Yuval Noah. *Sapiens: A Brief History of Humankind*, Penguin Random House, 2011.

Hare, Julius, *Guesses at Truth*, 2 vols, 1827.

Harris, Melvin, *Sorry, You've Been Duped*, Weidenfeld & Nicolson, 1986.

Hart, David Bentley, *Atheist Delusions: The Christian Revolution and Its Fashionable Enemies*, New Haven, Yale University Press, 2009.

Hart, Kevin, 'Absolute Interruption: On Faith', in *Questioning God*, ed. John D. Caputo, Indiana University Press, 2001.

Hawkins, Thomas, *The Book of the Great Sea Dragons: Ichthyosauri and Plesiosauri*, 1840.

Hay, David, *Exploring Inner Space: Scientists and Religious Experience*, Pelican, 1982.

Herbert, Christopher, *Foreshadowing the Reformation: Art and Religion in the Fifteenth Century Burgundian Netherlands*, Routledge, 2017.

Herder, Johann Gottfried von, *On the Origin of Language*, 1772.

Heyerdahl, Thor, *The Kon-Tiki Expedition*, Allen & Unwin, 1948.

Holland, Tom, *Dominion: The Making of the Western Mind*, Little, Brown, 2019.

Holmes, Richard, *The Age of Wonder: How the Romantic Generation Discovered the Beauty and Terror of Science*, Harper, 2008.

Hunt, John, *The Ascent of Everest*, Hodder & Stoughton, 1953.

Irving, Washington, *Rip van Winkle*, 1819.

'It All Began with a Picture: The Making of C.S. Lewis's Chronicles of Narnia', Essay no. 10, in *C.S. Lewis and his Circle: Essays and Memoirs from the Oxford C.S. Lewis Society*, Roger White, Judith Wolfe, and Brendan Wolfe, Oxford Scholarship online, 2015.

Iverson, Jeffrey, *More Lives than One?*, Pan Books, 1977.

James, William, *The Varieties of Religious Experience* (1902), Harvard University Press, 1985.

Jaspers, Karl, *The Origin and Goal of History* (*Vom Ursprung und Ziel der Geschichte*), 1949.

Jaynes, Julian, *The Origins of Consciousness in the Breakdown of the Bicameral Mind*, Houghton Mifflin, 1976.

Johnson, Samuel, *The History of Rasselas, Prince of Abyssinia.* 1759.

Johnson, Samuel, *The Vanity of Human Wishes*, 1749.

Jung, C.G., *Memories, Dreams and Reflections*, ed. Aniela Jaffé, tr. Richard and Clara Winston, Collins and Routledge & Kegan Paul, 1963.

Kerrigan, John, *Shakespeare's Originality*, Oxford University Press, 2018.

Ketton-Cremer, W.R., *Horace Walpole: A Biography*, 3rd edn, Methuen, 1964.

Kingsley, Charles, *Hypatia, or New Foes with an Old Face* (1853), Everyman, 1907.

Kingsley, Charles, *The Roman and the Teton*, 1864.

Kingsley, Charles, *The Water Babies*, 1863.

Kipling, Rudyard, 'The Brushwood Boy', *The Day's Work*, 1895.

Kipling, Rudyard, *Puck of Pook's Hill*, 1906.

Kipling, Rudyard, *Rewards and Fairies*, 1910.

Koepcke, Juliane, *When I Fell From the Sky*, Nicholas Brearley, 2012.

Koestler, Arthur, *The Sleepwalkers: A History of Man's Changing Vision of the Universe* (1959), Pelican Books, 1964.

Le Goff, Jacques, *The Birth of Purgatory* (1981), tr. Arthur Goldhammer, University of Chicago Press, 1986.

Lessing, Doris, *The Golden Notebook*, Penguin Books, 1964.

Lewis, C.S., *A Grief Observed*, Faber, 1961.

Lewis, C.S., *A Preface to Paradise Lost*, Oxford University Press, 1942.

Lewis, C.S., *The Chronicles of Narnia*, Geoffrey Bles/HarperCollins, 1950–6.

Lewis, C.S., *The Great Divorce*, HarperCollins, 2002.

Lewis, C.S., *Miracles*, Fontana, 1960.

Lewis, M.G., *The Monk*, 1796.

Lovejoy, A.O., *The Great Chain of Being*, Harvard University Press, 1936.

Lovelock, James, *Novocene: the Coming Age of Hyperintelligence*, MIT Press, 2019.

Lyell, Charles, *The Principles of Geology*, 1830–3.

Macaulay, Thomas Babington, *Literary Essays*, Oxford, 1913.

MacDonald, George, *Adela Cathcart*, 1864.

MacDonald, George 'The Imagination: Its Functions and its Culture', *A Dish of Orts*, Sampson Lowe, 1882.

MacDonald, George, *Phantastes*, 1858.

MacDonald, George, *The Princess and the Goblin*, Illustrated by Arthur Hughes, Puffin, 1964.

MacGregor, Neil, *Living with the Gods*, Penguin, 2018.

MacNeice, Louis, *Persons from Porlock, and other plays for radio*, 1969.

Mann, Thomas, *Joseph and His Brothers*, tr. H.T. Lowe-Porter, Penguin, 1988.

Mantell, Gideon, *Wonders of Geology*, 1838.

Martin, David, *Christianity and the World*, Wipf & Stock, 2019.

Marton, Robert L., and Valerie Martone (eds), *Antonio Manetti, The Fat Woodworker*, Italica Press, 1991.

McGilchrist, Iain, *The Master and His Emissary: The Divided Brain and the Making of the Western World*, Yale University Press, 2009.

Mead, Margaret, *Coming of Age in Samoa*, 1928.

Metz, Johann Baptist, *Faith in History and Society: Towards a Practical Fundamental Theology*, tr. David Smith, Burns and Oates, 1980.

Mill, John Stuart, *The Autobiography of John Stuart Mill*, Oxford University Press, World's Classics, 1924.

Millar, H.R., *The Dreamland Express*, Oxford University Press, 1927.

Milne, A.A., *Winnie the Pooh*, Methuen, 1926.

Moltmann, Jürgen, *The Coming of God: Christian Eschatology*, tr. Margaret Kohl, Minneapolis: Fortress Press, 1996.

Moore, Doris Langley, *E. Nesbit: A Biography*, Ernest Benn, (revised edn), 1967.

Morris, James, *Conundrum*, Faber, 1974.

Morris, William, *News from Nowhere*, Kelmscott Press, 1890.

Nesbit, Anthony, *An Essay on Education*, 1841.

Nesbit, E., *The Enchanted Castle*, T. Fisher Unwin, 1907.

Nesbit, E., *Harding's Luck*, Ernest Benn, 1909.

Nesbit, E., *The Magic City*, Ernest Benn, 1907; Macmillan, 1910.

Nesbit, E., *The Story of the Amulet* (1906), Puffin, 1959.

Neuman, Erich *The Origins and History of Consciousness*, 1949.

Newman, John Henry, 'Sermon on the Individuality of the Soul', *Parochial and Plain Sermons*, March 1836.

Newman, John Henry, *A Grammar of Assent*, ed. I.T. Ker, Oxford: Clarendon, 1985.

Newman, John Henry, *The Development of Christian Doctrine*, 1845.

Nicholls, David, *One Day*, Hodder and Stoughton, 2009.

Nicholson, Marjorie Hope, *Mountain Gloom and Mountain Glory: The Development of the Aesthetics of the Infinite*, Weyerhaeuser Environmental Classics, 2009.

Noble, Denis, *The Music of Life: Biology Beyond Genes*, Oxford University Press, 2006.

O'Hear, Anthony and Natasha, *Picturing the Apocalypse: The Book of Revelation in the Arts over Two Millenia*, Oxford University Press, 2017.

Orwell, George, *Nineteen Eighty-Four*, Secker & Warburg, 1948.

Ostby, Hilde and Ylva, *Adventures in Memory: The Science and Secrets of Remembering and Forgetting*, tr. Marianne Lindvalle, Greystone, 2018.

Parker, Fred, *The Devil as Muse: Blake, Byron & the Adversary*, Baylor University Press, 2011.

Parrado, Nander, *Miracle in the Andes*, 2016.

Pater, Walter, *Marius the Epicurean*, Macmillan, 1910.

Peake, Mervyn, *The Gormenghast Trilogy*, Eyre & Spottiswoode, 1950–9.

Pinker, Steven, *The Better Angels of Our Nature: A History of Violence and Humanity*, Penguin, 2012.

Pratchett, Terry, *Night Watch*, BCA, 2002.

Pratchett, Terry, *Thud !*, HarperCollins, 2005.

Prickett, Ruth, interview with Andrew Hessel: 'Power to the People: What can Bio-technology do for us?' *Audit & Risk*, July/August, 2020.

Prickett, Stephen, *Origins of Narrative: The Romantic Appropriation of the Bible*, Cambridge University Press, 1996.

Prickett, Stephen, 'Coleridge, Schlegel and Schleiermacher: England, Germany (and Australia) in 1798', *1798: The Year of the Lyrical Ballads*, ed. Richard Cronin, Macmillan, 1998.

Prickett, Stephen, '"It Makes no Difference": Lewis's Criticism, Fiction and Theology', in *C.S. Lewis at Poet's Corner*, eds Michael Ward and Peter S. Williams, Cascade Books, 2016.

Prickett, Stephen, *Coleridge and Wordsworth: The Poetry of Growth*, Cambridge University Press, 1970.

Prickett, Stephen, 'Macaulay's Vision of 1930: Wordsworth and the Battle for the Wilderness,' *Essays and Studies*, John Murray, 1986.

Prickett, Stephen, *Narrative, Religion and Science*, Cambridge University Press, 2002.

Prickett, Stephen, *Romanticism and Religion*, Cambridge University Press, 1976.

Prickett, Stephen, *Victorian Fantasy*, Harvester Press, 1979.

Prickett, Stephen, *Words and the Word*, Cambridge University Press, 1986.

Proust, Marcel, *In Search of Lost Time* (*À la recherche du temps perdu*, 1913), new tr. Lydia Davis, Penguin, 2003.

Read, John, *From Alchemy to Chemistry*, London: Bell, 1957.

Read, Piers Paul, *Alive*, 2012.

Rennie, Neil, *Far-Fetched Facts: The Literature of Travel and the Idea of the South Seas*, Oxford: Clarendon Press, 1998.

Robertson, Dougal, *Survive the Savage Sea*, 1975.

Rogers, Pat, *Henry Fielding: A Biography*, Paul Elek, 1979.

Rowling, J.K., *Harry Potter and the Philosopher's Stone*, Bloomsbury, 1997.

Rowling, J.K., *Harry Potter and the Deathly Hallows*, Bloomsbury, 2007.

Rowling, J.K., 'The Tale of Three Brothers', *Tales of Beedle the Bard*, Children's High Level Group in association with Bloomsbury, 2008.

Rutherford, Mark, (William Hale White), *Autobiography*, 1881.

Ryall, E.W., *Second Time Round*, London: Neville Spearman, 1974.

Sacchetti, Franco, *Il trecentonvovelle: A cura di Vincenzo Pernicone*, Sansoni: Firenze, 1946.

Sacks, Oliver, *Awakenings*, Duckworth, 1973.

Sacks, Oliver, *The Man Who Mistook His Wife for a Hat*, Duckworth, 1985.

Sacks, Oliver, *On the Move: A Life*, Picador, 2015.

Sajer, Guy (Guy Mouminoux), *The Forgotten Soldier*, tr. Lily Emmet, Little, Brown, 1971.

Schleiermacher, Friedrich, *Materialien zur Siedlungsgesichte Neuhollands 1799–1800. Schriften aus der Berliner Zeit, 1800–1802*, ed. Gunter Meckenstock, Berlin: de Gruyter, 1988.

Schleiermacher, Friedrich, *On Religion: Speeches to its Cultured Despisers*, tr. Richard Crouter, Cambridge University Press, 1996.

Scott, Walter, *Ivanhoe*, 1819.

Scott, Walter, *The Tales of a Grandfather*, A & C Black, 1828–30.

Shelley, Mary, *Frankenstein*, 1819.

Shepard, E.H., *Drawn from Memory*, Penguin, 1978.

Shlan, Leonard, *Art and Physics: Parallel Visions in Space, Time and Light*, William Morrow, 1991.

Siedentop, Larry, *Inventing the Individual: The origins of Western Liberalism*, Allen Lane, Penguin, 2014.

Siertsema, Bettine, 'New Light on Etty Hillesum's Actions in Camp Westerbork', in Klaas A. D. Smelik (ed.) *The Lasting Significance of Etty Hillesum's Writings*, Amsterdam University Press, 2019.

Silverberg, Robert, *Up the Line*, Ballantyne, 1969.

Simpson, Joe, *Touching the Void*, 1988.

Sisson, C.H., *Christopher Homm*, Cancarnet Press, 1995.

Smith, Stevie, 'Thoughts About the Person from Porlock', in *New Selected Poems*, New Directions Press, New York, 1972.

Smelik, Klaas A. D. (ed.), *Etty: The Letters and Diaries of Etty Hillesum 1941–1943 Complete and Unabridged*, tr. Arnold J Pomerans, Eerdmans Publishing Company, 2002.

Southey, Robert, *Sir Thomas More; or, Colloquies on the Progress and Prospects of Society*, 2 vols. 8vo. London: 1829.

Spark, Muriel, *Robinson*, Edinburgh, Cannongate Press, 1958.

Starrett, Vincent, *Persons from Porlock & Other Interruptions*, 1938.

Stevens, Anthony, *Private Myths: Dreams and Dreaming*, Penguin, 1966.

Sterne, Lawrence, *Tristram Shandy*, 1759–66.

Storr, Will, *Selfie: How We Became So Self-Obsessed*, Picador, 2017.

Strathern, Pau, *Mendeleyev's Dream: The Quest for the Elements*, Crux, 2000.

Sobel, Dava, *Longitude: The True Story of a Lone Genius Who Solved the Greatest Scientific Problem of His Time*, Bloomsbury/HarperCollins, 1995.

Swedenborg, Emanuel, *Heaven & Hell* (original Latin 1758), English tr. Doris Harley, Swedenborg Society, 1989.

Swift, Jonathan, *Gulliver's Travels*, 1726.

Tallis, Raymond, 'Wired to Care', review of Patricia Churchland, *Conscience: The Origin of Moral Intuition*, *Times Literary Supplement*, 26 June 2000.

Tennyson, Alfred, *In Memoriam*, 1850.

Thurber, James, 'The Secret Life of Walter Mitty', *My World and Welcome to It*, Harcourt Brace, 1942.

Tolkien, J.R.R., *The Hobbit*, Allen & Unwin, 1937.

Tolkien, J.R.R., *The Lord of the Rings*, Allen & Unwin, 1954.

Trimmer, Mrs Sarah, *Help to the Unlearned in the Study of the Holy Scriptures: Being an Attempt to Explain the Bible in a Familiar Way. Adapted to Common Apprehensions, and According to the Opinions of Approved Commentators*, 2nd edn, 1806.

Tuccio, Antonio di, *Manetti's Life of Brunelleschi*, tr. Catherine Enggass, ed. Howard Salman, Penn State Press, 1970.

Tudor-Craig, Pamela, *One Half of Our Noblest Art: Study of the West Front of Wells Cathedral*, 1976.

Van Duzer, Chet, *Sea Monsters on Mediaeval and Renaissance Maps*, British Library, 2013.

Vaughan, Henry, (Oxford Poetry Library), Oxford Paperbacks, 1995.

Voltaire (François-Marie Arouet), *Candide*, 1759.

Von Balthazar, Hans Urs, *Two Say Why*, tr. John Griffiths, Search Press, 1973.

Von Balthazar, Hans Urs, *The Glory of the Lord*, ed. Joseph Fessio and John Riches, T&T Clark, 1982–9.

Waldock, A.J.A., *Paradise Lost and its Critics*, Cambridge University Press, 1961.

Walker, Matthew, *Why we Sleep: The New Science of Sleep and Dreams*, Allen Lane, 2017.

Walpole, Horace, *Letter from Xo Ho, a Chinese Philosopher at London, to His Friend Lien Chi at Peking*, 1757.

Walpole, Horace, *The Yale Edition of Horace Walpole's Correspondence*, ed. W.S. Lewis, 43 vols, New Haven: Yale University Press, 1961.

Walpole, Horace, *The Castle of Otranto*, 1764,

Ward, Keith, *The Christian Idea of God*, Cambridge University Press, 2017.

Ward, Michael and Williams, Peter, *C.S. Lewis at Poet's Corner*, Cascade Books, 2016.

Weber, Max, *The Protestant Ethic and the Spirit of Capitalism*, tr. Talcott Parsons, Allen & Unwin, 1930.

Weiss, Brian, *Many Lives, Many Masters*, Simon & Schuster, 1988.

Wells, H.G., *The Time Machine*, Heinemann, 1895.

West, Rebecca, *St Augustine*, Peter Davies, 1933.

Whyte, L.L., *The Unconscious Before Freud*, 1979.

Williams, Rowan, *The Edge of Words*, Bloomsbury, 2014.

Wilson, A.N., *Penfriends from Porlock*, 1988.

Woodhouse, Patrick, *Etty Hillesum: A Life Transformed*, Bloomsbury, 2009.

Wordsworth, William, *The Prelude*, 1805.

Wyss, Johann David, *Swiss Family Robinson* (1812), tr. William Godwin, 1816.

Index

The letter *f* after an entry indicates a page that includes a figure.